The Queen and the Poet

Queen Elizabeth in 1584: a design by Nicholas Hilliard

The Queen and the Poet

by

WALTER OAKESHOTT

BARNES & NOBLE INC.

NEW YORK

1961

First published in U.S.A. 1961
Printed in Great Britain by
R. MacLehose and Company Limited
The University Press Glasgow
All rights reserved

Preface

When Raleigh's Victorian biographer was discussing the period of Raleigh's life that followed his disgrace in 1592, he spoke of him enjoying 'the rustic delight of Sherborne and the peaceful pursuits of planting and poem making'. It is not easy to fit these phrases to the tempestuous moods which the letters written at this period reveal. And in particular the idea that Raleigh was a poet for the sake of the enjoyment he got from writing poetry—that poetry was a hobby in which he indulged from time to time—can hardly be sustained. His poems were written for special occasions, the occasion most often being to please, or to pacify, the Queen. The evidence suggests that most of his poems had already been written before 1592. It is noteworthy that the list of books which he had with him in his later imprisonment in the Tower is representative of almost all his other known interests, but includes no work of English poetry. Assuming that his verses were written, therefore, for specific occasions, I have attempted here to study a group of them against the background of his life and letters during the years to which they may be attributed, and in the context of the literary history of the period.

The incident which led one whose specialist studies lie in a different direction to devote some of his time to this phase of Raleigh's life, is described in the introductory section. Otherwise Part I of the book is devoted to Raleigh's relationship with the Queen. In this first section the evidence of his letters and of other contemporary documents over the period 1580–97, is considered. The second section discusses evidence, different in character, drawn from the poems of Spenser, but bearing on those same relationships. In the third the question, much argued by editors of *Love's Labour's Lost*, of Shakespeare's concern with Raleigh in that play, is examined afresh.

The second part is an edition of the poems which can plausibly be associated with the Queen. They are printed in a version with modern spelling, and with some notes; and in the case of the long fragment known as the *XIth Book to Cynthia* a more elaborate interpretation is attempted, on the grounds that, the autograph being an unfinished draft, the non-specialist cannot be expected to read the work without such a commentary. This section includes several poems not yet recognised as belonging to the Raleigh canon and here suggested for inclusion in it in addition to the two new poems the attribution of which to Raleigh is certain.

I have been sadly conscious of the limitations under which the amateur who invades such a field is bound to labour. The decision to modernise is due only in part, however, to the lack of a specialist's training in Elizabethan literature. I have found that intelligent readers may be put off by the vagaries of Elizabethan spelling, and these are specially marked in Raleigh's own autographs where they exist. It is true that Spenser's spelling is part and parcel of his conscious archaisms. But it can at times make his work far more difficult for the modern reader than he intended it to be. It is true also that Raleigh's spelling, 'sythes'—to take one example—has a vividness (perhaps fortuitous) and a weight which 'sighs' does not. But these are irrelevant if the reader does not understand what it means. And when in one of the Elizabethan versions of the poem which appears on p. 166 it is printed thus:

> *Would I were chaung'd into that golden showre*
> *That so diuinely streamed from the skies,*
> *To fall in drops vpon the daintie floore,*
> *Where in hir bed, she solitarie lies. . . .*

the spelling is positively misleading. What the writer intended at the end of l. 3 was 'flower', not 'floor'. Some powerful arguments have recently been advanced for retaining some sort of Elizabethan spelling in any edition of Elizabethan texts (even, apparently, if, owing to the need for clearing up obscurities and correcting mistakes, that has to be a modern reconstruction), but, while I see the advantages of a 'simplified' Elizabethan spelling, in that it may help to preserve the atmosphere of the original, there are obvious dangers for the amateur in adopting it, and these seemed almost decisive. What clinched the matter was the existence of Miss Latham's scholarly edition which includes somewhere within its covers all but six of the poems here printed, and in which immense pains have been taken to print, literally transcribed, the best Elizabethan version she found available. Incidentally, I have also adopted a conventional spelling of Raleigh's name, and have not followed the writer himself in the varieties he discovers.

What is here attempted, therefore, with most of the poems, is a modernised interpretative edition. It is a different matter when an unknown text is being published for the first time, and in one instance when this book will provide the first readily accessible text, I have given complete information about the originals from which the text is taken. The author's autograph clearly has unique authority. Even so, an early copy may give a valuable indication of the way in which an obscure phrase or ambiguous spelling in the autograph were understood at the time (cf. p. 208). A manuscript which is not the author's autograph has no special claims as compared with an early printed text. Hence it has seemed to me justifiable to introduce certain emendations into the text of No. X, the authority for these modifications being an early printed version of a poem in which Raleigh material was incorporated. But a photograph of the manuscript text is reproduced so that the available evidence may be fully accessible. My quotations of Spenser are made from the Globe edition of the poems. Here too, I have modernised spelling and also some archaic forms (e.g. 'must' for 'mote'). But scansion or rhyme often make it necessary to keep the original form, so that the result must often seem somewhat arbitrary. Quotations from *Love's Labour's Lost* are made from the Cambridge Shakespeare text, though I have checked them against the Greg facsimile of the Quarto.

* * *

My thanks are due to a great number of friends who have helped me at various stages, especially to Professor Dover Wilson who saw an early draft of my conclusions about *Love's Labour's Lost*, urged me to develop them and later read the proofs; and to Miss Latham, whose edition of Raleigh's Poems is the basis of so much of my work. She helped me also over the indentification of the Raleigh notebook, and I only wish that her edition of the letters had been available. If I had not learnt that she was working on such an edition I should have been tempted to embark on it myself. As it is, my quotations from the letters, except where otherwise stated, are from Edward's edition; but I have here also (as with the poems) modernised the spelling. Miss Bradbrook helped to unravel the riddle of some characteristic Raleigh obscurities. My colleague Mr. W. W. Robson read some of the book in a

fairly early draft, and his comments led to a number of modifications. Professor C. S. Lewis made some suggestions which I used
to considerable advantage, and Mr. John Hayward read the book
at an early stage, looked through the proofs with his eagle eye,
and in general helped me with characteristic generosity. Professor
W. A. Jackson of the Houghton Library, Harvard University,
also read through the proofs and made a number of important
corrections and suggestions. Mr. Frank Howes, Professor J. A.
Westrup and Mr. Thurston Dart gave me their views on a theory
recently put forward about *The Triumphs of Oriana* which, if
generally accepted, would have invalidated an argument I use
about the dating of one of Raleigh's poems (see p. 207). The
present owners of the notebook, Mr. Philip and Mr. Lionel Robinson, could not have been more gracious in the way they have
made it accessible to me; and one of the new Raleigh poems (No.
X) is Mr. Philip Robinson's discovery rather than mine, for he
wrote drawing my attention to verses in another manuscript in
his collection (apart from the notebook) which he said had evidently something to do with Raleigh. Lord Salisbury has allowed
me to examine more than once the famous manuscript of the
'*XIth Book to Cynthia*' and I have used the chance to look also at a
number of the Raleigh letters in that amazing library. I learnt
much from a visit paid me by M. Pierre Lefranc, and more from
articles he has written about Raleigh, and both these comments
apply to Mr. Philip Edwards also. Reference to 'Edwards' in the
commentary on *Cynthia* are to his book, not that of the editor of
the *Life and Letters*. For the illustrations I have to thank Mr. Croft
Murray in the British Museum Print Room (and the Museum),
the authorities of the National Portrait Gallery, Professor Edward
Robertson (and the John Rylands Library), Mr. Neill (and the
Bodleian Library), Dr. Sayce at Worcester College, Oxford (and
the Provost and Fellows of Worcester), the authorities of the
Kunsthistorisches Museum in Vienna, and Miss Hanna Rott who
helped me to secure photographs from them; and Mr. Philip and
Mr. Lionel Robinson. Mr. R. L. Drage, Curator of Hatfield
House, and Miss Talbot its present Librarian, and Miss Crum
(whose index of first lines of manuscript poems in the Bodleian
is one of its treasures) are also owed my thanks. My secretary,
Miss Phyllis Alcock, has shown extraordinary patience and for-
bearance, when I have demanded from her revision after revision.

She made the index, and it would indeed have been impossible for me to write the book without her help.

It is scarcely necessary to add that none of those who have helped me is in any way committed to the views here put forward. But their assistance has been of exceptional value because the subject lay outside my own field. Perhaps it may be admissible to mention in this context Mr. Richard David, editor of *Love's Labour's Lost* in the *Arden Shakespeare* (revised edition), and Professor F. P. Wilson. Their criticisms, given at an early stage in the working out of Part I, ch. IV, modified its final pattern considerably. They will still find things with which they disagree—but not so many as if they had not looked at it then.

Oxford,   WALTER OAKESHOTT
Mareh 1960

Contents

List of Plates

S.W.R., to Sir Walter Raleigh. [It seems that particularly after 1597 Raleigh was anxious to avoid being associated with the writing of poetry and that the cancellation slip may therefore have been added at his request after the book had been printed; cf. pp. 149, 161. For his reluctance at an earlier date to allow publication, see p. 79.]

FIGURES IN THE TEXT

PART I

THE QUEEN AND
THE POET

Introduction

In the summer of 1935 a sale of printed books and manuscripts took place at Sotheby's, the catalogue of which came into the hands of the writer of this study. He was at that time a schoolmaster, comparatively young, and impecunious as always; but his eye was nevertheless caught by one item in it, a manuscript commonplace book which had once belonged to the renowned library of Sir Thomas Phillipps. It was called by the cataloguer a 'geographical dictionary' of Egypt, Palestine and other adjacent regions, was dated about 1600, and was described also as containing some manuscript maps. This last point interested that particular reader of the catalogue, for he owned already a few sixteenth- and seventeenth-century maps, and as librarian of Winchester College had access to Mercator's great atlas, to Hariot's account of Virginia, published in 1589, to the 1600 edition of Hakluyt, and other such treasures which had added fuel to his passion for the history of exploration in the Elizabethan age. Was there any chance of acquiring the commonplace book? He wrote to a London bookseller friend, who reported that the maps were of moderate quality; that if anyone else was after it, it might run up to £40, but that it might go (as many things then used to do) quite cheaply. It went for £4 15s., and so he became the possessor of a book which contained a dozen maps of varying quality, and carried out with varying amounts of detail; all no doubt secondary in character (copied that is from printed originals, not made on the ground); but nevertheless manuscript maps of about the year 1600 and, as such, to him highly desirable.

From the first this notebook, a large quarto in size, with its original vellum covers and tattered green silk ties for tying the covers closed, was a satisfactory possession. The geographical dictionary had a limited interest. Its compiler had evidently read many of the biblical commentaries published in his day and jotted down in it under alphabetical heads scraps of information about places or rivers or other geographical features in Palestine, Egypt and so on. He had also added his library list, or actually two lists; the first apparently an abortive draft, the second a detailed list, the scope of which coincided in many ways with the interests of its modern owner. The man who collected the library had evidently been interested in travel. He also had his copy of Hakluyt, and his books about Virginia. He had been interested in Science, and (most unusually) had a Copernicus on his shelves. He had had some medieval books also and a number of historical and political books, including some Machiavelli. Literature, however, was—disappointingly—hardly represented. Nevertheless he was evidently not wholly unresponsive to it, for on the last flyleaf was a set of verses in the writer's most crabbed and difficult hand. On a first reading they seemed no more important than many other such verses which so often are to be found on old endpapers.

Unfortunately, the new owner's interests were soon dissipated in other fields. He was, not much later, plunged into a sociological study of unemployment, which took him away from school-mastering for a time. After it his fortunes became in due course involved in those of a great London school, and he was left little opportunity for the study of sixteenth-century seamen; or for his other inordinate passion, twelfth-century illumination. So the notebook was laid aside. At one exciting juncture of the war, in 1943, the two interests were curiously combined in a journey to America. But that is another story.

After the war the notebook was often taken down and the pages casually turned. It was exhibited once or twice as an example of seventeenth-century map making. But the possibility that its original compiler might be identifiable never occurred to its owner—obvious though the answer now is. So that, in 1952, when it became necessary to sell some books in order to help pay the family bills, this was picked out, with others, for sacrifice. It might, perhaps, by this time have realised £40 or £50 (for prices had greatly appreciated) which would have helped. So it was taken, with the rest, to another London bookseller, a specialist in maps, and as no one happened to be there to make an actual offer, the books were left there temporarily, while their owner went off to solace himself with the form of stimulus which is his chief addiction. For him, being something of an oddity, this was not a whisky and soda, nor a gin and It., but a visit to the British Museum, where he would of course find a few twelfth-century illuminated manuscripts (though none indeed of the highest quality) on view, and probably quite a batch of maps and travel books.

Some god, however, as the ancient poet said, must have guided his steps. For there was, at that moment, set out in the King's Library in the British Museum, a Raleigh-Hakluyt quatercentenary exhibition. He had seen stray letters of Raleigh before. But this was something different, an exhibition which contained examples of Raleigh's letters, beginning with one written from Ireland in 1587 and ending with one written perhaps thirty years later, asking for the loan of some books needed for his work, the *History of the World*. There was other important material also. The effect of a brief glance at this great series of autographs was like that of the ringing of an alarm-bell, an alarm that grew more and more insistent. Were not those the hands of the writer of the notebook? Did not the list of books at the end of it tally with Raleigh's known interests? Must not the geographical glossary be connected with the *History of the World*, be in fact working notes for it? It was difficult to suppress the intense excitement of the next forty-eight hours. The bookseller was told that the notebook was not, after all, for sale. It was recovered and examined side by side with the *History*. Correspondence between the phrasing of the notes and the printed word left no doubt that there was a connection between the two. And at that stage, since the study of sixteenth- and seventeenth-century hands is a matter for experts rather than amateurs, the notebook was taken to London, and shown to Mr. A. J. Collins, at the time Keeper of the Department of Manuscripts in the British Museum. The owner explained, gasping with a mixture of excitement and embarrassment, what he believed the notebook to be. He was greeted with the kind of look which Keepers of the Department of Manuscripts normally reserve for leading Baconians. But Mr. Collins (being a kindly man) kept the notebook for examination by his department. And in due course their reply was received. They confirmed that the hand was Raleigh's, as certainly as such a judgement can be made. But Mr. T. C. Skeat had found proofs more convincing than the handwriting. It had already become clear that there was a connection between the notebook and some passages in the *History of the World*. But the writer of the notebook might conceivably have jotted them down from the history—until Mr. Skeat showed that in one passage the printer had misunderstood his copy, and that the right reading could be restored from the notebook. And he found, too, what had escaped the owner's notice, that in a section dealing with a lake of pitch in the Near East, the writer says 'I have seen the same in Trinidado'. We know when that happened, for Raleigh describes the sight in the first few pages of his *Discoverie of Guiana*, his account of his first voyage to Trinidad and South America, published in 1596. So it was established that this was a notebook compiled by Raleigh himself while he was writing the *History of the World*, during the long imprisonment in the Tower which preceded the final voyage to Guiana and his execution on his return from it.

At this point the owner began to take a new interest in the stanzas on the flyleaf. They began

> *Now we have present made*
> *To Cynthia.* ....

The owner remembered dimly having read of that remarkable literary mystery, Raleigh's poem addressed to Queen Elizabeth as 'Cynthia'; of the long fragment in Lord Salisbury's library, written in Raleigh's autograph, and proclaiming itself as part of this poem; but which seemed to have been written in 1592 or after, by which date Raleigh's poem to Cynthia had already been highly praised in print by an Elizabethan literary critic, and already praised, also in print, by Edmund Spenser himself. How did the verses on the flyleaf connect with Raleigh's poem to Cynthia, and what could be found out about that poem? Out of that enquiry this book has developed.

II

The Twelve Years' War and its Sequel

*'Twelve years entire I wasted in this war,
Twelve years of my most happy younger days
But I in them, and they now wasted are
Of all which past, the sorrow only stays.'*

The 'Cynthia' fragment at Hatfield, lines 120–4

(i) 1581–1588

The first task to be undertaken is one for which the information available unfortunately is inadequate. Raleigh's rise to favour is something about which strangely little detailed record, in any form, has survived. In looking back over his years at Elizabeth's court, Raleigh when he wrote the *XIth Book to Cynthia*, talked of the 'war' on which those years had been wasted. That war was, as the poem shows, Raleigh's love for Queen Elizabeth. This chapter is concerned with the evidence (apart from Raleigh's own poems which will be discussed at a later stage) for these years; and our purpose is to find out what may have been in his mind when he spoke of them as 'war'.

The evidence is in many respects unsatisfactory. A number of Raleigh's own letters belonging to the period has survived, but that number is comparatively scanty for the crucial years 1578–88, and not until well into the nineties do the surviving letters become comparatively frequent. Moreover those that are available are often difficult to interpret. Raleigh had a habit of dating his letters by the month and day (if he dated them at all) leaving out the all-important detail of the year, and though something can be done by bibliographical methods, in particular by the examination of watermarks, to group letters together and so define some dates which would otherwise be doubtful, the method has only a limited application. Apart from his own letters, there are mentions in other correspondence which may be of the greatest importance. Yet behind Raleigh's own letters and other men's talk about him, the truth of what was happening remains elusive. If it can be established at any given time what he was trying to get his correspondents, or the Queen, to believe about himself, or even if it can be established what his detractors were saying, that is often as far as we are likely to reach.

As is well known, the famous stories of Raleigh's rise to favour are first found in seventeenth-century writers and lack documentary support from Raleigh's own day. The legend about the cloak spread for Elizabeth's feet in the mud, is first told by Fuller in his *Worthies of England*. He says that Raleigh was 'bred in Oriel College, Oxford, and thence coming to Court found some hopes of the Queen's favour reflecting upon him. This made him write in a glass window obvious to the Queen's eye

Fain would I climb, but I fear to fall.

Her Majesty either espying or being shown it did under write:

If thy heart fail thee, climb not at all.

However, he at last climbed the stairs of his own desert. But his introduction to the Court bare an elder date. From this occasion: this Captain Raleigh coming out of Ireland to the English Court in good habit (his clothes then being a considerable part of his estate) found the Queen walking, till meeting with a plashy place, she seemed to scruple walking thereon. Presently Raleigh cast and spread his new plush cloak on the ground, whereon the Queen trod gently, rewarding him afterward with many suits for his so free and seasonable tender of so fair a footcloth.'

The story has generally been disbelieved on the grounds that Fuller is unreliable and that the story is too picturesque to be true. A curious detail however may give support to it. Early in 1585 Raleigh adopted a seal as Governor of Virginia. It carries the date 1584, but this must be an 'old reckoning' date, and must indicate some time in the narrow period between 6th January, 1585 when he was knighted—the seal calls him 'Miles'—and 25th March that year, since according to the old reckoning of date, it was on March 25th that the new year began. The seal bears the motto AMORE ET VIRTUTE: By love, and by courage. The 'love' by which he has risen to his position is certainly the love of Elizabeth: his love for the Queen, or hers for him, or more probably both. The mantling of the crest is a cloak so curiously realistic that it strikes the eye at

Raleigh 'the Queen's dear minion'; 1581–1586

Raleigh the Statesman; 1588

once as being significant.[1] It must be said, however, that in the heraldic achievements of this time or in the years just subsequent to this, the form of mantling is often a cloak, though it is normally highly stylised, and a cloak so naturalistically designed as this seems to be unusual to say the least of it. It is unsafe to build much confidence on this possible fragment of evidence. But at least the use of the motto on the seal shows that Raleigh was already early in 1585 claiming the Queen's special favour.

Another seventeenth-century writer, Aubrey, has a different story of the way in which Raleigh first came to the Queen's notice.

'He went into Ireland, where he served in the wars, and showed much courage and conduct, but he would be perpetually differing with (I think) Grey, then Lord Deputy; so that at last the hearing was to be at Council table before the Queen, which was that he desired; where he told his tale so well and with so good grace and presence that the Queen took especial notice of him and presently preferred him.'

Now it is true that in 1581 Raleigh was serving in Ireland, and that there were strong differences of opinion between him and Grey, the Lord Deputy; for chance has preserved letters written by each of them at that date, which contain allusions to the other. 'I have spent some time here' writes Raleigh to Leicester in the summer apparently of that year, 'under the Deputy, in such poor place and charge as, were it not for that I knew him to be one of yours, I would disdain it as much as to keep sheep.' In that same year Grey wrote to Walsingham, 'For mine own part, I must be plain: I neither like his [Raleigh's] carriage nor his company; and therefore, other than by direction and commandment, and what his right can require he is not to expect at his hands.' Aubrey's story goes back at least to Sir Robert Naunton, who though Raleigh's junior by some twenty years, knew him personally. But the incident cannot explain the *first* notice of Raleigh by the Queen, since there is a royal warrant drawn in his favour, in eulogistic terms, early in April, 1582, while Grey did not return to England till a few months later. In this story, then, there is something less than an accurate account, but nevertheless some substance, if only in the background of hostility between the two men and their differing advice given to the Queen; for another letter

[1] See Pl. II b.

of Grey's, this time to Burghley, speaks of a plan 'delivered by Captain Raleigh unto her Majesty for the lessening of her charges here in the province of Munster, and the disposing of the garrisons according to the same, the matter at the first indeed offering a very plausible show of thrift and commodity'—a plan which Grey proceeds, claiming the authority of his council, roundly to condemn. In 1582 Raleigh was one of a distinguished party of noblemen and gentlemen who escorted the Duke of Alençon on his return to Antwerp. After the return of Leicester (who headed the mission) to England, Raleigh met William the Silent who charged him with a message for the Queen, SUB UMBRA ALARUM TUARUM PROTEGIMUR. That protection was to prove, alas, all too weak.

The young Raleigh, then, was by 1582 in an important position. And by May, 1583, Raleigh was already undoubtedly enjoying the intimate confidence of the Queen. For on that date he wrote a letter to Burghley, who had evidently appealed to him to speak to the Queen in commendation of his ward, the Earl of Oxford. The letter is remarkable. 'This evening', it begins, 'after receipt of your Lordship's letter, I spake with Her Majesty; and ministering some occasion touching the Earl of Oxford, I told Her Majesty how grievously Your Lordship received Her late discomfortable answer.' It goes on to report the Queen as saying that her censure had been intended only as a warning to the Earl; and concludes by stressing Raleigh's own desire to serve Burghley: '. . . I am content, for your sake, to lay the serpent before the fire, as much as in me lieth, that having recovered strength, myself may be most in danger of his poison and sting.' By this date then, it was already worth the Lord Treasurer's while to ask Raleigh to speak a word in the Queen's ear on his behalf. Raleigh was at this date aged about thirty-one. He had had no title of nobility to commend him, and his rise, however it had begun, had been unusually, if not dramatically, rapid.

Nor was Raleigh simply the oracle which the Queen constantly consulted for advice. A letter written by Raleigh to his half-brother, about to set out on a voyage of western discovery in March, 1583, gives a different impression. 'Brother, I have sent you a token from her Majesty, an anchor guided by a lady as you see; and farther, her Highness willed me to send you word that she wished you as great good hap and safety to your ship as if herself were there in person; desiring you to have care of yourself as of that which she tendereth; and therefore, for her sake, you must provide for it accordingly.

'Farther, she commandeth that you leave your picture with me. For the rest, I leave till our meeting, or to the report of this bearer who would needs be the messenger of this good news. So I commit you to the will and protection of God, who send us such life or death, as he shall please, or hath appointed. Richmond, this Friday morning. Your true brother, W. Raleigh.'

This letter, written to Sir Humphrey Gilbert, gives a glimpse not of an adviser, but rather of a personal *aide*; of a man who enjoys the complete confidence of his mistress, and is sure of his position. Here again is incontrovertible evidence of the strength of that position at Court in 1583.

A letter written to Leicester in 1586 shows Raleigh still in the inner counsels of the Queen, and once more, so it seems, mediating with her on behalf of one of the greatest figures of the time. Its famous postscript reads: 'The Queen is on very good terms with you and, thank be to God, well pacified; and you are again her sweet Robin.' And in the following year another letter to Leicester speaks of leave having been procured by Raleigh 'with much ado' from her Majesty for Drake to visit Leicester in the Low Countries. In 1587 Raleigh succeeded Hatton, who had become Lord Chancellor, as Captain of the Queen's Guard. This appointment brought him back more often to Court, after an interim during which offices conferred on him in 1585 in the West Country had put him in charge of the preparations to resist Spanish invasion, in Cornwall and Devon. His leaving for the West seems to have been the occasion of a recently discovered poem in the *Cynthia* Series [No. X].

Thus by 1583 Raleigh was already in the Queen's confidence, kept at court for her company, moving round with her on her progresses, and in a position of influence in which for a time he had no rival. But he was not the first man at Elizabeth's Court with whom her relations had given cause for malicious comment. When she was still a girl, there had been slanderous reports of her association with Seymour, and she had lived for a time under the threat of the fate that Seymour had suffered. He was a man old enough to be her father, but ambitious, and no doubt ready to exploit her for his own ends. But she had an old head on young shoulders, and somehow she survived the ruthless cross-examina-

tion designed by her accusers to induce a confession. In the first
months of her reign, the air had been full of talk of a marriage with
some foreign prince. But it soon became clear that it was an
Englishman, already married, who attracted her; Robert Dudley,
this same Leicester, her sweet Robin—whose father and grand-
father before him had been executed for treason. The story of the
affair between them is, in outline, well known. There is no doubt
that he hoped to marry her, and that the suicide of his wife,
though it may in fact have made the marriage a final impossibility
owing to the horror, linked with the suspicion of murder, that
it caused, in another sense removed the only obstacle to it. Nor
is there any doubt that for years the Queen was greatly attracted
by him, and not till her reign was ten years old did the spell lose its
force. She never had the same feelings for any other man. But
there is no good reason for accepting the story, which was current
in almost every European court, that she had taken him as a lover.
The evidence is rather that once he was free to marry her she could
not bring herself to make up her mind. She was not in the last
resort prepared to face an outcry in which she knew there would
be justification. Yet what kept the question still alive with her
was this hatred which his ambitions brought upon him, and of
which she was perversely determined to take no notice. Eventually
he married again and, though the secret was kept from the Queen
for a time, when she came to know of it she visited him with the
same unreasoning anger which she was to show to others of her
admirers when they turned their eyes elsewhere. But in spite
of such outbursts, the 1570's are in some ways the lyrical period of
her reign. She was on terms of delightful intimacy with many of
her administrators and courtiers: not only with Robert Dudley,
'her eyes', but with her 'spirit', Burghley; her 'Moon', Walsingham; and with her 'Mutton' or 'Bell-wether', Hatton. Into this
charmed circle Raleigh had now broken. But things were changing as Elizabeth grew older. Hatton found reason to suppose that
Raleigh, whom she nicknamed 'Water', was replacing him in her
affections. She sent her Bell-wether a reassurance 'that the beasts of
the field were so dear unto her that she had bounded her banks so
sure as no water or floods could be able ever to overthrow them'.
But what had been enchanting flirtations when she was still in
her thirties began, in her fifties to look like infatuation. There
came a time when some one man, Raleigh it might be, or later

Essex, was universally recognised to have attained a dominating, if hazardously insecure position, and when the Court rivalries assumed the aspect of a girls' school rather than of an adult society.

Raleigh was twenty years younger than the Queen. He came of a comparatively undistinguished, and in no sense aristocratic family. But from the moment he entered on a career at Court, he played its game. His first reckless gesture had caught her attention immediately, and though she had had other admirers with that same swaggering pride which she so much enjoyed, she had none with anything like his imaginative gifts. These she was quick to appreciate, and as his motto shows she allowed him to claim a passionate devotion to her; and he began to write verses to her, which if they were part of the courtly game, had sometimes a vein of seriousness in them which reached out beyond the elegant accomplishments of flattery:

> *Calling to mind mine eye long went about*
> *T'entice my heart to seek to leave my breast;*
> *All in a rage I thought to pull it out*
> *By whose device I lived in such unrest.*
> > *What could it say to purchase so my grace?*
> > *Forsooth that it had seen my Mistress' face.*

But most of what has survived and can be dated to this early period is on an altogether more conventional level, though it has a certain witty sparkle. He used the same clichés about the Queen as many others were to use in the later years of her reign, picturing her as Diana, the changeless Queen of the heavenly spheres, beyond time; or praising those features which, in their day, had had indeed power to attract—the 'crispèd hairs', the 'dainty hands', the 'wit that turns huge Kingdoms upside down'. There is no reason to suppose that he, or she, put a higher value on such writing than it deserved. Its justification was that she enjoyed it. And it had not yet become that fantastic web of hypocrisy which much of the poetry addressed to her in the 1590's was going to be. There is no indication in the extant poems that he shared with her the profound, and often dangerously profound, intellectual interests which make him an unusual figure in this world of brilliant entertainment and extravagant luxury. Not until estrangements had come between them did he try to use poetry to move her deeply. It was designed at first simply to capture her fancy. And its commendation by contemporaries suggests that in this it succeeded.

*   *   *

For some indication of the time when things began to change, it is necessary to turn to that incomparable collection of Elizabethan letters and documents preserved at Hatfield which formed the archive of the Cecils, Elizabeth's great administrators. It contains two letters sent by Mary Queen of Scots' servant, Thomas Morgan, to his mistress and intercepted by Burghley's secret agents, which show the popular estimate of the trend of Raleigh's relationships with the Queen at this period. The first, written in April, 1585, speaks of Raleigh as 'the Queen's dear minion, who daily groweth in credit'. The second, written almost exactly two years later (two years during which Raleigh's absences in the West had, as has been seen, been comparatively frequent), says that the Queen now has a younger favourite, who might for age be her grandson. 'Either Raleigh, the minion of her of England, is weary of her, or she is weary of him.' Another correspondent writing two months later, mentions names. 'When she is abroad, nobody near her but my Lord of Essex; and at nights, my Lord is at cards, or at one game or another, with her, till the birds sing in the morning.' Just after this Essex himself is found writing to Sir Edward Dyer, to describe how he had accused Elizabeth of slighting both Essex and his sister, 'only to please that knave Raleigh. . . . From thence, she came to speak of Raleigh, and it seemed she could not well endure anything to be spoken against him. . . . As near as I could I did describe unto her what he had been and what he was.'

The writer does not go into details. But some of the topics which he discussed, although he knew that Raleigh, on duty as Captain of the Guard, might be able to overhear him, are indicated. He will indeed hardly have branded Raleigh, in the terms used by a Jesuit writer (a year or two later), as one among Elizabeth's '*suavissimos Adonides*' since Essex himself was already one of them. But he certainly dilated on Raleigh's plebeian origins ('what he had been and what he was'), on his arrogance, on his avarice, perhaps also on his atheism.

For Raleigh had not been a mere courtier during the previous six or seven years. The Queen's favour had made him a man of wealth, and he was already using that wealth in the patronage of

Raleigh claiming himself as the Queen's lover; seals of 1587 (*a*) and 1585 (*b*), showing his use of the motto 'Amore et Virtute'

discovery and of learning. And it appears probable that the rise of Essex in one respect was an advantage to Raleigh—who does not seem to have realised at first the nature of the threat which it implied. For what this made possible was a greater freedom of movement. Elizabeth's favourites were tied to her apron strings. We do not know precisely to what Raleigh was referring, when, looking back in 1592, he wrote of some expedition:[1]

> '*To seek new worlds, for gold, for praise, for glory,*
> *To try desire, to try love severed far;*
> *When I was gone she sent her memory*
> *More strong than were ten thousand ships of war*
> *To call me back, to leave great honour's thought*
> *To leave my friends, my fortune, my attempt,*
> *To leave the purpose I so long had sought. . . .*'

It looks as if she had prevented him from going on one of the American expeditions which embodied some of his highest ambitions. By 1587 however there are signs that the chains which had fettered him to the Court were being loosened. He was, in that year, given the appointment of Lieutenant-General of Cornwall, Deputy-Lieutenant of Devon, and Warden of the Stannaries. This was no sinecure at a time when the impending threat of the Armada was believed to carry danger to the western counties, and Raleigh's extraordinary reputation in those parts, to be shown by the events of the autumn of 1592, was no doubt built up by his work in Armada year.

When the campaign itself began Raleigh joined Howard, at sea, once it became clear that the Spaniards were not intending to force a landing in the west. And as with many other incidents in his career, there is a pertinent comment included by him in his *History of the World* (in his description of the Roman siege of Agrigentum) which suggests the part he played in the tactics of the action without making any explicit claims for himself. 'To clap ships together without consideration belongs rather to a madman than to a man of war. By such an ignorant bravery was Peter Strozzi lost at the Azores, when he fought against the Marquess of Santa Cruz. In like sort had Lord Charles Howard, Admiral of England, been lost in the year 1588, if he had not been better-advised than a great many malignant fools that found fault with

[1] See note on p. 179.

his demeanour. The Spaniards had an army aboard them, and he had none. They had more ships than he had, and of higher building and charging; so that, had he entangled himself with those great and powerful vessels, he had greatly endangered the Kingdom of England. For twenty men upon the defence are equal to a hundred that board and enter. Whereas then, contrarywise, the Spaniards had an hundred for twenty of ours, to defend themselves withal. But our admiral knew his advantage and held it; which had he not done, he had not been worthy to have held his head.' Raleigh understood Drake's advice, to take the offensive, and his voice may have been decisive in getting its acceptance. In many later naval actions his own advice, as at Cadiz, came to be regularly sought and accepted. He saw the series of Armada actions in 1588 through, at sea, to the finish. And his comparative freedom enabled him to run his own privateering ventures in the following few years with lack of scruple which more than once brought him into dispute with the Council. They brought him great profits; and may already have been one of the charges which Essex brought against him when he unburdened himself to the Queen.

But it was the exploration of Virginia that was the most important of the fruits of Raleigh's work in this period. Much of the detailed history of this discovery is lost, and the way in which Raleigh, writing in the mid-1590's to Cecil about Guiana, emphasises the need for secrecy, shows why so little documentary material survives relating to the analogous project of the eighties. But in the year of the Armada, there appeared Thomas Hariot's *Brief and True Report of the Newfound land of Virginia*. Hariot was a brilliant mathematician who was one of Raleigh's most intimate friends, from these early years up to and during the time of Raleigh's imprisonment in the Tower in the reign of King James I. He was as it were Raleigh's Lord Cherwell, and was himself one of the Virginia pioneers, so that the *Brief and True Report* is a first-hand document. It made Raleigh famous on the Continent, where it was reprinted with engraved illustrations of fine quality, and texts in Latin, English, German and French. In a sense, it was a 'prospectus' of the new territory of which the Queen had made Raleigh Governor, and over which she had granted him extensive rights. He intended to make money out of the venture, by getting Virginia settled with colonists, as he and others were making money out of

Irish plantations. Virginia was to prove in practice, however, a continual, and formidable, financial drain on his resources. But his interest had been aroused and the enterprise was more than a financial speculation. Hakluyt, in one of his prefaces, wrote of Raleigh as the 'Joshua' who was leading to the promised land, for with Hakluyt also maritime enterprise was an article of faith rather than simply a commercial proposition. It is possible that Raleigh had himself at an early date taken part in one of the transatlantic voyages. But the probabilities are that the role he played was that of the prime mover of this undertaking rather than that of a participant in any of the voyages. And though no permanent settlement was achieved by Raleigh in Virginia, for our present purpose what is important is the picture of Raleigh working during the 1580's in the promotion of discovery and settlement in America, and in the building up of his own fortune, during the time when he was enjoying the Queen's intimate friendship. Towards the end of the decade, however, the picture has begun to change, as this rival, much younger, of aristocratic family and with royal blood in his veins begins to win favour. Raleigh's upstart arrogance was part of Essex's theme when he spoke to the Queen on this occasion, as the words of his letter to Dyer show. He was *nouveau riche*. The earl may have poured scorn (as he and his associates were to do over Guiana, eight years later) on the bogus nature of the Virginia enterprise which Raleigh's enemies regarded as what might be called in the slang of today an 'advertising stunt'.

Other material for slander may have been Raleigh's pretensions to learning. The foundations of the intellectual interests, which were to come to fruition not only in such technical investigations as shipbuilding, but in a great variety of speculative work and finally in that masterpiece, the *History of the World*, had already been laid at Oxford.[1] These intellectual interests have been the subject of a number of specialist studies, one of the most important being Professor E. A. Strathmann's *Sir Walter Raleigh: A Study of Elizabethan Skepticism*. Professor Strathmann has investigated what lies behind the charge of atheism levelled against Raleigh, whose name was already being associated with 'atheism' in the early

[1] One of the most moving of benefactions the University has ever received is Raleigh's gift of £50, made within a few weeks of his imprisonment, to the Bodleian Library; it suggests that Oxford continued to claim a share of his devotion.

1590's, and who, at his trial in 1603, was denounced as a 'damnable atheist' by Coke: 'You have been taxed by the world, Sir Walter Raleigh, with holding heathenish, blasphemous, atheistical and profane opinions.' Strathmann makes it clear that Raleigh was a theist; and that though sceptical of the means by which Pharoah's magicians had tried to convince their opponents, and confident that a modern conjurer could do better, he was deeply aware of the working of God in Creation. But it seems likely that already in the second half of the decade 1580–90, he was being criticised as an atheist and a follower of Machiavelli.

His literary friendships, which are unfortunately more thinly documented, have been considered by Miss M. C. Bradbrook in her *School of Night*. The phrase she has adopted as title for her book comes from a passage in the earliest text of *Love's Labour's Lost*, in which the phrase used to be emended, but is now sometimes accepted as being the original text: a nickname for Raleigh and his circle of intimates, Hariot the mathematician, and Chapman the poet among them, whose dark studies, it is assumed, were satirised by Shakespeare in that play. If the reference is indeed to Raleigh's circle (and to this question we shall return later) the time will be the 1590's. It is worth quoting here, however, a passage from Spenser's *Mother Hubberd's Tale*, an allegory of Court life, which describes the invasion of the Court by the Fox and the Ape. *Mother Hubberd's Tale* was published in 1591. In the dedication, Spenser says that it was 'long since composed in the raw conceit of my youth'. We know, however, from his handling of *Colin Clout's Come Home Again* that his habit was to work over and make additions to such poems when the time came to send them to the printer, so that it cannot be said for certain when the particular lines were composed; only that they were printed by 1591. He has been talking of the Ape at Court, persuading any courtiers who might hold chivalrous ideals to abandon them and mocking at any who devoted themselves to intellectual pursuits:

> But if perhaps into their noble sprights
> Desire of honour or brave thought of arms
> Did ever creep, then with his wicked charms
> And strong conceits he would it drive away
> Ne suffer it to house there half a day.
> And whenso love of letters did inspire

Their gentle wits, and kindle wise desire,
That chiefly doth each noble mind adorn,
Then would he scoff at learning, and eke scorn
The sectaries thereof as people base
And simple men, which never came in place
Of world's affairs, but in dark corners mew'd
Muttered of matters as their books them shew'd
Ne other knowledge ever did attain
But with their gowns their gravity maintain.

The passage suggests particular references. When it was written, Spenser (who by the year of its publication at any rate was on intimate terms with Raleigh) may have been thinking of Raleigh and his scientific and literary associates, in some ways an incongruous appanage of the glistering life of the Court. The scholars 'in dark corners mew'd' sound curiously similar to 'The School of Night'. It is certain that in the later years of the decade 1580–90 Raleigh's scientific interests were already beginning to find scope in his association with Hariot. In the year 1576 he was already a friend of George Gascoigne the poet, and wrote commendatory verses for his book, *The Steele Glass*, which appeared in that year. After Gascoigne's death Raleigh sometimes used his motto, *Tam Marti quam Mercurio*, to emphasise his interest in learning, just as his other motto, *Amore et Virtute*, emphasises the favour of the Queen. In 1582 Raleigh put in a word with the Queen on behalf of the poet Churchyard, who recalled the favour in a preface six years later. We shall see Raleigh's own verse handsomely commended by a literary critic in 1589, by which year he was already a friend of Spenser. Their association demands a chapter to itself. Thus a strong interest in literature and science must already be assumed as part of Raleigh's life at this period.

Nothing has yet been said of his contacts with Marlowe in which both interests were associated. Raleigh is mentioned in depositions made in the enquiry into Marlowe's atheism at the time of Marlowe's death in 1593, when one of the witnesses claimed that Marlowe had read Raleigh his 'atheist lecture'. It seems difficult to explain away these depositions, connecting Marlowe with Raleigh and his associates, completely, in spite of their obviously gossipy character. The detail may be inaccurate, but the connection was there. One witness 'said and verily believed that one Marlowe is able to show more sound reasons for atheism than any divine in England is able to give to prove divinity, and that Marlowe told him that he had read the atheist lecture to Sir Walter Raleigh and others'. Another asserted that Marlowe had said that 'Moses was but a juggler and that one Heriots (i.e. Hariot) being Sir W. Raleigh's man can do more than he'. Marlowe and Raleigh share an interest in Machiavelli, another forbidden topic in Elizabeth's reign. Scepticism about any personal relationship between them seems extravagant. A connection between them is suggested (though perhaps not proved) by Raleigh's famous answer, 'The Nymph's reply to the Shepherd', made to Marlowe's verses 'The Passionate Shepherd to his Love' :[1]

THE PASSIONATE SHEPHERD TO HIS LOVE

Come live with me, and be my love,
And we will all the pleasures prove,
That Vallies, groves, hills and fields,
Woods, or steepy mountain yields.

And we will sit upon the Rocks,
Seeing the Shepherds feed their flocks,
By shallow Rivers, to whose falls
Melodious birds sing Madrigals.

And I will make thee beds of Roses,
And a thousand fragrant posies,
A cap of flowers, and a kirtle,
Embroidered all with leaves of Myrtle.

A gown made of the finest wool,
Which from our pretty Lambs we pull,
Fair lined slippers for the cold:
With buckles of the purest gold.

A belt of straw, and Ivy buds,
With Coral clasps and Amber studs,

[1] Since for our purpose the dating of Raleigh's 'moods' in verse is important, it may be worth noticing that there is an allusion to the Marlowe song in his *Jew of Malta*. That play has been dated between the years 1588 and [Feb] 1592, at which latter date it is mentioned in Henslow's diary. If the allusion implies that the song was new and popular, and if (as is here suggested) Raleigh's answer is a direct personal response to Marlowe's poem, the period 1588–90 would seem the likely date for Raleigh's reply.

And if these pleasures may thee move,
Come live with me, and be my love.

The Shepherd Swains shall dance and sing,
For thy delight each May-morning,
If these delights thy mind may move;
Then live with me, and be my love.

THE NYMPH'S REPLY TO THE SHEPHERD

If all the world and love were young
And truth in every Shepherd's tongue,
These pretty pleasures might me move,
To live with thee, and be thy love.

Time drives the flocks from field to fold,
When Rivers rage, and Rocks grow cold,
And Philomel becometh dumb,
The rest complains of cares to come.

The flowers do fade, and wanton fields,
To wayward winter reckoning yields,
A honey tongue, a heart of gall,
Is fancy's spring, but sorrow's fall.

Thy gowns, thy shoes, thy beds of Roses,
Thy cap, thy kirtle, and thy posies,
Soon break, soon wither, soon forgotten:
In folly ripe, in reason rotten.

Thy belt of straw and Ivy buds,
Thy Coral Clasps and Amber studs,
All these in me no means can move,
To come to thee, and be thy love.

But could youth last, and love still breed,
Had joys no date, nor age no need,
Then these delights my mind might move,
To live with thee, and be thy love.

The charm of Marlowe's verses, and the deeper undertones of
Raleigh's suggest a direct and personal response, and I find the
contention that Raleigh did not know Marlowe impossible to accept. They shared, among other things, a suspicion of orthodoxy,

and the interest in Machiavelli already noted—at the time, something less than respectable. Thus the vitality and versatility of this remarkable man, shown in these many contacts, can hardly fail to impress us, though so many of his contemporaries laughed at it. He was not one who suffered fools gladly, and the evidence for his overbearing arrogance is unanswerable. So his contemporaries mocked him, and hated him. Not until the time of his imprisonment by James I did he become the popular hero that he was to continue to be, alive and dead, for the next three hundred years.

Certainly as a young man he was disliked heartily. We have already heard the Deputy in Ireland saying 'I like neither his carriage nor his company'. Sir Robert Naunton says that the Queen 'took him for a kind of oracle, which nettled them all'. From the time of the Virginian voyages he and his associates were subject to the calumnies of those who were jealous of them, and these are already mentioned by Hariot in the *Brief and True Report*. Calumny was going to be no stranger to him in the following decades.

(ii) 1588–1592

The next phase in Raleigh's relationship with the Queen is best studied in association with those poems of Spenser which have a bearing in it. This study is attempted in another chapter. Here all that will be done is to indicate what is known, from sources outside Spenser's work, of the change which occurred. Edwards in his *Life of Raleigh* speaks of this change as a 'passing cloud'. But that is an understatement for the disturbance in their association which Spenser suggests. The phrase used by him in *Colin Clout* is to the effect that Cynthia 'debarred' Raleigh, 'faultless, from her presence'.

Popular opinion ascribed Raleigh's discomfiture to Essex. The rivalry which we have observed beginning in 1587 reached a climax late in 1588, when Essex challenged Raleigh to a duel. Efforts were made by the Council to suppress the story of their quarrel, but the rivalry persisted and in August, 1589, Sir Francis Allen wrote to Anthony Bacon: 'My lord of Essex hath chased Mr. Raleigh from the court, and hath confined him to Ireland.' Raleigh's comment on what must be the same incident is given in a well-known letter, now in the Library of Lambeth Palace, written to his cousin, Sir George Carew:

'Cousin George,

For my retreat from the court, it was upon good cause to take order for my prize. If in Ireland they think that I am not worth the respecting, they shall much deceive themselves. I am in place to be believed not inferior to any man, to pleasure or displeasure the greatest; and my opinion is so received and believed as I can anger the best of them. And therefore, if the Deputy be not as ready to stead me as I have been to defend him—be it as it may.

When Sir William Fitzwilliam [the Deputy] shall be in England, I take myself far his better by the honourable offices I hold, as also by that nearness to Her Majesty which still I enjoy, and never more. I am willing to continue towards him all friendly offices, and I doubt not of the like from him, as well towards me as my friends. This much I desire he should understand; and for my part, there shall be nothing wanting that becometh a friend; neither can I but hold myself most kindly dealt withal hitherto, of which I desire the continuance. I have deserved all his courtesies in the highest degree. For the suit of Lismore, I will shortly send over order from the Queen for a dismiss of their cavellations; and so, I pray, deal as the matter may be respited for a time; and commend me to Mr. Solicitor with many thanks for his friendly dealing therein; and I assure you, on mine honour, I have deserved it at his hands in place where it may most stead him. For Harding, I will send unto you money by exchange with all possible speed, as well to pay him (if he suffer the recovery) as all others; and till then, I pray, if my builders want, supply them.

I look for you here this spring, and if possible I may, I will return with you. The Queen thinks that George Carew longs to see her; and therefore see her. Farewell, noble George, my chosen friend and kinsman, from whom nor time nor fortune nor adversity shall ever sever me.

The 27 of December.   W. RALEIGH.'

The next extant letter from Raleigh seems to have been written nearly a year later. It is concerned with some details about prizes captured by a certain John Watts, and is dated from Raleigh's London residence, Durham House, 16th October [1590]. There is accordingly considerable uncertainty about Raleigh's movements, as well as about what lay behind them.

What sequence of events does Raleigh's letter to Carew imply?

It seems to be a 'retreat from the Court', involving a visit to Ireland where Raleigh was undoubtedly staying in the summer of 1589; the visit designed, according to Raleigh, to make arrangements about a ship taken by his privateers, but due, according to London gossip, to the growing influence of Essex with the Queen. News that he is out of favour has evidently spread in Ireland, and after Raleigh's return, Carew (at the time Master of the Ordinance in Ireland) is given by Raleigh the task of making it clear to the Deputy that he will assume Raleigh to be in disgrace at his peril. For by December, when he writes this letter, Raleigh is clearly back in England, and he claims to be 'near' the Queen again. The tone of the letter suggests that the writer is rattled. But he expresses himself as confident that he can persuade the Queen to give a ruling in the Lismore incident which will bring about the end that he desires, provided that Carew can for the moment postpone action. And he issues a warning that his position at Court still makes it possible for him to do a good turn, or a bad turn, to whomsoever he pleases. We can perhaps detect in the last few phrases, a suggestion that events have taken a serious shift, and that Raleigh foresees the approach of adversity; but this interpretation is not necessary, even if made more probable because these phrases have no ready parallel in the series of Raleigh letters which survive.

There is no evidence that Raleigh went back to Ireland in the spring of 1590, as he said he might. Certainly it was at least as early as the summer of 1589,[1] and not at some later date, that he formed the friendship with Spenser some of the fruits of which are decribed in the next chapter; and late that autumn, they came back to England together. The first three books of the *Faerie Queene* were entered at Stationers' Hall on 1st December, 1589, while the preface is dated 23rd January of the following year. The preface was addressed to Raleigh, the work dedicated to Elizabeth, and there are seventeen sonnets addressed to various English dignitaries, including one dedicated to Essex. The poem was an immediate success. Spenser is spoken of as the new Laureate and was granted a pension by the Crown. It might seem on the face of it that the reconciliation between the Queen and Raleigh was complete, if the reception of his protégé could be taken as a criterion of it.

[1] Edwards's statement 'In 1590 we see Raleigh in exile and are told that Essex drove him thither' seems to be simply a mistake.

One of the reasons why Raleigh won his way back at least temporarily into favour was Essex's marriage, in 1590. The venture was given by Elizabeth the devastating reception that she tended to give to her favourites' matrimonial excursions, and when Essex returned to court, she made the condition that his wife be left behind in the country. This temporary fall from grace explains why, according to a note written by one of the government's agents, Essex 'makes Raleigh join him as an instrument from them [the Puritans] to the Queen upon any particular occasion of relieving them'. The note was made early in 1591. One such joint intervention was apparently made on behalf of the Puritan John Udall who had been condemned to death for advocating Church Reform. He appealed to Essex as well as to Raleigh, and Udall's case may be that to which the note of 1591 refers. This seems to be the only example which has survived from 1590 or 1591 of representations made by Raleigh to the Queen, such as he made freely at an earlier time. On the other hand he enjoyed some signal marks of her patronage. Early in 1592 he obtained, through her, the lease of Sherborne Castle. It was said that Elizabeth had left the see of Salisbury vacant for three years because she could not find a new bishop sufficiently accommodating to assure the alienation to Raleigh of Sherborne Castle, the property he desired, and for which he came to have such a deep affection; and said also that when the gift at last materialised he gave her a jewel worth £250 in thanks.

Yet it may be that the Raleigh of these years wore her favour with a difference. We shall see later that Spenser is anxious in the first three books of the *Faerie Queene* to emphasise to her Raleigh's humility; as if Raleigh himself had become convinced that he must show the Queen his awareness that he had flown too high. At some date which is not recorded, the young Arabella Stuart came to London and dined with the Lord Treasurer. Raleigh was one of the party, as was also the Lady Arabella Stuart's uncle, Sir Charles Cavendish. In describing the incident, Sir Charles writes: 'Sir Walter Raleigh is in wonderful declination, and labours to underprop himself by my Lord Chancellor and his friends.' He goes on to contrast Raleigh's former pride with his present too great humility, and guesses that he will never rise again. There are some circumstances (in particular an allusion to Arabella Stuart's age) which suggest that this meeting took place before Raleigh's 'exile' in Ireland; it may have been as early as 1587, when the rise of Essex had already begun.

What makes this noteworthy is Cavendish's contrast between the old Raleigh and the new. Some of the poems (such as the justly famous 'Like truthless dreams, so are my joys expired') undoubtedly belong to this new phase, after Essex's arrival in Elizabeth's court had darkened the skies for Raleigh:

> *Like truthless dreams, so are my joys expired*
> *And past return are all my dandled days;*
> *My love misled, and fancy quite retired,*
> *Of all which past, the sorrow only stays.*
>
> *My lost delights now clean from sight of land,*
> *Have left me all alone in unknown ways*
> *My mind to woe, my life in fortune's hand,*
> *Of all which past the sorrow only stays.*
>
> *As in a country strange without companion*
> *I only wail the wrong of death's delays,*
> *Whose sweet spring spent, whose summer well nigh done,*
> *Of all which past, the sorrow only stays.*
>
> *Whom care forewarns, ere age and winter cold*
> *To haste me hence, and find my fortune's fold.*

Several facts help to account for the contrast between the sad *obbligato* of this poem and of others that belong to the same phase, and the slick performance, the assertive assonances, the tripping rhythms and the witty allusions, rather awkwardly introduced ('in manger oft for spite') of earlier work:

> *Thus hope brings hap: but to the worthy wight,*
> *Thus pleasure comes; but after hard assay*
> *Thus fortune yields, in manger oft for spite;*
> *Thus happy state is none without delay.*

Raleigh, like his cousin Sir Arthur Gorges, who may have written verse actually in association with him, had been reading Desportes. Nor had English poetry stood still, with Sidney's sonnets in circulation, and Spenser's *Shepheardes Calendar* going into three editions in the 1580's. But more significant than these is the change in Raleigh's own experience. In his poetry he is now not only speaking to the Queen, but speaking to himself. He can move the Queen only by showing himself; not as the conventional puppet lover of the conventional love song, but from depths of feeling the genuineness of which need not be doubted. Thus the change is not simply one of poetical technique, but a change of background; the change from the 'dandled days' of the early 1580's to a rudderless loneliness. He is saying goodbye to the spring. The summer itself is almost over. And the oppressiveness of the realisation is already marked, and will indeed be seared into the verse of the next phase. It is unfortunate that there is so little which is precisely datable written at this time. But, assuming that our date, 1592, for the long *Cynthia* fragment (a date now widely accepted) is right, 'Like truthless dreams' belongs to a period some time earlier than that—say to 1589 or early 1590; while the answer to Marlowe which bears traces of the same mood and was written between 1588 and 1592 helps to date the group with which 'Like truthless dreams' is associated. This group so clearly forms a single whole that even the mere fragment of it which the surviving poems represent gives a vivid impression. Its characteristics were an anxiety for the future, sometimes akin to depair; an awareness that the carefree delights of youth are over; and a growing sense that his devotion to Elizabeth has been a fool's paradise. The poet's cruel mistress and her disdain are conventions which might mean nothing. But the reader is left in no doubt that this cruelty has a cutting edge. What Edwards called the 'passing cloud' in their relations was at first a cloud the size of a man's hand, but now the skies were overcast. She might give Raleigh Sherborne, but she had given her heart to Essex, and Raleigh was being paid off. The verse that he wrote now showed that he was well aware what was happening.

(iii) 1592–1593

Essex spent some of the year 1591 overseas. He was recalled early in 1592, and though many details of the incidents which were to lead to Raleigh's imprisonment are obscure, it is impossible not to connect some of the disasters which fell on Raleigh during the following months with his rival's presence at court and his desire to make certain that Raleigh would never again cause trouble. What is sufficiently clear is the popular account of the circumstances. Camden says that Raleigh's disgrace was due to his wronging one of Elizabeth's maids of honour, Elizabeth Throckmorton, and that later (presumably when the facts became apparent) Elizabeth forced them to marry, and they were both imprisoned in the Tower. A letter of Robert Cecil's, written just after Raleigh's release (a release sanctioned to enable him to undertake a particular mission which it was thought that he alone could hope to fulfil successfully) speaks of Raleigh's 'brutish offence'. This is the popular version of what happened.

It is desirable, however, before the genuine evidence is discussed further, to clear aside a Victorian forgery which, though it was rejected by Brushfield and more recently by Miss Latham, the editor of Raleigh's poems, continues to darken counsel. Payne Collier who achieved notoriety later with his Shakespearian forgeries published what he claimed to be a letter written in 1592, referring to Raleigh's imprisonment. As printed in Mr. Edward Thompson's *Life of Raleigh* (1935) it runs as follows:

'S.W.R., as it seemeth, have been too inward with one of Her Majesty's maids; I fear to say who, *but if you shall guess E.T., you may not be far wrong.* The matter hath only now been apparent to all eyes, and the Lady hath been sent away, *but nobody believes it can end there.* S.W.R. hath escaped from London for a time; he will be speedily sent for, and brought back, where what awaiteth him nobody knoweth save by conjecture. All think the Tower will be his dwelling, like hermit poor in pensive place, where he may spend his endless days in doubt. *It is affirmed that they are married*; but the Queen is most fiercely incensed, and *as the bruit goes threateneth the most bitter punishment to both the offenders. S.W.R. will lose it is thought all his places and preferments* at Court with the Queen's favour; such will be the end of his speedy rising, and now he must fall as low as he was high, at the which many will rejoice. *I can write no more at this time, and do not care to send this, only you will hear it from others. All is alarm and confusion at this discovery of the discoverer, and not indeed of a new continent but of a new incontinent.*'

That Payne Collier should have been able to carry off this forgery (the italicised passages surely being enough in themselves to proclaim its character) is an indication of the way in which a high reputation can get away with almost anything. Mr. Thompson rightly rejects another forgery, purporting to be a letter from

Raleigh to his wife written just after his imprisonment by James I. In Payne Collier's forgery, the allusion to Raleigh's

> *Like to a hermit poor in place obscure*
> *I mean to spend my days of endless doubt*

may have been suggested to him by a letter at Hatfield, written by Lady Raleigh in 1596: 'I oft wish it with her [the Queen], else is a hermit's cell most fit for me and my mind at this time.' But he was determined that his allusion should be still more explicit.[1]

Nothing in this letter then which is not otherwise confirmed has any authority. The idea that Raleigh 'escaped from London' seems to be the misrepresentation, or misunderstanding, of an absence connected with the command of a privateering expedition, his recall from which was apparently in the first instance a mark of royal favour rather than the reverse. We are left, however, with the rumour of a liaison with one of the maids of honour, for which Camden is a witness, and the imprisonment of the offending couple in the Tower. 'If you have anything to do with Sir Walter Raleigh' (wrote Sir Edward Stafford to Sir Anthony Bacon on 30th July)[2] 'or any love to make to Mrs. Throckmorton, at the tower tomorrow you may speak with them, if the countermand come not tonight, as some think it will not be, and particularly he that hath charge to send them thither.'

The first heard of this matrimonial venture in Raleigh's existing correspondence is in a well-known letter among the Hatfield papers, written to Sir Robert Cecil on 10th March, 1592. Raleigh was at the time involved in the preparations for an expedition, in which the Queen and others were associated with him in providing the necessary finance, an expedition directed against the Spanish treasure fleet. Raleigh had spent already as much as and more than he thought he could afford.

'Sir,

I received your letters this present day at Chatham, concerning the wages of the mariners and others.

---

[1] Brushfield found among the papers of Payne Collier what was apparently a draft of this forged letter.

[2] M. Pierre Lefranc has shown that this date is correct and that Gorges's letter, dated 26th July and referring to Raleigh's imprisonment should actually be dated a fortnight later: *Etudes Anglaises*, 1946, p. 207 *seq*.

For mine own part, I am very willing to enter bond, as you persuaded me, so as [provided that] the Privy Seal be first sent for my injoining the third [underwriting a third share of the enterprise]; but I pray consider that I have laid all I am worth, and must do, ere I depart on this voyage. If it fall not out well, I can but lose all, and if nothing be remaining, wherewith shall I pay the wages? Besides, her Majesty told me herself that she was contented to pay her part, and my Lord Admiral his, and I should but discharge for mine own ships. And further, I have promised her Majesty that if I can persuade the companies to follow Sir Martin Frobisher, I will without fail return; and bring them but into the sea but some fifty or three score leagues; for which purpose my Lord Admiral hath lent the *Disdain*; which to do her Majesty many times with great grace bad me remember, and sent me the same message by Will Killigrew, which, God willing, if I can persuade the companies, I mean to perform; though I dare not be acknown thereof to any creature [sc. I dare not admit so much to anyone]. But, Sir, for me then to be bound for so great a sum, upon the hope of another man's fortune, I will be loth; and besides, if I were able, I see no Privy Seal for my thirds. I mean not to come away as they say I will for fear of a marriage, and I know not what. If any such thing were, I would have imparted it to yourself before any man living; and therefore I pray believe it not, and I beseech you to suppress, what you can, any such malicious report. For I protest before God there is none on the face of the earth, that I would be fastened unto. And so in haste I take my leave of your Honour. From Chatham, the 10th of March

Yours ever to be commanded

W. RALEIGH.'

This letter shows a number of important things. Its primary object is to question financial proposals which Raleigh thought would operate to his disadvantage. The famous reference to rumours of an entanglement reads in its context almost like an afterthought. The letter shows however that rumour was already involving Raleigh in the scandal which eventually led to his imprisonment five months later. It shows also that Raleigh's recall from the voyage was at the express direction of the Queen, and suggests that it was a mark of favour rather than a punishment. She had persuaded him 'with great grace' to hand over the command to Frobisher, and Raleigh in reply no doubt told her that to hand over to Frobisher might be difficult. He was one of the most unpopular of sea captains. This is why in the letter Raleigh avows the need for disguising his intentions of returning to court. He actually sailed with the expedition, after this letter was written, as far as the north Cape of Spain (a memorandum drawn up by him later and assessing the results of the voyage shows this) and then returned. On 31st July he was thrown into the Tower.

M. Pierre Lefranc, a brilliant young French Raleigh scholar, has recently published a document which purports to give a date, or an approximate date, to Raleigh's marriage.

> ... *Posteaque scilicet Vicesimo die Februarii Anno Regni dictae dominae Elizabethae Reginae Tricesimo vel eo circiter praedicta Elizabetha Throckmorton cepit in virum suum Walterum Raleigh militem. . . .*

(And thereafter, that is to say on 20th February in the thirtieth year of the said Queen Elizabeth, or thereabouts, the said Elizabeth Throckmorton married Walter Raleigh, Knight. . . .)

The information occurs, however, in a document drawn up thirty years after the events in question. M. Lefranc claims that it was taken out of an earlier conveyance, which he thinks must have been made in 1596. But the phrase, *vel eo circiter*, is surely significant; and the date 1588 for the marriage is surely incredible. It is true that the Queen's violent reaction would be readily explicable if she found that Raleigh had been married for more than four years. But that such a secret could have been kept for four years to Queen Elizabeth's court seems to be stretching the imagination too far. What appears likely is that one of the family, many years later, knew the day on which the wedding anniversary was celebrated, but did not know the year. But M. Lefranc's discovery confirms a conjecture already substantiated by the existence of a letter written by Lady Raleigh in the Tower and subscribed, not E.T., but E.R: that the marriage had already taken place when the pair were incarcerated. Its date may have been 20th February, 1592, just before Raleigh sailed.

'Lying', says Miss Latham, 'was a sixteenth-century accomplishment.' Whatever the date of Raleigh's marriage, there is hardly room for doubt that by the time he wrote to Cecil on 20th March (when, on the supposition made above, he had been married just over a fortnight) he was already deeply involved with Elizabeth Throckmorton. Such of their correspondence as has survived, Lady Raleigh's being notable for spelling of a delightful extravagance, suggests that the marriage was an exceptionally happy one. If she is the 'Serena' of 'Now Serena, be not coy'—and she may be, for we shall find that an allusion to Raleigh in the *Faerie Queene* associates him with a Serena—that poem must have been written not many months away from the violent despair of the *Cynthia* fragment, and during the period when the letters to Cecil continue to show Raleigh in unrelieved dejection. This is only one of the many contradictions which no biographer of Raleigh has been able completely to resolve. His life was lived in separate compartments. The Queen's displeasure frustrated his ambitions and his ambitions were always inordinate. But while frustration and distress were genuine enough, he found time for a family life and for what would be called nowadays a parliamentary career which are the antithesis of the inaction and despair that some of the letters to Cecil suggest.

For Raleigh's moods following this rigorous action taken by the Queen are mirrored in a number of letters and other documents coming from his hand during the next four years. He is to be found, in them, at first in a state which seems to be bordering on madness, and was doubtless calculated to give that impression; calculated, like the attempted 'suicide' when Raleigh was first imprisoned by James I, or the feigned madness during the last desperate months, excused by Raleigh himself on the grounds that David had had recourse to a similar subterfuge. The story of this first attack is recorded by Sir Arthur Gorges. Raleigh had been committed to the guard of a relative, Sir George Carew, the 'Cousin George' of a letter already quoted. Queen Elizabeth proceeded down the river, in her state barge, at which Raleigh 'brake out into a great distemper'. He said that his enemies had planned the procession to break his gall in sunder with Tantalus's torment, and begged for a boat so that he might row out to get a sight of the Queen herself. He came to blows with his guardian, and they scrambled and brawled 'like madmen'. The scene delighted Sir Arthur Gorges till he saw daggers drawn. Then he intervened to try to 'appease the fury'. And he tells Cecil in conclusion that 'Sir Walter Raleigh will shortly grow to be "Orlando Furioso" if the bright Angelica persevere against him a little longer'.

46

This was one mood. Reason has recently been given for dating this outburst to 9th August, Raleigh's imprisonment having begun on 31st July.[1] How this same mood developed, after the Queen's procession had passed, is reflected in a passionate letter, which though it bears no date was undoubtedly written within a short time of the incident just mentioned. It begins sensibly enough. Raleigh was still Captain of the Guard, and he retained the office throughout the period of his disgrace. Arrangements had to be made for payments for uniforms, and Sir Robert Cecil is asked to do this:

'Sir,

I pray be a mean to her Majesty for the signing of the bills for the Guards' coats which are to be made now for the Progress, and which the Clerk of the Check [Exchequer] hath importuned me to write for.

My heart was never broken till this day, that I hear the Queen goes away so far off[2]—whom I have followed so many years with so great love and desire, in so many journeys, and am now left behind her in a dark prison all alone. While she was yet near at hand, that I might hear of her once in two or three days, my sorrows were the less: but even now my heart is cast into the depths of all misery. I that was wont to behold her riding like Alexander, hunting like Diana, walking like Venus, the gentle wind blowing her fair hair about her pure cheeks like a nymph; sometimes singing like an angel; sometime playing like Orpheus. Behold the sorrow of this world! Once amiss hath bereaved me of all. O glory that only shineth in misfortune, what is become of thy assurance? All wounds have scars but that of fantasy; all affections their relenting but that of womankind. Who is the judge of friendship, but adversity? Or when is grace witnessed, but in offences? There were no divinity but by reason of compassion; for revenges are brutish and mortal. All those times past, the loves, the sighs, the sorrows, the desires, can they not weigh down one frail misfortune? Cannot one drop of gall be hidden in so great heaps of sweetness? I may then conclude, *Spes et fortuna, valete*. She is gone in whom I trusted, and,

[1] Lefranc in *Etudes Anglaises*, Vol. IX, no. 3 (July–September, 1956). It was in this article that M. Lefranc published the discovery quoted above, p. 45.

[2] The Queen started on progress before the middle of August and did not return to London till October.

of me hath not one thought of mercy, nor any respect of that that was. Do with me now therefore what you list. I am more weary of life than they are desirous I should perish; which if it had been for her, as it is by her, I had been too happily born.

> Yours, not worthy of any name or title
>
> W.R.'

It is theatrical. But that is not all. For us its particular interest lies in its relationship to the longest of Raleigh's existing poetical works, the draft of the XIth and the opening of the XIIth books of the *Ocean to Cynthia*. This relationship will be examined later. But a critic who said that the XIth book was devoid of feeling would be himself lacking in perception. It is written with an exceptional intensity; an intensity which was developed, perhaps, out of the attitude struck in this letter, but which makes the draft something of real power. And it is an intensity which this letter in some degree, for all its theatricality, already shows.

When the letter was written, Raleigh was representing his fault as something comparatively insignificant. 'Once amiss hath destroyed all.' A single step, wrongly placed, has brought destruction. 'One frail misfortune.' Four years later, when the *Discoverie of Guiana* was published, the cloud of the Queen's displeasure still showed no signs of lifting, and in the Preface Raleigh took a different view: 'as my errors were great, so they have yielded very grievous effects, and if ought might have been devised in former times to have counterpoised any part of the offences, the fruit thereof (as it seemeth) was long before fallen from the tree, and the dead stock only remained.' In the interim, his letters are weighed down with the sense of the Queen's displeasure (partly because so large a proportion of those that survive was written to the Queen's Secretary of State or to other members of the Council) and it is only the Cadiz voyage in 1596 that at last restores to Raleigh his spirits.

Meanwhile, however, while Raleigh was in the Tower there were other moods than that of the despairing lover trying to belittle his faults. Letters which were written soon after his imprisonment began, refer with resentment to his 'disgraces having crossed the seas' and being 'highly commended' to the Deputy in Ireland who is then making trouble for Raleigh's settlers there. He speaks bitterly of a prophecy of rebellion in Ireland, to which the Queen scorned to listen; a rebellion from which she and Essex were destined to reap the whirlwind. In a letter to Howard, in which he alludes to the reason for his imprisonment as 'this unfortunate accident', he speaks with an irony which has often been misunderstood: 'It is more profitable to punish my great treasons than that I should either strengthen the fleet or do many other things than lie in the ditches.' He asks that he 'be stayed no one hour from all the extremity that either law or precent can avow. And if that be too little, would God it were withal concluded that I might feed the lions, as I go by, to save labour.[1] For the torment of the mind cannot be greater. . . .' And throughout, there seems to be an underlying conviction that his enemies are taking the opportunity that has been offered finally to dispose of him. 'I see there is a determination to disgrace me and ruin me.' 'I am more weary of life than *they* are desirous I should perish.'

The details of the affair in connection with which Raleigh was released from the Tower are briefly these: the expedition which he was to have commanded, which he left Frobisher to lead, and which he had largely financed, scored a splendid success in the capture of the *Great Carrack*. She was described as the richest prize ever taken. But the removal of Raleigh's leadership had impaired discipline in the ships' crews. Each captain and each sailor was for himself, and the wealth of the prize vanished into thin air. Hawkins advised that the only man who could get matters under control was Raleigh, and on 16th September, when Raleigh wrote to Burghley, he had been provisionally released and was already on his way down to the west. It is a fair guess that the loss the Queen suffered, or rather, the fact that her profits were not so large as they would have been (and especially perhaps the circumstance that the comparative lack of success was directly due to her own orders that Raleigh should be imprisoned) was a contributory cause to her implacable refusal, for four years, so much as to see Raleigh. At first, though released, he regarded himself as 'the Queen's poor captive'. The same letter which gives this phrase, a letter written by Robert Cecil to his father, on 21st September, 1592, gives the impression of a chastened Raleigh 'whose heart is broken'. But his eagerness to show repentance did not extend to

[1] There had been lions kept in the Tower since medieval times. King James I once paid them a characteristic visit. For an account of them (and this visit) see Stow, *Survey of London*, 1720 ed., p. 118.

giving away financial concessions easily over his share in the profits of the expedition. The Queen seems to have treated him unfairly, and he did not hesitate to complain bitterly about this to Cecil and Burghley.

Raleigh did not, so far as is known, return into the Tower in 1592. He was not apparently taken back into custody, though he was certainly not received back into favour. In December he was at his own town house, Durham House. And one of the many paradoxes about his career as has already been mentioned is the contrast between the impression given by his correspondence in the next four years, that his career is ruined and his life hopeless, and the growing part he played in parliamentary debates, in which, in 1593, he was already conspicuous. In May, 1593, he writes, from Sherborne, 'I am tumbled down the hill by every practice.' 'I am myself here at Sherborne' he concludes, 'in my fortune's fold.' It is where his fortunes, his career, his life will be folded to rest, like a shepherd's flock.[1]

As time goes on, a more desperate note comes into his correspondence with the Cecils. He has now begun to consider the possibilities of a last overseas expedition to restore his fortune. Expeditions to the east as well as to the west were in his mind, as a letter of Lady Raleigh's shows. But another possibility was to serve with Howard who had remained his friend throughout. 'I hope I shall stand your Lordship in the place of a poor mariner or soldier. I have no other desire but to serve her Majesty. And seeing I deserve nor place nor honour nor reward, I hope it will be easily granted—if I be not condemned to the grave; no liberty nor hope left that either time or the giving of my life may recover, or be a sacrifice for, my offences. I hope your Lordship will not forget my desire, or that I am evermore your poor kinsman to serve you.' He succeeded eventually in both projects. His service with the fleet was a disappointment, and offered no real opportunity. The expedition to Guiana was a different matter. He came back with a magnificent story, even if there were few new tangible assets. But it was not till the Cadiz expedition of 1596 that he clearly felt his offence to have been expiated. And the famous account he wrote of that adventure has a new ring to it. To some extent, at least, the Queen then at last accepted his view.

[1] The phrase is an allusion to one of Raleigh's own poems, 'Like truthless dreams': see p. 170.

'I am tumbled down the hill by every practice.' One form which the attack on Raleigh took is so marked that (though this is not the place to consider in detail the many unsolved problems which it involves) it must be mentioned. It is the enquiry held at Cerne Abbas in March 1594, into atheistical practices in Dorset. The papers which have survived with the account of this enquiry contain the 'interrogations to be administered unto such as be examined in her Majesty's name by virtue of her Highness' commission for causes ecclesiastical'. Such enquiries could be held under an edict of 1591 that was directed primarily against the Jesuits. The drawing up of the 'Interrogations' however shows that this particular enquiry was directed precisely against Raleigh, the questions being highly specific in some instances. The Commissioners are to enquire of witnesses 'whom do you know or have heard to be suspected of atheism or apostasy and in what manner do you know or have heard the same, and what other notice can you give thereof?' That is general enough. But when they are told also to put the question 'whom do you know or have heard that hath blasphemously cursed God, as in saying one time (as it rained when he was hawking) if there be a God a pox on that God which sendeth such weather to mar our sport or such like . . . ? Do you know any to have said when he was dead his soul should be hanged over the top of a pole and run God run devil and fetch it that would have it or to the like effect; or that hath otherwise spoken against the being or the immortality of the soul?' the questions have been framed to catch a particular victim. The enquiry elicited a fascinating account of a conversation over dinner in which the nature of the soul had been discussed by Raleigh with some of his friends. And in the evidence there seems material for further proceedings, according to the standards of the day. No proceedings were taken, however, and in fact Raleigh is found within a month co-operating with one of the Commissioners (who were local men) in the arrest of a Jesuit. The explanation may be that Raleigh had not only enemies, but also friends, at court. His enemies could add to his disgrace. But they could not complete his ruin.

* * *

Three poems which are, by any account, among Raleigh's most important works can be connected with the imprisonment in the Tower. 'The Lie' is known in a manuscript copy at least as early as

1600. Willmott's edition of Percy's *Reliques*, 1867, quotes 'a manuscript of 1593' as being in existence. Its reference therefore in the fifth and sixth lines to impending execution—

> *Go, since I needs must die,*
> *and give the world the lie*

—must belong to this imprisonment, and not to his incarceration in the reign of James I. We have already seen allusions, in a letter written during his imprisonment to Lord Howard, to the possibility of his execution (above, p. 49). Whether he seriously anticipated such a fate, it is difficult to say. But he certainly wrote of it, and 'The Lie' is his superb act of defiance:

THE LIE

Go soul the body's guest
upon a thankless errand,
Fear not to touch the best
the truth shall be thy warrant:
Go since I needs must die,
and give the world the lie.

Say to the Court it glows
and shines like rotten wood,
Say to the Church it shows
what's good, and doth no good;
If Church and Court reply,
then give them both the lie.

Tell Potentates they live
acting by others' action,
Not loved unless they give,
not strong but by affection;
If Potentates reply
give Potentates the lie.

Tell men of high condition
that manage the estate,
Their purpose is ambition,
their practice only hate,
And if they once reply
then give them all the lie.

The Twelve Years' War and its Sequel

Tell them that brave it most,
though they beg for more by spending,
Who in their greatest cost
seek nothing but commending.
And if they make reply,
then give them all the lie.

Tell zeal it wants devotion
tell love it is but lust
Tell time it metes but motion,
tell flesh it is but dust.
And wish them not reply
for thou must give the lie.

Tell age it daily wasteth,
tell honour how it alters.
Tell beauty how she blasteth,
tell favour how it falters;
And as they shall reply,
give every one the lie.

Tell wit how much it wrangles
in tickle points of niceness,
Tell wisdom she entangles
herself in over wiseness.
And when they do reply
straight give them both the lie.

Tell Physic of her boldness,
tell skill it is prevention:
Tell charity of coldness,
tell law it is contention,
And as they do reply
so give them still the lie.

Tell fortune of her blindness,
tell nature of decay,
Tell friendship of unkindness,
tell justice of delay.
And if they will reply,
then give them all the lie.

53

> *Tell Arts they have no soundness,*
>   *but vary by esteeming,*
> *Tell schools they want profoundness*
>   *and stand too much on seeming.*
> *If Arts and schools reply,*
>   *give arts and schools the lie.*
>
> *Tell faith it's fled the City,*
>   *tell how the country erreth,*
> *Tell manhood shakes off pity,*
>   *tell virtue least preferreth;*
> *And if they do reply*
>   *spare not to give the lie.*
>
> *So when thou hast as I*
>   *commanded thee, done blabbing,*
> *although to give the lie,*
>   *deserves no less than stabbing.*
> *Stab at thee he that will,*
>   *no stab thy soul can kill.*

It is unique in that it does not even spare 'Potentates', and it shows Raleigh in a passion of reckless bitterness. The closeness of the mood to that of the Howard letter is unmistakable. The second work belonging to this phase is the long draft amounting to more than 500 lines headed *The XIth and last Book of the Ocean to Cynthia*, a draft followed by twenty lines or so of a twelfth book and preceded by two shorter sets of verses. The second of these is one of the finest things that Raleigh wrote:

> *My body in these walls captived*
> *Feels not the wounds of spiteful envy;*
> *But my thralled mind, of liberty deprived,*
> *Fast fettered in her ancient memory,*
> *Doth naught behold but sorrow's dying face;*
> *Such prison erst was so delightful*
> *As it desired no other dwelling place.*
>
> *But time's effects, and destinies despiteful,*
> *Have changèd both my keeper and my fare.*
> *Love's fire, and beauty's light, I then had store.*
> *But now close kept as captives wonted are*
> *That food, that heat, that light I find no more.*

> *Despair bolts up my doors, and I, alone,*
> *Speak to dead walls, but those hear not my moan.*

The poem is a contrast between the previous fate of his mind as Elizabeth's prisoner, prisoner to a love than which he desired nothing more; and the dead walls in which his body is now close kept. The intricacy of the construction by which in the first seven lines three captivities—his old enthralment with Elizabeth, the fetters of those memories which still bind him fast, and his bodily imprisonment—are interconnected, is strikingly effective, and the tremendous finality of the phrase 'Despair bolts up my doors' is magnificent.

The first of the two prefatory sets of verses has proved a considerable puzzle, particularly to those who have tried to date the series to some other period of Raleigh's life. It has an air of doggerel about it, which may be intentional, like the doggerel with which Spenser prefaces his cantos. But the poet's feelings have got the better of him, and what ought to have been doggerel become something more serious:

> *If Cynthia be a Queen, a princess and supreme,*
> *Keep these among the rest, or say it was a dream;*
> *For those that like expound, and those that loathe express*
> *Meanings, according as their minds are movèd more or less.*
> *For writing what thou art, or showing what thou were,*
> *Adds to the one disdain, to th' other but despair.*
> *Thy mind of neither needs, in both seeing it exceeds.*

The poet is addressing himself. If Cynthia is really Queen, and his whole love be not mere imagining, he is to keep these verses with the rest that he has written to her. Whether we like or loathe, our meanings are expressed more or less successfully, according to the power of the feelings that move us. To write what he is now or what he used to be will be to add disdain to the past, despair to the present (and, the implication seems to be, since he has written passionately, it would be devastatingly effective). His mind needs neither; in both it has more than enough. The argument (if in an utterance of this intensity we can talk of argument) seems to be that he should hoard up his verses, and remember that, if he offers them to the Queen, what he has written with such intensity and such explicit purpose will only add to the disdain he suffers and the despair he feels.

The main text of the draft is indeed written, in many passages, under the stress of extreme feelings. It is not a consecutive account of the last phases of his love for Elizabeth (of which the earlier phases would perhaps have been treated in the first ten books);[1] but rather a series of impressions, many of them intensely vivid, which, as the evidence seems to suggest, would have been broken up in any final version into short sections of irregular length. He is addressing as it were one dead—yet one whose death to him he will not accept; for she is not only lost, but found, and ever fair. She whom he has lauded in the past as a goddess, is now a stranger to him; actually bent on improving his misfortune. He is alone, friendless, forsaken; the blossom has fallen, the sap is gone from the tree. In this evening, this sad winter, he is due to pay the balance of sorrow for the joys he once had.

These themes of age, withered leaves, the sorrow-worn face, and of others enjoying the happiness which once was his, recur and the suggestion seems to be that it is the passing of youth that has lost him Cynthia's love. But he recurs also to the theme that unlike Cynthia's love, his is not of time, is eternal; and there bursts out from time to time protestations of physical passion which suggest that he is struggling to bear what is intolerable.

How much of this is genuine the reader must judge for himself.

> *'And as a man distract, with treble might*
> *Bound in strong chains, doth strive and rage in vain*
> *Till tired and breathless, he is forced to rest,*
> *Finds by contention, but increase of pain. . . .'*

We are reminded of the incident a few days before, when Raleigh, seeing the Queen's barge go by from the Tower, struggled like a madman with his guardian and cried that the procession had been planned to 'break his gall with Tantalus's torment'. We are reminded of the closing words in a letter written to Cecil possibly that same day, though the exact date is not precisely ascertainable: 'So I leave to trouble you at this time, being become like a fish cast on dry land gasping for breath, with lame legs and lamer lungs.' We are reminded of this incident, and compelled to question again how much of it, and how much of that, was genuine. And the answer is not easy. We cannot doubt that this man,

[1] But see also p. 141. He might perhaps have planned to arrange these earlier verses into books.

with his overleaping ambition, was oppressed and appalled by
events which could hardly mean anything other than the end of
his hopes and aspirations. He was conscious that he had aged since
he won Elizabeth's favour, and that her preoccupation with Essex
was due in part at least to his youth and charm. He had persuaded
himself that his feelings for Elizabeth were the feelings of love. But
it is when he writes of her that there seems to be artificiality about
what he says. When he speaks of the withering of his own life, and
the wastage that there has been already, the writing is genuine, and
individual lines and phrases have extraordinary power.

The other poem that can most reasonably be attributed to this
time is a justly famous version of the ballad 'Walsingham'.

> '*As you came from the holy land,*
>   *Of Walsingham,*
> *Met you not with my true love*
>   *By the way as you came?*
>
> *How shall I know your true love*
>   *That have met many one*
> *As I went to the holy land*
>   *That have come, that have gone?*
>
> *She is neither white nor brown*
>   *But as the heavens fair*
> *There is none hath a form so divine*
>   *In the earth or the air.*
>
> *Such an one I did meet, good sir,*
>   *Such an angelic face*
> *Who like a queen, like a nymph did appear*
>   *By her gait, by her grace.*
>
> *She hath left me here all alone*
>   *All alone as unknown*
> *Who sometimes did me lead with herself*
>   *And me loved as her own.*
>
> *What's the cause that she leaves you alone*
>   *And a new way doth take,*
> *Who loved you once as her own,*
>   *And her joy did you make?*

> *I have loved her all my youth,*
> *But now old, as you see,*
> *Love likes not the falling fruit*
> *From the withered tree.*
>
> *Know that love is a careless child*
> *And forgets promise past,*
> *He is blind, he is deaf when he list*[1]
> *And in faith never fast.*
>
> *His desire is a dureless content*
> *And a trustless joy,*
> *He is won with a world of despair*
> *And is lost with a toy.*
>
> *Of womenkind such indeed is the love*
> *Or the word love abused*
> *Under which many childish desires*
> *And conceits are excused.*
>
> *But true love is a durable fire*
> *In the mind ever burning;*
> *Never sick, never old, never dead,*
> *From itself never turning.'*

This lovely poem is of course made out of an earlier ballad, 'writ o'er' in Shakespeare's phrase. Professor C. S. Lewis has no doubt that the early stanzas of 'Walsingham' 'owe all their beauty to that model'. (It is, incidentally, another version of this ballad that Ophelia sings in *Hamlet*, Act IV, scene iii.) He may indeed be right; at present unfortunately the original is not known. But the beauty of the poem overflows from its opening into the marvellous fifth, sixth, seventh, or indeed the last, stanza; and as a technical achievement the capture of the free ballad rhythms throughout is singularly successful. The poet's loneliness in stanza 5, with its parallel in the *XIth and last Book*:

'*Alone, forsaken, friendless on the shore*'

is of course comparatively a commonplace; but the image of the 'falling fruit from the withered tree' is like the 'withered leaves left

---

[1] *list* = likes.

on the tree' or 'the blossoms fallen, the sap gone from the tree' of
Cynthia, and is much more unusual; he was going to return to it
not many years later in the Preface to the *Discoverie of Guiana*. In
both *Cynthia* and 'Walsingham' these notions of Cynthia's love as
having been lost, as her lover lost his youth, and of his love being
enduring and unchanging, but hers transient, are dominant
themes. But the difference between this and *Cynthia* is important.
Cynthia is a fierce and passionate protestation. In 'Walsingham',
partly perhaps under the inspiration of the ballad, the sadness is in
a sense accepted; not so much recollected in tranquillity as seen as
part of human experience. *Cynthia* is Raleigh writing about himself. In 'Walsingham' he is writing about something far wider and
more generalised. And thus if the descriptions of Elizabeth in
Cynthia:

> *O hopeful love, my object and invention,*
> *O true desire, the spur of my conceit,*
> *O worthiest spirit, my mind's impulsion*
> *O eyes transpersant, my affection's bait,*
> *O princely form, my fancy's adamant*

and so on; or

> *This did that Nature's wonder, Virtue's choice*
> *The only paragon of time's begetting,*
> *Divine in words, angelical in voice*

—if such passages be compared with such a stanza as this:

> *Such an one did I meet, good Sir,*
> *Such an angelic face,*
> *Who like a queen like a nymph did appear*
> *By her gait, by her grace.*

the quality of this ballad, unique in Raleigh's poetry, is apparent.
It is attributed to Raleigh on good early manuscript authority.
Professor F. P. Wilson and Miss Latham have drawn attention to
the parallels between this and other works of Raleigh, especially
Cynthia; the evidence for his authorship seems to me unanswer-
able, and I think it dates from a phase a few weeks later than
Cynthia, when its tempestuous, and at times hectic, violence has
given way to a mood that was more gentle and reflective; like

Raleigh's insistence, on his temporary release, that he was the 'Queen of England's poor prisoner'.

(iv) The Guiana Enterprise

The Guiana enterprise is relevant to our purpose in that it is a phase in Raleigh's relationships with the Queen. It was planned and carried through during a period when Elizabeth would not consent to see him, but it was nevertheless intimately concerned with those relationships. During the 1580's the Virginian enterprise had presented itself to him partly as a way to the prestige he lacked if he was ever to attain the highest position. But it had ended in failure. One settlement had struggled on for a year and then the colonists had come home. In 1587 there had been a more ambitious, but even less fortunate attempt, and nothing certain was ever heard of the fate of the hundred and fifty colonists then established there. The Guiana plans were conceived with a similar object at a time when he was in disgrace; though in Guiana the will-o'-the-wisp which he followed was rather the hope (still alive in the minds of many Spaniards also) that there were rich and unknown civilisations, such as Pizarro and Cortes had found in Peru and in Mexico, seventy years before, to be discovered. 'I hope I shall be thought worthy' Raleigh wrote to Cecil in November 1595, after his return from Guiana '. . . to govern that country which I have discovered and hope to conquer for the Queen.' And as he set out on the original voyage, he subscribed his letter to Cecil 'Even so, only gazing for a wind to carry me to my destiny'. It was his last hope.

Raleigh's moods during the months following his imprisonment, alternated (as we have already seen from his letters) between anger and resentment on the one hand, and humility and despair on the other. Late in 1592, at the time of his conditional release in the affair of the *Great Carrack* Cecil, who had been sent down to Plymouth in advance of Raleigh, wrote to his father, Lord Burghley. 'Sir Walter Raleigh' he says, 'arrived with his Keeper, Mr. Blount. I assure you, Sir, his poor servants, to the number of a hundred and forty goodly men, and all the mariners, came to him with such shouts and joy, as I never saw a man more troubled to quiet them in my life. But his heart is broken; for he is very extreme pensive longer than he is busied, in which he can toil terribly. The meeting between him and Sir John Gilbert was with tears on Sir John's part. Whensoever he is saluted with congratulations for liberty, he doth answer, No; I am still the Queen of England's poor captive. I wished him to conceal it, because here it doth diminish his credit, which I vow to you before God is greater among mariners than I thought for. I do grace him as much as I may, for I find him marvellous greedy to do anything to recover the conceit of his brutish offence.' A letter written by Raleigh himself in the following May shows him in a different mood: 'Every fool knoweth that hatred are the cinders of affection, and therefore to make me a sacrifice shall be thankworthy.' To damage him was to win favour from Essex and from the Queen. But to judge from the letters to Cecil which are frequent, it was the mood of despair that predominated: 'From this desolate place I have little matter; from myself less hope: and therefore I think the shorter the discourse, the better welcome.' Those words were written actually after his return from Guiana, when he found himself encountering, instead of the enthusiasm he had expected, the slanders of those who said he had never been to Guiana at all.

There still exists a letter written by Lady Raleigh to Cecil in February, 1593, when the Guiana plan had not yet been formulated in detail. Lady Raleigh, who had received from Cecil some token or 'tablets' with a motto inscribed in the form of an anagram or puzzle, was anxious to enlist his help in diverting her husband from his plans. He was talking at times of going to the East Indies, at times of going to Guiana. Lady Raleigh disliked both plans equally. It would be of the utmost interest if we could understand precisely her reference to the Queen, who 'will read her own destiny in a plain alphabet'; and to the breaking of faith with herself. Raleigh's faith? Presumably; but how and when? In any event, on an occasion which caused no malice between her and her husband.[1]

'I received your tablets of no less rare device than the sentence within was comfortable. If faith were broken with me, I was yet far away. But I fear that my Mistress—if all hearts were open and all desires known—might, without so great curiosity of deciphering, read her own destiny in a plain alphabet. But we are both

[1] Just possibly, perhaps, Cecil had mentioned the writing of the *XIth and last Book to Cynthia*, in the Tower (see below, p. 136). This might be represented as a breach of faith with his newly married wife. See the note especially on line 339 of that book, p. 193.

great believers,[1] and therein we flatter ourselves, and nourish our own minds with what we would. Now sir, for the rest, I hope for my sake, you will rather draw Sir Water[2] towards the East than help him forwards towards the sunset, if any respect to me, or love to him, be not forgotten. But every month hath his flower, and every season his contentment; and you great counsellors are so full of new counsels as you are steady in nothing. But we poor souls that have bought sorrow at a high price, desire, and can be pleased with, the same misfortune we hold; fearing alterations will but multiply misery. I know only your persuasions are of effect with him, and held as oracles tied to them by love. Therefore I humbly beseech you, rather stay him than further him.'

The drift is clear. Lady Raleigh is content to let things be. They are through the worst; a change now would not necessarily be for the better. But Raleigh is continually scheming, and only Cecil's advice may serve to deflect him from his purpose. Throughout the years of disgrace Cecil remained loyal (as did also Lord Howard) to Raleigh. Raleigh reckoned that he owed everything to him. 'I shall be your debtor' he wrote to Cecil just before the start of the Guiana voyage, 'and most yours of all living.'

Raleigh's own reactions to the criticism he encountered when he got back from Guiana are to be observed in the preface to the account of the voyage which he wrote for publication. He had taken infinite pains, as he was always capable of doing in any cause which interested him, to win the confidence of the native chieftains, in the belief that a permanent settlement ought to be attempted there and that the help of the chieftains or 'kings' would be invaluable in any such project. He had found a region which he describes in lyrical terms; and he had heard rumours, which thenceforward deeply infected his mind, of the wealth of the city of Manoa, and of the gilded man, 'el Dorado'. The voyage, finally achieved during the summer of 1595, to him appeared as a reconnaissance of great promise. Thus on 13th November, 1595, sending Cecil a copy of his narrative, or *Relation*, he wrote:

'Sir,

You may perceive by this *Relation* that it is no dream which I have reported of Guiana. And if one image hath been brought

---

[1] Both Lady Raleigh and also the Queen.
[2] For the wording here, see p. 82, n. 3.

from thence weighing 47 quintals—which cannot be so little worth as 100 thousand pound—I know that in Manoa there are store of these. If the *Relation* sent to the Spanish King had been also taken, you should therein have found matter of great admiration. But howsoever this action be respected, I know that the like fortune was never offered to any Christian prince. I know it will be presently followed both by the Spanish and French, and if it be foreslowed by us, I conclude that we are cursed of God.

In the meantime I humbly beseech you to move her Majesty that none be suffered to soil the enterprise; and that those kings of of the borders which are by labour, peril and charge won to her Majesty's love and obedience, be not by other pilferers lost again. I hope I shall be thought worthy to direct those actions that I have at mine own charges laboured in; and to govern that country which I have discovered and hope to conquer for the Queen without her cost. I am sending away a barque to the country to comfort and assure the people, that they despair not nor yield to any composition with other nations.

I know the plot [map] is by this time finished which if you please to command from Hariot, that her Majesty may see it. If it be thought of less importance than it deserveth, her Majesty will shortly bewail her negligence therein, and the enemy, by the addition of so much wealth, wear us out of all.

Sir, I pray esteem it as the affair requireth, if you love the Queen's honour, profit and safety. If I be thought unworthy to be employed, or that because of my disgrace all men fear to adventure with me—if it may not be otherwise—I wish some other of better sufficiency and grace might undertake it, that the Queen lose not that which she shall never find again.

You find that there are, besides gold, both diamonds and pearl. And I brought with me, taken up among the sands, a stone which being cut, is very rare. I pray you do me the favour to command Peter Vanlore to deliver you those two which I gave him to prove, which he made little account of. But I will have them cut by Pepler, who is skilful, and dwells here with A. Gilbert. I have sent you one which was cut here which I think is amethyst, and hath the strange blush of carnation. But I assure myself that there are not more diamonds in the East Indies than are to be found in Guiana; which you see also verified by the relation of the Spanish letters.

I have another, cut, of another sort, and if it be no diamond, yet it is exceeding any diamond in beauty. But these stones bear witness of better, and there is enough for all the world if we have the grace. But we must cast so many doubts; and this dolt and that gull must be satisfied, or else all is nothing. If the Spaniards had been so blockish and slothful, we had not feared now their power, who by their gold from thence vex and endanger all the estates of Kings. . . .

I rest your assured to be commanded, poor or rich

W. RALEIGH

Sherborne, this Wednesday morning, an hour after the receipt of your letter; the 13 of November.'

By this time Raleigh already knew that his own estimate of the possibilities in Guiana had not been generally accepted.[1] 'This dolt and that gull' had to be dislodged from their positions before anything else could be done. Three days before this letter was written, he had said to Cecil: 'What becomes of Guiana, I much desire to hear, whether it pass for a history or a fable?' The answer was fable. But his own faith remained unshaken, and was so to remain till 1618. And a fortnight later he was pressing Cecil for an answer as to whether he might in 1596 follow up his reconnaissance with a full-scale expedition; which if it was to take place that summer must be prepared at once. 'I beseech you let us know whether we shall be travellers or tinkers; conquerors or crones. For if the winter pass without making provision, there can be no victualling in the summer; and if it now be foreslowed, farewell Guiana for ever. Then I must determine to beg or turn away. Honour and gold and all good, for ever hopeless.

'I do not hear how you like the white stone; I have sent for one of each; and as soon as they come you shall have them.'

In the event, Raleigh was not destined to make the Guiana attempt for another twenty years. But the summer of 1596 brought him a different chance in the Cadiz expedition. He took it with both hands, and thanks to his success in it, his position was, after four years of disgrace, restored. But Guiana still stayed in his mind, reckoned by him as the most romantic of all his offerings to Cyn-

[1] It is worth noting that an appropriate date for *The Merry Wives of Windsor*, Act I, scene iii, l. 66 (Falstaff speaking about Mistress Page) 'She's a region of Guiana: all gold and bounty' would undoubtedly be the winter of 1595. The Quarto did not appear till 1602.

Raleigh the pioneer of overseas settlement; (*a*) a map prepared for
him of part of Virginia, 1589
(*b*) Raleigh in conference with a native chief in Guiana, 1595

thia. Cynthia's own reckonings were somewhat more down to earth. The white stones were not diamonds. What concerned her most—and who will say that she was wrong?—was pounds, shillings and pence. If they *had* been diamonds, her attitude would have been different. Raleigh had designed the expedition to win back the Queen's favour. From that point of view, its failure was complete.

(v) Raleigh and Essex 1592–1601

If the plans for the Guiana voyage concern us because they were the expression of Raleigh's endeavours to win back Elizabeth's favour, his varying relations with Essex are also bound up with the same story. The differences between the two men were often temporarily composed, but they were in fact rivals to the end, and at no period was their hostility more violent than in the closing months of Essex's life. It was then evident that one or other of them must go to the wall. Raleigh has often been criticised for a letter which he wrote to Cecil while the Earl was in custody, in answer to Cecil's enquiry as to how Essex should be treated. Raleigh's advice was that now Essex was down, he should be kept down.[1] It is not always remembered, as this is quoted against Raleigh, that when Essex and his followers tried to rouse the citizens of London to rebellion against the Government and the Queen, they shouted that their real enemies were Cobham and Raleigh. If the revolt had succeeded Raleigh would certainly have lost his life. He came near to losing it because of his personal success in the Islands Voyage of 1597, under Essex's command.

The steps taken by Essex against Raleigh during the first years of Raleigh's disgrace are largely a matter of conjecture. Was Essex responsible for the incident in 1594, already mentioned, when an attempt was made to use the weapon of the commission against atheism to complete Raleigh's ruin? We do not know; though we know that Raleigh had friends as well as enemies at court. It must have been Cecil who saw that the effort to discredit him was not pressed home. For the commission collected evidence which could have been used to bring a definite accusation against him. Its terms of reference are clearly drafted (as has already been seen) with a particular individual, his habits, and his way of talking, in mind,

---

[1] See below, p. 77, for the text.

and other men were drawn in only so far as they appeared to be his associates. If the ally at court was Cecil, almost as certainly the enemy was Essex. There is a curious letter written by Raleigh to Cecil late in 1594. That to which it was a reply has been lost like all Cecil's to Raleigh; Raleigh's answers alone are available. 'My carelessness' this says 'in losing the copy of the letter I cannot excuse, but it concerned nobody but myself, and therefore the less matter. But how it came into the Earl's hand, I beseech you learn by some means; that I may but know where it were lost or otherwise embezzled. . . .' Thus Raleigh's affairs were being watched continuously. His correspondence was tampered with, and a false step might have brought final disaster. But by 1594 Raleigh had already seen the impossibility of a return to the Queen's good graces if he did not conciliate the reigning favourite. Five days after writing to Cecil the words just quoted, he wrote on behalf of 'Charles who was sometime his page' to Cecil: 'I would be glad he would sue to serve the Earl of Essex, to which I have persuaded him.' And a striking feature of the documents of the next six years is Raleigh's commendations of the Earl. There is, on paper at any rate, no criticism. He accepts Essex's superior position, though occasionally it may be suspected that his commendations are consciously exaggerated.

The occasion for re-establishing his position came with the expedition to Cadiz in 1596 and the Islands Voyage in 1597. Elizabeth was already making some tentative approaches to him, through Lady Raleigh, in the spring of 1596. The evidence is provided by Lady Raleigh, writing to Cecil in March of that year. 'I thank my honourable mistress' she says—Cecil was evidently being used as the intermediary—'for wishing me near her. To do her service and to enjoy both your companies, I oft wish it with her; else is a hermit's cell most fit for me and my mind at this time, being for a time thus dissevered from him that I am.' Lady Raleigh's letters unlike her husband's or those of other Elizabethan statesmen give the impression that they are always honest. She was devoted to him, and one experience of Elizabeth's anger was enough. It was a full year after this approach was made before Raleigh himself actually returned to court, and there seems to be no evidence that his wife ever attended Elizabeth again.

Nor is there anything to show precisely how Raleigh came to be designated, with Lord Thomas Howard, as a member of the

Council of War for the 1596 expedition, of which Essex and the old Lord Howard of Effingham were in joint command. But Elizabeth was already beginning to be afraid of Essex (though her feelings for him may be fairly described still as intermittent infatuation) and this may have made it easier for Raleigh's friend, Lord Howard of Effingham, to suggest Raleigh's name to her. Howard had remainded loyal to Raleigh through the locust years, and had been at one point actually dissuaded by Raleigh from in-intervening with the Queen on his behalf on the grounds that it was useless to do so. The plan now was to attack the Spaniards in their home waters, and as Raleigh like Drake had consistently advocated this policy, to associate him with it made excellent sense, provided that he and Essex could work together. For this expedition was Essex's 'show'. 'I have racked my wit to get this commission', Essex told one of his friends: 'and my means to carry that with which to do the feat as they say. I will either go through with it, or of a general become a monk, at an hour's warning.' The young Bacon observed 'my Lord's crosses are many'. He may have been alluding to Raleigh's designation as one of the commanders.

And at the outset there were misunderstandings, Raleigh being accused of delaying the expedition for some subtle reason of his own. 'Sir Walter Raleigh's slackness and stay by the way is not thought to be upon sloth, but upon pregnant design.' In view of the eagerness which Raleigh showed in the operations at Cadiz, these accusations may be discounted. His side of the story is shown in letters to Cecil, where he speaks of the difficulty of collecting sailors. 'As fast as we press men one day, they come away another.' He was sailing from North Kent. If he had been working in his own West Country the problem might have been easier. He blamed also, probably rightly, adverse winds. On 16th April, the Lord Admiral wrote impatiently to Cecil (and a few days later in the same strain to Raleigh himself), 'I pray you hasten away Sir Walter Raleigh.' Essex was writing in the same vein. On 3rd May Raleigh wrote to Cecil 'more grieved than ever I was, in anything of this world for this cross weather'; and on the following day he appealed to the judgement of one of the old naval conservatives, William Borough: 'Sir by the living God' (he wrote to Cecil) 'there is nor King nor Queen nor general nor any else can take more care than I do to be gone. But I humbly pray you but to speak with Mr. Borough, and let him be sent for afterward, before my Lord Chamberlain, that they may hear him speak whether any man can get down with this wind or no; which will satisfy them of me.' Meanwhile Essex's impatience was growing. 'If I seem impatient', he wrote to Cecil, 'think how many things concert to move my patience. Sir Walter Raleigh with the rest of our fleet is not come, and yet he hath had (if the winds be the same as they are here) all the wished winds he could desire, both to bring him out of the river and after he was in the channel along to this place.' It is fashionable to decry Raleigh's seamanship. I doubt whether this attitude can be justified. The old professional seamen, that great leader Drake, the able but cautious Hawkins and the steady unimaginative Borough are all found in close contact with him, Hawkins, for example, making the suggestion that Raleigh is the man to deal with the problems of the *Great Carrack*, even if it means releasing him from the Tower; and it is noteworthy how in the expeditions of '96 and of '97 the commanders rely on him for an estimate of the naval situation, once the fleets have sailed.

Raleigh's own vivid account of the Cadiz action waited a hundred years for publication[1]—unlike his account of the last fight of the *Revenge* in which he had not been involved (though the *Revenge* was his ship), which was published soon after the events it described had taken place. His part in the planning of the attack, and also in its execution, was decisive. There was rivalry for the lead in the assault, but Raleigh won for himself the most dangerous position, and but for his advice when the fleet was still outside Cadiz harbour, the expedition might have failed completely. As it was the King of Spain suffered an even greater disaster to his shipping than he suffered in 1588.

Raleigh was wounded in the leg. There is no suggestion of disagreement between him and the Earl of Essex in the planning of the assault. Rather it seems that Lord Howard of Effingham made difficulties about the plan which was finally adopted—that of entering the harbour without previously attempting to take the city by sending the soldiers in, in boats, from the sea—and that Raleigh's judgement coincided with that of Essex. And Sir George Carew (Raleigh's kinsman and friend, it is true, whose views may therefore be coloured in his favour) wrote from Cadiz: 'Many words in Sir W. R's commendation would not do well from me,

[1] As it is not easily accessible, it is here reprinted (Appendix II).

wherefore I do leave him to the vulgar, saving, in a few words, I do assure your honour his service was inferior to no man's, and so much praiseworthy as those which formerly were his enemies do hold him in great estimation.' It is not surprising therefore that later in the year Essex was telling Cecil that he proposed to suggest to the Queen that Sir Walter Raleigh 'be named among others for a meeting of such persons as were experienced in martial cases. . . .' Nevertheless Essex is on record criticising his colleagues before the voyage was over. While the document[1] that contains this criticism carries neither date nor place of origin, the last sentences make it clear that it was written by Essex on the homeward voyage. It is a defence of his own dispositions and an attack on those of the Lord Admiral and Raleigh which is querulous and partial, giving the impression that he was frustrated throughout by his older colleagues. The Earl's gallantry and enthusiasm went with a jealousy of Raleigh that was never far below the surface.

Our immediate concern however is with the sense of relief, and release, that can be read in Raleigh's letter, written when the fleet was still off Cadiz:

'Sir,

This bearer, Sir Anthony Ashley, that hath seen all can better report all than any letter or discourse. The XXI of June we beheld the city of Calize (Cadiz) the fleet of the King, and that of Nova Hispania; all which we mastered the same day.

Of every man's desert, both for counsel and performance, let it be delivered with what device soever, yet I doubt not but all shall have right. I was not second to any in the fight against the galleons and galleys; wherein I was hurt, and could not be first at the taking of the town as at the rest.

There hath been good agreement between the Generals. The victory was carried with great honour and mercy. There hath been much gotten by the land commanders; although I do think little possessed by the Generals themselves. The King of Spain never so much dishonoured; neither hath he ever received so great loss.

The Earl hath behaved himself, I protest unto you by the living God, both valiantly and advisedly in the highest degree; without pride; without cruelty; and hath gotten great honour and much love of all.

[1] BM Cotton Julius F VI, fol. 280. *'The first and greatest occasion . . .'* etc.

For particulars, your Honour shall receive by others—which I had rather should so be written you, [than] by me.

I hope her most excellent Majesty will take my labours and endeavours in good part. Other riches than the hope thereof I have none; only I have received a blow[1] which now I thank God is well amended;—only a little eyesore will remain. If my life had ended withal, I had then paid some part of the great debts which I owe her. But it is but borrowed, and I shall pay it, I hope, to her Majesty's advantage, if occasion be offered.

Sir, I humbly beseech you to excuse me that I write thus briefly for the present, and that you will vouchsafe also to excuse me to my Lord your father. And I will remain evermore to be commanded by you as your servant.

W. RALEIGH

To the westward of Calize, some x leagues, the 7 of July.'

And a month later he was writing from 'the port of Plymouth, coming in, this 6th of August', 'Sir, I hope her divine Majesty is well; the report wherof hath encountered us all with infinite joy.' But alas! The financial results of the expedition were meagre. Raleigh had to wait months yet before Cynthia would receive him.

The documents already mentioned, one in which Essex criticises the conduct of his associates in the Cadiz action and one in which he suggests that Raleigh's advice on the Spanish question would be valuable, are all that we have to indicate the relationship between him and Raleigh during this winter. The state of affairs they suggest is that Raleigh's proffered armistice was not fully acceptable and that Essex's jealousy continued. From time to time Essex would 'keep his chamber' sulking like Achilles (the comparison is used during the following winter by a contemporary, but the fact was already apparent this winter); and it was said that the Queen had been heard to exclaim 'I will break him of his will, and pull down his great heart'. It was Cecil's influence which at last brought Raleigh back to court, in June 1597. 'Yesterday, my lord of Essex rode to Chatham. In his absence Sir Walter Raleigh was brought by [Cecil] to the Queen, who used him very graciously, and gave him full authority to execute his place as

[1] He was wounded in the leg; see above, p. 68.

captain of the Guard[1] which immediately he undertook and swore many men into the places void. In the evening he rode abroad with the Queen, and had private conference with her; and now he comes boldly to the Privy Chamber, as he was wont.' Unfortunately the series of Raleigh's letters now dwindles. One letter of Raleigh's, undated originally, and dated wrongly to a considerably earlier period by the secretary who eventually came to file it, must belong to this time. It cannot belong to 1590 as the filing note suggests, since it is addressed to 'Sir Robert Cecil, Knight, Principal Secretary to her Majesty [Edwards, Letter LXXXVI]. Cecil did not hold that office till 1596, as Edwards in his edition of the letters observed. This letter shows Raleigh writing, on behalf of the Queen as he used to do before his disgrace, a letter of commendation. But nothing in this or in his other letters which survive from this phase, gives any positive hint of the character of his relations with Essex.

Yet if there is doubt about the relations of Raleigh and Essex in the winter of 1596–7, the situation during the following summer shows that strange fluctuations were taking place. When Raleigh went back to court at the beginning of June, the implication seems to be that Essex absented himself in dudgeon. Only a month later, however, Essex, Cecil and Raleigh appear to be on terms of exceptional intimacy. During that spring a new expedition was being planned to follow up the success at Cadiz. On 6th July, when the preparations for the expedition were at their height, and those at court were noticing the new intimacy between the three men, Raleigh wrote to Cecil a letter which gives rise to one of the most fascinating problems of literary history.

'In this haste and confusion of business among so many wants and so great haste, I hope you will pardon me if I write little, and that confusedly. We have all written for supply. I beseech you to further it, or to look for nothing at our hands; for the time, together with the multitude of men's bodies,[2] hath such an advantage over us as we shall not be able to reach the place of our greatest hope. I acquainted the Lord General [Essex] with your letter to me, and your kind acceptance of your entertainment; he was also wonderful merry at your conceit of *Richard the Second*. I hope it

[1] It had been exercised by deputy in the intervening years, August, 1592–May, 1597.
[2] He means that the size of the force makes provisioning slow.

shall never alter, and wherof I shall be most glad of, as the true way to all our good, quiet, and advancement, and most of all for Her sake whose affairs shall thereby find better progression. Sir, I will ever be yours; it is all I can say, and I will perform it with my life and with my fortune.

Weymouth, the 6 of July.   W. RALEIGH.'

Raleigh and Essex have been entertaining Cecil, and out of the entertainment some idea, or jest, has arisen associated with *Richard the Second*. The point becomes one of first-class interest when it is remembered that at the examination of Essex after the rebellion, the Government brought up against him the fact that someone had arranged for *Richard II* to be performed on the evening before the rebellion broke out. Shakespeare's play had been printed during these years, 1597–8, in at least three editions, one dated 1597, two dated 1598. From all these editions the famous abdication scene was omitted. That was first printed in 1608 when the play appears, as advertised on one of the variant title-pages, 'with new additions of the Parliament scene and the deposing of Richard II'. Queen Elizabeth was sensitive about this deposition scene for reasons that can be imagined, and it was in deference to her that the scene was omitted from the earlier printed versions, not because it was not acted. Thus the acting of this scene on the eve of the rebellion's outbreak was a serious count in the charge against Essex later. Was Shakespeare's play the entertainment which the three men saw together early in July, 1597; and what was Cecil's idea about it which caused the Earl so much pleasure? We do not know. But it looks as if they were involved in a plan which boded no good for Elizabeth. The second half of the letter gives no real clue, since it was vitally important to any letter-writer at this time to avoid any remark on paper that might be held against him. The three men may have discussed the possibility of the Queen's abdication as the best solution for her as well as for everyone else. It was some time later than this meeting, when Essex was in Ireland, that Shakespeare mentioned his absence in a prologue written to Act V of *Henry V*:

> *Were now the general of our gracious empress—*
> *As in good time he may—from Ireland coming,*
> *Bringing rebellion broachèd on his sword,*
> *How many would the peaceful city quit*
> *To welcome him!*

We shall consider later the evidence for another connection between the Earl and Shakespeare. But in Raleigh's letter of 1597, no such connection is necessarily implied, though arguments that the item referred to was not Shakespeare's play are hardly credible in view of the later connection with Essex.

But Raleigh and Essex were at odds again not long after this entertainment, though Raleigh was emphasising in public at least, his admiration for the General. An incident early in the Islands Voyage illustrates this. The fleet was driven back by storms—'that gale' which as Donne described it 'like shot, not fear'd till felt' assailed them. Essex having ventured further than Raleigh, recovered the English coast some days later than he. The reception of a letter from Raleigh with assurance of the Earl's safety is thus reported back to Essex by Howard who remained at court:

'I protest before God I never did see creature receive more comfort than she [the Queen] did when she saw by Sir W. Raleigh's letter that your person was safe. She showed the dear love that she beareth for you, for with joy the water came plentiful out of her eyes.'

Raleigh had insisted on taking the Earl into his own ship when he returned. While the storm was still raging he had written to Cecil 'I beseech you to work from her Majesty some comfort to my Lord General who I know is dismayed by these mischances, even to death; although there could not be more done by any man upon the earth, God having turned the heavens with that fury against us. . . .' Six days later he was reassuring: 'My Lord General is my guest in the Wastspight'. . . . 'And now her Majesty may be sure his Lordship shall sleep somewhat the sounder, though he fare the worse by being with me; for I am an excellent watchman at sea. We only attend the wind; having repaired as much as we can our bruises.' It is almost as much as to say to the Queen (for the letter is obviously intended for her eyes) 'Your favourite is safe. I am looking after him!'

The detail of the voyage must again be omitted. Some of it has been immortalised by Donne in his two verse letters, 'The Storm' and 'The Calm', for he was with Essex, in his service. The squadrons, their movements hampered by the weather, became separated. At an early stage Essex's associates (including the Earl of Southampton, Henry Wriothesley, to whom in 1593 *Venus and Adonis* had been dedicated and in 1594 *Lucrece* and who was now in command of the *Garland*) tried to kindle the Earl's suspicions against Raleigh. These suspicions burst into flame after Raleigh's assault on Fayal, an assault undertaken without Essex's help or authority, after Raleigh had waited some time in vain for him to arrive. It was successful. But Sir Gilly Merrick (who was later to be associated with the treasonable production of *Richard II*), and others, Southampton probably being among the party actually in Essex's cabin, represented that Raleigh's action was a breach of faith that ought to be punished with death; and, says Gorges 'if my Lord who by nature was timorous and flexible had not feared how it would be taken in England, I think Sir Walter had smarted for it'. Throughout his narrative Gorges takes the view that Gilly Merrick, with Blunt at his side 'and others', was the evil genius of the weak Essex. When Raleigh entered Essex's cabin, on Essex's arrival at Fayal, 'after a faint welcome, the General began to challenge him with a breach of the order of articles. To whom the Rear Admiral answered that he knew not of any such breach. My Lord replied that there was an article that none should land any troops without the General's presence or his order.' Raleigh's defence was a clause in the articles which Essex had omitted to quote, that such a landing should not take place without directions from the General *or some other principal commander*, upon pain of death. Raleigh was himself a principal commander, and his defence was unassailable. His crime had been to achieve the one notable success in this ill-fated expedition. The difference between the two men was patched up by Lord Thomas Howard. It is true that on 30th October, Raleigh wrote from Plymouth, reporting information received from the continent: 'This captain reported unto us of his own voluntary that the Earl our General hath as much fame and reputation in Spain and Italy as ever, and more than any of our nation had.' It is true also that early next year Cecil, Essex and Raleigh were sometimes seen together in the same sort of intimate conference that had been remarked in July, 1596. But the Islands Voyage perhaps marks the parting of the ways. Thereafter Raleigh knew that England was not large enough for both of them. There were intervals of truce, but the war was to the death.

With its final phases we cannot concern ourselves in detail, but because of the date on the title-page of *Love's Labour's Lost* which we shall examine later, it is important to know what was happening in the late autumn of 1597. The answer is that there was still in progress that strange lovers' war between the Queen and Essex, in which she alternated between a furious determination to humiliate him, and a passionate desire for reconciliation. Her love of 'scenes' became at this period in her life almost pathological, while he found it increasingly difficult to curb his tongue when she crossed him.

In spite of this infatuation and the scenes it brought with it, it is impossible to withhold sympathy for the Queen. 'Mr. Speaker,' she was to reply, in her speech to her last Parliament, 'we perceive your coming is to present thanks unto us; know I accept them with no less joy than your loves can have desire to offer such a present—and do more esteem it than any treasure or riches; for those we know how to prize; but loyalty, love, and thanks, I account them invaluable. And though God hath raised me high, yet this I account the glory of my crown, that I have reigned with your loves.' She had indeed, from the day of her succession to the throne, been in love with her people and they with her. For many years her charm had enchanted them, as it enchanted also the members of her court; and in the last resort she had resisted the powerful attraction which she had felt towards individual admirers and towards Leicester in particular, for fear perhaps that the wider spell would be broken. The love between her and her people was the deepest emotion of her life. As she grew old, she feared that the bond was weakening. She was alone, and friendless. To name her successor would have been to invite defection and treachery. Many would have turned to worship the rising star, as some of those whom she most trusted, in the end actually did. Her infatuation for Essex was a desperate attempt to re-establish the personal ascendancy which had earlier come to her so easily. Late in the year 1597, she made Charles Howard, the Lord High Admiral, Earl of Nottingham. This gave him precedence over Essex, which was no doubt its main purpose. No doubt also the Queen anticipated that Essex would take it hardly, and that there would be yet another scene followed by a reconciliation. Essex adopted his technique of retiring like Achilles to his tent; he withdrew from the court, said he was indisposed, and said that he had a violent throbbing in the temples when exposed either to cold or to long speeches. He indicated however that he would come back again 'if her Majesty should be pleased to command his services'. Her reply was that his place and duty were sufficient to command him. There was however a long negotiation, in which Raleigh took some part—particularly in that branch of the negotiations which concerned his friend Howard—the result of which was to restore Essex's precedence, and about Christmas he returned to court. On 7th December Essex was still 'a prey to melancholy'. By 22nd December the negotiations with Cecil which were to give him the Earl Marshal's office with the precedence he desired were far advanced; and they were certainly completed before the end of the year. Raleigh was certainly in London in January, 1598, since there is a letter from him written in Durham House on 16th January. The possibility that Essex's reconciliation with the Queen was celebrated by a fresh performance of *Love's Labour's Lost* (modified from an earlier version) at Essex House before Twelfth Night cannot be ruled out. The reconciliation had certainly taken place. But the part Raleigh had played in smoothing the way (even though that does not seem to have brought him directly in contact with Essex again) perhaps makes it unlikely.

But as with Raleigh's relations with Essex, so with the Queen also, the decisive moment was now past. It was inevitable that after more of the same manoeuvres—Essex in the Queen's black books in September, 1598, a return to the court and reconciliation by mid-October—the day would come when Essex said words which he could not recall. He took the commission in Ireland, failed, returned in disgrace, and at some point told her that 'her conditions were as crooked as her carcase'. This, as Raleigh observes, writing many years later, was what sealed his fate. He became convinced that the only hope for him lay in a successful *coup d'état*. The rising took place. Essex rode through the City of London appealing for support. But he got none and the attempt collapsed. Elizabeth may have been longing for yet another scene and yet another reconciliation in spite of it. But she could not bring herself to take the initiative and so give him the victory; and he went to the block.

Raleigh's enemies said that he sat smoking his pipe watching the execution of his rival. This may or may not be slander. It was asserted, and was hotly denied. What we have got, however, is the letter he wrote to Cecil during the Earl's arrest. It is undated, and the date put on it when it was filed by a secretary some time later, '1601', is probably not right. It is more likely to have been written some time in the summer of 1600.

'Sir,

I am not wise enough to give you advice; but if you take it for good council to relent towards this tyrant, you will repent it when it shall be too late. His malice is fixed, and will not evaporate by any your mild courses. For he will ascribe the alteration to her Majesty's pusillanimity and not to your good nature; knowing that you work but upon her humour, and not out of any love towards him. The less you make him, the less he shall be able to harm you and yours. And if her Majesty's favour fail him, he will again decline to a common person.

For after revenges, fear them not; for your own father that was esteemed to be the contriver of Norfolk's ruin, yet his son followeth your father's son, and loveth him. Humours of men succeed[1] not; but grow by occasions and accidents of time and power. Somerset made no revenge on the Duke of Northumberland's heirs. Northumberland that now is thinks not of Hatton's issue. Kelloway lives, that murdered the brother of Horsey; and Horsey let him go by, all his lifetime.

I could name you a thousand of those; and therefore afterfears are but prophecies—or rather conjectures—from causes remote. Look to the present, and you do wisely. His son shall be the youngest Earl of England but one; and if his father be now kept down, Will Cecil shall be able to keep as many men at his heels, and more too. He may also match in a better house than his; and so that fear is not worth the fearing. But if the father continue, he will be able to break the branches and pull up the tree; root and all. Lose not your advantage; if you do, I rede your destiny.

Yours to the end

W.R.

Let the Q. hold Bothwell while she hath him. He will ever be the canker of her estate and safety. Princes are lost by security, and preserved by prevention. I have seen the last of her good days, and all ours, after his liberty.'

*   *   *

If we enquire what form Raleigh's poetry took during the period which followed his release from the Tower, the short

---

[1] i.e. do not pass into the next generation.

answer seems to be that it dried up at the source. Its prime object had always been the Queen, and he could no longer hope to reach her with it. The charming poem (No. XIX in Miss Latham's edition) addressed 'to his Love when he had obtained her';

> *Now Serena be not coy;*
> *Since we freely may enjoy*
> *Sweet embraces; such delights*
> *As will shorten tedious nights*

may indeed have been addressed to his wife at this time, but a more likely date would seem to be between their marriage and its discovery. 'Nature that washed her hands in milk' (No. XX in Miss Latham's edition) has a deeper undertone, and one line seems at first to be a reminiscence of 'The Lie', but might be a chance anticipation of it:

> *But Time which nature doth despise*
> *And rudely gives her love the lie,*
> *Makes hope a fool, and sorrow wise,*
> *His hands doth neither wash nor dry,*
> *But being made of steel and rust*
> *Turns snow, and silk, and milk to dust.*
>
> *The Light, the Belly, lips and breath*
> *He dims, discolours and destroys,*
> *With those he feeds, but fills not, death,*
> *Which sometimes were the food of joys;*
> *Yea Time doth dull each lively wit,*
> *And dries all wantonness with it.*
>
> *O cruel Time which takes in trust*
> *Our youth, our Joys and all we have,*
> *And pays us but with age and dust*
> *Who in the dark and silent grave*
> *When we have wandered all our ways*
> *Shuts up the story of our days.*

This is more difficult to date, but perhaps for it also a date before Raleigh's imprisonment—not far distant from the Answer to Marlowe—is more plausible than one after it. And if this is so, we are left with virtually nothing for the Sherborne period and the last decade of Elizabeth's reign. Raleigh had always been reluctant to see his poems in print, if we are to believe what Puttenham said in 1589 and Spenser in 1591. But the *Arte of English Poesie* had attributed certain lines to him by name. When we find some of his poems printed in an anthology in 1600, and a cancel slip pasted down over his initials 'SWR' it looks as if he was taking steps to eliminate the very idea of his having been a writer of poetry; and the Library list that survives from his second imprisonment in King James I's reign contains not a single entry of English poetry[1]— not even the *Faerie Queene*. 'Give me my scallop shell of quiet' was written under threat of immediate execution, from which he was reprieved at the last moment (when the first of James I's supposed three victims was already on the scaffold); when Raleigh thought that

> *Blood must be my body's balmer*
> *No other balm will there be given . . .*

and ended with his

> *eternal plea*
> *To him that made heaven, earth, and sea*
> *Seeing my flesh must die so soon*
> *And want a head to dine next noon,*
> *Just at the stroke when my veins start and spread,*
> *Set on my soul an everlasting head.*
> *Then I am ready like a palmer fit*
> *To tread those blest paths which before I writ.*

Like all Raleigh's poems, this was written for an occasion, and this was the kind of occasion that he found irresistible, and to which he rose with superb poise and humour. There are indeed other poems, written during the later years. Most of them demonstrably were written after 1603. None can be shown to belong to the period 1593–1603. It seems that for some reason, conceivably the mockery of his opponents, his Muse was for these years almost silent.

Almost; but in spite of the indications that Raleigh wrote no verse during the years 1591–1603, having turned his back on such

[1] I say English, because there are two separate Petrarch entries in the list: *Petrarch de remedio fortunae* and *Opera Petrarchae*. I hope to publish the list shortly.

things, I am inclined to regard a date about 1599 or 1600 as the most probable for 'the poem in the notebook' which clearly belongs to the *Cynthia* series, and may be read as a sort of epilogue to it. Raleigh was to recall it later, in the Tower, and inscribe it among the working notes for his *History of the World*. One of its lines is so closely similar to the line of an earlier poem quoted in the *XIth Book to Cynthia* that there is an argument for its having been that very poem, and written in the eighties. But the poem was put to music, and was included in a set of part songs,[1] many of which belong to the latter part of Elizabeth's reign, being addressed to her as 'Oriana' and published as *The Triumphs of Oriana* in 1601. Raleigh's was not included in the printed series, for he was avoiding publication for his verse. But it was clearly written for some sort of entertainment presented to Elizabeth perhaps at the same time as the Oriana songs were first sung in her honour; since it begins with the line: 'Now we have present made To Cynthia....' He returned, in it, to the old themes—Elizabeth's mind as the eternal binding-force of the universe, the 'vestal fire that burns, but never wasteth', and so on; but the third stanza speaks, if the reader looks between the lines, as if to an ageing Elizabeth:

> She as the valley of Peru
> Whose summer ever lasteth
> Time conquering, all she mastreth
> By being always new.

It is as if he had been bidden to write once again for Cynthia, and this set of verses, in a strange metre, with their curiously tentative ending, was the result. For what kept his attention at this time was his splendid prose works, the *Discoverie of Guiana*, his account of the Cadiz expedition, and others which have been lost. Prose was now, he seems to have decided, to be his medium. The poetic spell was broken. The words of Mercury were harsh after the songs of Apollo. But they were more suited to a counsellor and Man of War. And it was in these roles that he now saw himself.

[1] For details and a fuller discussion see below, pp. 206–7.

III

Raleigh and Spenser

The earliest mention of Raleigh's poetry occurs in 1589, in *The Arte of English Poesie*. After naming Raleigh with Sir Philip Sidney, in a list of gentlemen who have written excellently well and whose merits would appear if only their poetry could 'be found out and made public', the author (probably as we have seen George Puttenham) speaks of Raleigh with commendation. 'For ditty and amorous Ode', he writes, 'I find Sir Walter Raleigh's most lofty, insolent and passionate.' He quotes three passages from Raleigh's poems as examples of particular figures of speech. The poem from which two come has only recently been discovered, but the third was published anonymously, in an anthology called *The Phoenix Nest* which appeared in 1593. It had already been written, as Puttenham's allusion shows, by 1589.

In another mention occurring in a manuscript note made somewhat later by Spenser's friend Gabriel Harvey, Raleigh's name is linked with that of Sir Edward Dyer. 'His Amaryllis, and Sir Walter Raleigh's Cynthia, how fine and sweet inventions.' But the most important early documentation of Raleigh's poems comes from the poet Spenser himself, from his poem *Colin Clout's come home Again*, which when it was published was prefaced by a letter to Raleigh; and from the *Faerie Queene*, also prefaced by a letter to Raleigh. This preface (covering only the first three books of the *Faerie Queene*; the next three did not appear till 1596) is dated 23rd January, 1589 (i.e. January, 1590, new reckoning). The date of the allusion in *Colin Clout* is more difficult to determine. It was not printed till 1595. But the prefatory letter is dated, from Spenser's estate in Ireland, 27th December, 1591. The poem contains allusions to well-known figures under fictitious names, as was Spenser's practice, and one such allusion belongs to the period between 1591 and 1595—to a date therefore subsequent to that of the prefatory letter. The explanation widely accepted is that when Spenser prepared his poem for publication, he retouched it in places and the later allusion is one instance of this revision.

It is reasonable therefore to accept the date December, 1591, as that when the first version of *Colin Clout* was originally sent to Raleigh.

Colin Clout's come home Again is set in a framework of narrative, and describes a visit made by the poet, Colin Clout, who is Spenser himself, to London, under the auspices of Raleigh. The dramatic setting of the first lines is a gathering of shepherds in Ireland, who ask Colin to tell them what happened to him during his recent absence. He describes how one day as he sat piping a 'strange shepherd' found him out:

> '*Whom when I askèd from what place he came,*
> *And how he hight,[1] himself he did ycleep[2]*
> *The Shepherd of the Ocean by name[3]*
> *And said he came far from the main-sea deep.*
> *He, sitting me beside in that same shade,*
> *Provokèd me to play some pleasant fit;[4]*
> *And when he heard the music which I made,*
> *He found himself full greatly pleas'd at it:*
> *Yet aemuling[5] my pipe, he took in hond[6]*
> *My pipe, before that aemulèd of many,*
> *And played thereon; (for well that skill he cond;)[7]*
> *Himself as skilful in that art as any.*
> *He pip'd, I sung; and, when he sung, I pipèd;*
> *By change of turns, each making other merry;*

---

[1] *hight* = was called.   [2] *ycleep* = name.

[3] It has always been clear that the Shepherd of the Ocean in *Colin Clout* is Raleigh, and since the discovery, three-quarters of a century ago, of the long fragment of *Cynthia*, in the library at Hatfield in Raleigh's autograph, we have Raleigh's own assertion of the name—the books *of the Ocean to Cynthia*—in his own hand: see below, p. 133 seq. Elizabeth's pronunciation of his name as 'Water' may be an allusion to this 'Ocean'; certainly in the exchange between Elizabeth and Hatton the name and the element were both in her mind: see above, p. 26. And, though it might only be another example of Lady Raleigh's unorthodox spellings, she calls her husband 'Watar' in a letter about him to Cecil: see the quotation from it on p. 62. For what the observation is worth, this spelling *Watar* is unique in her letters, in this passage only. Her normal spelling is *Wattar*. Her secretary writes *Walter*, a form which she also is once recorded as using, in a letter I have been unable to check with the original, written after his death.

[4] *fit* = a musical piece.   [5] *aemule* = to rival, emulate.
[6] *hond* = hand.   [7] *cond* = knew.

> *Neither envying other, nor envièd,*
> *So pipèd we, until we both were weary.'*

The shepherds then ask what was the theme of Colin's own song, which he proceeds to describe. They ask further what did the other shepherd sing: what, in other words, was the character of Raleigh's poetry:

> '*That shall I eke[1] (quoth he) to you declare:*
> *His song was all a lamentable lay*
> *Of great unkindness and of usage hard*
> *Of Cynthia, the Lady of the Sea,*
> *Which from her presence faultless him debar'd.*
> *And ever and anon, with singults[2] rife*
> *He cryèd out to make his undersong;*
> "*Ah my love's Queen, and goddess of my life,*
> *Who shall me pity when thou doest me wrong?*"
>
> *Then gan[3] a gentle bonny lass to speak*
> *That Marin hight: "Right well he sure did plain[4]*
> *That could great Cynthia's sore displeasure break,*
> *And move to take him to her grace again. . . ."* '

Colin goes on to say how the Shepherd of the Ocean persuaded him to go to England, and he tells of the terrors of the journey. The Shepherd of the Ocean describes to him on the way the herds of Cynthia, with their chief shepherd, Triton, and others; and (the Shepherd of the Ocean continues):

> *. . . I among the rest, of many least,*
> *Have in the Ocean charge to me assigned;*
> *Where I will live or die at her beheast,*
> *And serve and honour her with faithful mind.*

At last they come to the Court where Colin enumerates the poets, among whom Raleigh is once again mentioned:

> *And there that Shepherd of the Ocean is*
> *That spends his wit in Love's consuming smart:*
> *Full sweetly tempered is that muse of his*
> *That can enpierce a Princess' mighty heart.*

[1] *eke* = also. [2] *singults* = sighs.
[3] *gan* = began. [4] *plain* = complain, lament.

Here there is a second mention already in this one poem, of Raleigh's verses addressed to the Queen. The maids of the Court are then described, not long after which the other side of the Court's life is also discussed:

> *that same place*
> *Where each one seeks with malice and with strife*
> *To thrust down other into foul disgrace*
> *Himself to raise.*

From this the theme passes to the praise of Love and Beauty and of Colin's own Rosalind, and so moves to its close.

Raleigh's visit to Ireland, where he met Spenser, is one of which we have already heard (above, pp. 36-8). *Colin Clout* shows that, when it happened in 1589, Raleigh was already composing his poem or poems to Cynthia, his theme being that of the rejected lover. He had, though 'faultless', been debarred from Cynthia's presence. The implication seems to be that Cynthia was moved by his appeal to let him return, and that thus with Spenser he came to make the journey back to London.

It was during this stay in London that the first three books of the *Faerie Queene* were published, and they throw further light on the *Cynthia* poems. The close relationship between Spenser and Raleigh is shown by the addressing of the introductory letter 'expounding the author's whole intention in the course of this work' to Raleigh. Moreover, Raleigh's is the first of the commendatory sonnets addressed to the author, a splendid piece, often and rightly praised:

> '*Methought I saw the grave where Laura[1] lay*
> *Within that temple where the vestal flame*
> *Was wont to burn; and passing by that way*
> *To see that buried dust of living fame,*
> *Whose tomb fair love, and fairer virtue kept,*
> *All suddenly I saw the Fairy Queen:*
> *At whose approach the soul of Petrarch wept*
> *And from thenceforth those graces were not seen;*
> *For they this Queen attended, in whose stead*
> *Oblivion laid him down on Laura's hearse.*
> *Hereat the hardest stones were seen to bleed*

[1] *sc.* Petrarch's 'Laura'.

84

> *And groans of buried ghosts the heavens did pierce:*
> *Where Homer's spright did tremble all for grief*
> *And cursed the access of that celestial thief.'*

This is followed by 'Another of the same', a curious sing-song in the manner of one of Raleigh's earlier poems. In the complimentary sonnets, addressed by Spenser to 'various noblemen etc', that to Raleigh comes eighth. It is important for our purpose. In it Spenser returns the compliment to Raleigh:

> *To thee, that art the summer's nightingale*
> *Thy sovereign Goddesses most dear delight*
> *Why do I send this rustic madrigal*

and we hear moreover of

> *the streams, that like a golden shower*
> *Flow from they fruitful head of thy love's praise.*

We hear too of a theme which has already presented itself to us in Puttenham's complaint about the work which would be so good if only it could be found out and made public:

> *Yet till that thou thy Poem wilt make known*
> *Let thy fair Cynthia's praises be thus rudely shown.*

The passages mentioned complete the allusions to Raleigh in the introductory matter of the *Faerie Queene*. But when, in Book III, the poet comes to handle 'the legend of Britomartis, or of Chastity', there is an invocation to Elizabeth, in which, once again, Raleigh's poetry is praised:

> *But if in living colours and right hue*
> *Thyself[1] thou covet to see picturèd,*
> *Who can it do more lively, or more true,*
> *Than that sweet verse, with Nectar sprinkelèd,*
> *In which a gracious servant picturèd*
> *His Cynthia, his heaven's fairest light?*

Thus we have from publications of the years 1589, 1590, and 1591 a coherent picture. Raleigh has been writing a poem, or poems addressed to Elizabeth, under the name of Cynthia. Some of this verse was the lover's complaint for his lady's harshness.

---

[1] Spenser is addressing the Queen.

Other was descriptive of her charms. We are given no indication
however of continuity. Nothing in the nature of an epic seems to
be suggested; and when Gabriel Harvey writes of Sir Edward
Dyer's 'Amaryllis' and Raleigh's 'Cynthia' in one breath, as fine
and sweet inventions, it is fairly clear that he is simply using the
name to which the poets' lyrics are addressed as one might talk of
Catullus's 'Lesbia'. Taking the allusions in conjunction, they seem
to fit the picture already outlined of a phase during which Raleigh
was in some sort of disgrace, and, whether faultless or not, debarred or virtually banished from Elizabeth's presence; and a
phase when he was restored to favour, at least to some limited extent. 'So' wrote Spenser in his letter of 23rd January, 1590, 'crav-
ing the continuance of your happiness, I humbly take my leave.'
The first three books had been intended to play their part in the
re-establishment of that happiness. It seems that in some degree
they, or time or (if we are to believe Spenser) Raleigh's own
poetry, healed at least temporarily the breach between Raleigh and
the Queen. If we seek to find out more, from Spenser, than this,
it means embarking on the hazardous seas of interpreting the
veiled allusions which the books themselves contain. But other
evidence is so scanty that if anything can be gained from that risk,
it is worth taking.

*   *   *

Though the interpretation of Spenser's personal allusions is
hazardous, unless the reader is aware of them, he is missing one of
the calculated effects of the *Faerie Queene*, while in *Colin Clout* the
personal allusions are an equally large element in the poet's intentions. The list of the poets of Elizabeth's court in *Colin Clout* with
the characterisation of each of them is intended to be understood,
just as much as is the identity of the Shepherd of the Ocean. In expounding the intention of the *Faerie Queene* in the prefatory letter
published with it Spenser points out that the poem is written on
several levels. It is an allegory of the virtues. Sir Guyon is the virtue of Temperance. So 'in that Faery Queen I mean glory in my
general intention, but in my particular, I conceive the most excellent and glorious person of our Sovereign the Queen, and her
Kingdom in Fairy Land. And yet', he continues, 'in some places
else, I do otherwise shadow her.' This is important. A single
character in the poem does not always 'shadow' one individual,

and Queen Elizabeth turns up for instance in Belphoebe ('fashion-
ing her name' says Spenser to Raleigh, 'according to your excellent conceit of Cynthia, Phoebe and Cynthia being both names of
Diana') and also in Mercilla, to mention only two of her guises;
and the reader who is unaware of the allusion misses something
which the poet intended him to catch. Harvey, in his introductory
verses, talks of

> *that fair Island's right*
> *Which thou dost veil in type of Faery Land,*
> *Eliza's blessed field, that Albion hight.*[1]

while in Spenser's own complimentary sonnets, he draws attention
(when addressing Lord Howard of Effingham, Elizabeth's supreme commander in the Armada campaign,) to an allusion, otherwise not altogether obvious, to his great victory, and in another
sonnet he proclaims his plan to celebrate Essex in some later book;
in yet another he indicates an allusion in the *Faerie Queene* to the
Earl of Oxford's ancestry and upbringing. So also, in the introduction to Book II the poet says that he is enfolding the Queen's
glory 'in covert veil', and wrapping it 'in shadows'. But they are
'shadows light', and if the reader inquires more of Fairy Land

> *By certain signs, here set in sundry place*
> *He may it find.*

This is no matter of a Shakespearian cryptogram, designed for
the literary detective, but is part of the excitement and delight of
the original reader. And the Raleigh allusions have a special importance. To Raleigh the introductory letter of the poem is addressed. Raleigh himself writes two of the sets of commendatory
verses, and those verses are given pride of place. A complimentary
sonnet is addressed to him, and if it no longer takes pride of place,
this is for the excellent reason that Raleigh was not a nobleman as
were so many of the others similarly honoured, and his comparatively humble birth is an important feature of the treatment of his
story in the poem. Nor is this complimentary sonnet the last formal
allusion to Raleigh, whose 'Cynthia' is again praised in the fourth
of the introductory stanzas to Book III, the book in which, as will
be seen, the Raleigh allusions play a major part. The *Faerie Queene*
is, in one aspect, an enormous piece of flattery of Elizabeth. It has

---

[1] *hight* = called.

also a serious didactic purpose in its treatment of the courtly virtues. It is a work, for those who get to know it, of singular charm, and as such it had great vogue in its own day. It is also a work of extensive and interesting allusions to contemporary events, and in some instances (as in the execution of Mary Queen of Scots) of weighty comment on them.

These allusions, apart from the devastating glances at Mary Queen of Scots under the character of the witch Duessa (allusions which called forth a protest from the future James I in 1596) are generally designed to flatter or to please. But those to Raleigh, in the character of Timias, seem to have a wider purpose: that of assisting in the process of reconciliation between Raleigh and the Queen. This may have seemed feasible when the first three books were published in 1590, but it must have looked a more uphill job when the next instalment appeared in 1596. And the elusive nature of the method is to be observed (for instance) in the fact that at one moment we leave Timias embracing Amoret, in circumstances which we have every reason to connect with an important incident in Raleigh's life, and not so long afterwards he is found in company with Serena, who in real life was undoubtedly the same lady. So we shall not be able to assume that everything that happens to Timias is a precise allegory of, or even an allusion to, incidents in Raleigh's life. All that can be done is to examine what Spenser says in the light of what we already know of Raleigh's life, and consider how far the one may throw light on the other.

*   *   *

The principles involved are so important to our argument that it may be profitable to examine them in more detail by way of example in the allusions to Mary Queen of Scots as the witch Duessa. A change of standpoint takes place between 1590, when the first three books were published, and 1596 when the later books appeared. In the first books she is heaped with abuse, the description of Duessa, stripped of her fineries, at the end of the Canto VIII of Book I being thoroughly horrible. In her trial in Book V, however, so many advocates rise to plead for her that Arthur is strongly swayed in her favour. The intention of the latter passage as a whole is to praise the mercy of Elizabeth, and to emphasise the deep reluctance—the 'more than needful natural remorse' with which Elizabeth regarded the policy of Mary's execution. For this to be effective, the victim has to be a human being, not the filthy hag, clothed in a borrowed beauty, of Book I.

But while many of the references to Duessa in Book I are a mere travesty, there are also precise allusions to Mary in that character. Thus we are reminded of her betrothal, 'in the first flower of my freshest age'—she was actually five years old—to the Dauphin 'the only heir of a most mighty king, most rich and sage'. In the various and indiscriminate bestowal of her favours we are reminded of Mary's lovers, and, though it is not easy to say which is which, that unattractive but robust giant Orgoglio who is credited with one of the most rapid conquests, carries an allusion to Bothwell. The coarse, uncouth giant is in fact for a moment Duessa's Bothwell; but for the story's sake, his rival has not to be killed but to survive, and indeed (being the Knight of Holiness who has at this juncture been led badly astray), the rival in the poem bears no relation to Darnley—however highly we might rate the character of that unfortunate and foolish young man. The leading astray of the Knight of Holiness is in itself an allusion to the position Mary inevitably occupied vis-à-vis the reformed English church which she 'plotted' to lead back to Catholicism, and Duessa's claim to the allegiance of this same Redcross Knight at the moment of his betrothal to Una, in Canto XII, with the allegation that he has already been affianced to her, is a reference to Mary's claim to the English throne. The Catholic view that Elizabeth was illegitimate once being accepted, that claim was powerful. On the other hand, when Duessa rescues Sansjoy from the Redcross Knight in a mist of darkness, and goes to beg Night to save him, the story has taken control; it carries here no allegorical meaning beyond that of the association of Mary with the powers of darkness. These allusions were not incomprehensible to the original reader, nor did the poet intend that they should be so.

*   *   *

The 'certain signs here set in sundry place' are not far to seek, when in Book III the first major allusion in the text to Raleigh is made. The introductory stanzas to Book III, with their mention of the verses written by the 'gracious servant' picturing his 'Cynthia', give a first hint that this book may contain matter relating to Raleigh. And when in Canto V, we hear the story of the Squire Timias, we are left in no doubt. For Belphoebe has already been explained in the introductory letter to Raleigh as Elizabeth, his Cynthia; and when Timias is grievously wounded, and Belphoebe appears to minister to him so that when he opens his eyes, he is struck by that

> *unwary dart which did rebound*
> *From her fair eyes and gracious countenance*

and falls despairingly in love with her, the intention is inescapable. Raleigh was not, indeed, the only Elizabethan to be so enthralled. But so that there may be no mistake, an obvious clue is given at an early stage of the incident. When Belphoebe finds the sorely wounded squire, she withdraws into the woods to seek for the right herbs for his treatment.

> *There, whether it divine Tobacco were*
> *Or Panachaea, or Polygony,*
> *She found, and brought it to her patient dear. . . .*

Raleigh's special association with tobacco was a byword. It was a novelty brought back from his Virginia. The squire in this version languishes without revealing his love for Belphoebe (unlike Raleigh who had addressed love poems to the Queen), and the Canto ends without his having confessed it to her. But this tampering with the facts does not work dramatically, for the next incident in which Timias and Belphoebe are concerned, in Canto VII of Book IV, implies precisely that Belphoebe had accepted the pledge of Timias's faith. Otherwise there would have been no grounds for her complaint against him.

We can, then, tentatively explore the first of these passages further, for any added light which it might throw on the relationship between Raleigh and the Queen. Specially noticeable are two things. One is the emphasis on the squire's 'meek and lowly place'. This has already been indicated by the poet, in that Timias is a squire, not a knight like most of the heroes of the poem. He is indeed a special kind of squire:

> *Now God thee keep, thou gentlest squire alive*

the poet apostrophises. Nevertheless, a squire he is, and this lowly estate is a cause of hesitation and grief to him:

> Still when her excellences he did view
> Her sovreign bounty and celestial hue
> The same to love he strongly was constrained.
> But when his mean estate he did review
> He from such hardy boldness was restrained. . . .

So a few lines later he addresses himself as

> Thou a mean squire of meek and lowly place. . . .

Here we are on to something which is one of the keys to the understanding of Raleigh's career in the period from 1580 to 1591. He was inordinately ambitious. He was aspiring to the heights. But he had one fatal handicap from which the greatest of his rivals, Leicester, Oxford and Essex did not suffer. He was, compared with them, of humble origin. He hoped, perhaps, that some stroke of fortune like that which had blessed the Spanish adventurers in the new world three-quarters of a century before would leave him a prince with dazzling riches at his command. He made the most of such successes as he had. Though he never achieved his ambitions he became indeed a rich man, and the ostentation of his personal adornment was one of the many features that earned him hatred. It is to be explained by the need to raise himself in Elizabeth's eyes, from his 'mean estate'. According to a well-known tradition, the Queen had encouraged him at the outset so to raise himself. But he found that the handicap was one which he could not overcome.

Another point suggested by Book III, Canto V is that Raleigh's love for the Queen did not begin and end with an insubstantial platonic admiration. There was, we are told, only one possible cure for the squire's malady. The gracious lady spared no pains to find remedies. Yet that one remedy she denied him:

> But that sweet cordial which can restore
> A love-sick heart she did to him envy;
> To him, and to all th' unworthy world forlore,
> She did envý, that sovereign salve in secret store.

And the poet goes on to emphasise that she was bound to deny it, and praises her chastity in a series of stanzas that, like so much of this canto, are of particularly fine workmanship. This indication of the character of Raleigh's 'love' may be important when the attempt is made to discover what was the nature of his estrangement from Elizabeth in 1589.

The passage contains further significant material for our present purpose. *Colin Clout* describes the song of the Shepherd of the Ocean:

> *His song was all a lamentable lay*
> *Of great unkindness, and of usage hard,*
> *Of Cynthia the Lady of the Sea,*
> *Which from her presence faultless him debarred.*
> *And ever and anon, with singults rife,*
> *He crièd out, to make his undersong*
> *Ah! my love's queen, and goddess of my life,*
> *Who shall me pity, when thou dost me wrong?*

In the *Faerie Queene*, the tenor of the song is given differently, though the undersong or refrain of the three stanzas reminds us of Colin's description:

> 'Unthankful wretch,' said he,[1] 'is this the meed,
>   With which her sovereign mercy thou doest quite?[2]
>   Thy life she savèd by her gracious deed;
>   But thou dost ween[3] with villainous despite
>   To blot her honour and her heavenly light:
>   Die; rather die than so disloyally
>   Deem of her high desert, or seem so light:
>   Fair death it is, to shun more shame, to die
> Die; rather die than ever love disloyally.
>
> 'But if, to love, disloyalty it be,
>   Shall I then hate her that from deathës door
>   Me brought? ah! far be such reproach from me!
>   What can I less do than her love therefore,
>   Since I her due reward cannot restore?
>   Die; rather die, and dying do her serve;
>   Dying her serve, and living her adore;
>   Thy life she gave, thy life she doth deserve:
> Die; rather die than ever from her service swerve.
>
> 'But, foolish boy, what boots thy service base
>   To her, to whom the heavens do serve and sew?

---

[1] Timias is addressing himself.   [2] *quite* = quit.
[3] *ween* = think.

> *Thou, a mean Squire of meek and lowly place;*
> *She, heavenly born and of celestial hue.*
> *How then? of all Love taketh equal view:*
> *And doth not Highest God vouchsafe to take*
> *The love and service of the basest crew?*
> *If she will not, die meekly for her sake:*
> *Die; rather die than ever so fair love forsake!'*

If indications are being sought as to the character of Raleigh's relationships with the Queen at this period, these two passages are not to be neglected.

The intention of this canto can perhaps fairly be summed up thus. The poet is presenting to the Queen an episode with Raleigh (that episode, whatever it was, which led to Raleigh's visit to Ireland in 1589) in a new light. 'Here is a poor Squire' he says, 'whom you have wounded to the heart. His humble station means that his love always was and always must be hopeless. But it was you who wounded him. Would it not be fair to restore him to favour rather than to pursue him with the royal displeasure?' And, as has been seen, the evidence is that *something*—Raleigh's own poems, the first three books of the *Faerie Queene*, or a change of heart on Elizabeth's part—did in fact cause him to be accepted once again to the court, though it was not to be for long.

*   *   *

Timias comes on the scene again in Canto VII and Canto VIII of Book IV, not published till 1596 and written therefore presumably during the time of Raleigh's disgrace, following his imprisonment in the Tower. Here once again he encounters Belphoebe. He has rescued Amoret from the lustful embraces of a 'wild and savage man' but in the course of the fight for her rescue she has been dangerously wounded. Belphoebe, appearing on the scene, chases the 'carle' to his den, and slays him there. But when she returns, she finds, astounded, that Timias is embracing Amoret:

> *Thence she them brought toward the place where late*
> *She left the gentle Squire with Amoret:*
> *There she him found by that new lovely Mate,*
> *Who lay the while in swoon, full sadly set,*
> *From her fair eyes wiping the dewy wet*

Which softly stole, and kissing them between,
And handling soft the hurts which she did get:
For of that Carle she sorely bruised had been,
And of his own rash hand one wound was to be seen.

Which when she saw with sudden glancing eye,
Her noble heart, with sight thereof, was filled
With deep disdain and great indignity,
That in her wrath she thought them both have thrilled[1]
With that self arrow which the Carle had killed:
Yet held her wrathful hand from vengeance sore:
But drawing nigh, ere he her well beheld,
'Is this the faith?' she said—and said no more,
But turned her face, and fled away for evermore.

He, seeing her depart, arose up light,
Right sore aggrievèd at her sharp reproof,
And followed fast: but, when he came in sight,
He durst not nigh approach, but kept aloof,
For dread of her displeasure's utmost proof:
And evermore, when he did grace entreat,
And framèd speeches fit for his behoof,
Her mortal arrows she at him did threat,
And forced him back with foul dishonour to retreat.

At last, when long he followed had in vain,
Yet found no ease of grief nor hope of grace,
Unto those woods he turnèd back again,
Full of sad anguish and in heavy case:
And, finding there fit solitary place
For woeful wight,[2] chose out a gloomy glade,
Where hardly eye might see bright heaven's face
For mossy trees, which covered all with shade
And sad meláncholy; there he his cabin made.

The allusion now is plainly to the incident of 1592. 'Is this the faith?' In view of Spenser's version in these two books, we can offer a hypothetical reconstruction of what happened on both occasions. Seeing his position threatened by the ascendancy of a rival, Raleigh in 1589, had chanced his hand, and had made a

---

[1] *thrilled* = pierced.   [2] *wight* = man.

bolder approach to the Queen. His passion can hardly have been genuine—the only answer to that riddle is Raleigh's own poetry, and it will be read differently by different readers—but was his one hope of the highest advantage; and he perhaps suggested it only in the equivocal form of a poem. One which is attributed to Raleigh —the authorship is discussed later; it is also claimed for Sir Arthur Gorges—is a possible candidate; and the hypothesis is made more acceptable by the fact that it would be easier to present such a poem as being a translation (this comes from Desportes), than Raleigh's own original work, in which case it must surely have given immediate offence:[1]

> *Would I were changed into that golden shower,*
> *That so divinely streamèd from the skies,*
> *To fall in drops upon my dainty flower,*
> *Where in her bed, she solitary lies,*
> > *Then would I hope such showers as richly shine,*
> > *Would pierce more deep than these waste tears of mine.*
>
> *Else would I were that plumèd Swan, snow white,*
> *Under whose form was hidden heavenly power,*
> *Then in that river would I most delight,*
> *Whose waves do beat against her stately bower,*
> > *And in those banks, so tune my dying song,*
> > *That her deaf ears would think my plaints too long.*
>
> *Or would I were Narcissus, that sweet boy,*
> *And she herself, the fountain crystal clear,*
> *Who ravish'd with the pride of his own joy,*
> *Drenchèd his limbs, with gazing over near:*
> > *So should I bring my soul to happy rest,*
> > *To end my life in that I lovèd best.*

And this becomes perhaps a fair conjecture rather than a mere romantic idea when we recall that Spenser, in his sonnet addressed to Raleigh at the opening of the *Faerie Queene*, repeats this striking phrase,[2] *golden shower*, in talking of the poems Raleigh has addressed to Elizabeth:

[1] This version is modernised from that in Sandison, *Poems of Sir A. Gorges.*

[2] The phrase is further discussed in a note on p. 168 when the poem, No. XIX, occurs in its series: see that note for the question of priority in its use between Raleigh and Spenser.

the streams that like a golden shower,
Flow from thy fruitful head of thy Love's praise.

It is as if, after the reconciliation, Spenser were reminding the Queen of the poem that had caused the temporary estrangement, and giving as it were his hall-mark to its poetic quality. And in Book III of the *Faerie Queene* Spenser certainly represents Timias's love for Belphoebe, and her refusal to him of her favours, as the reason for Timias's distress. We have to seek an explanation that will satisfy the facts we know of the Queen's changing attitude to Raleigh at this time. It is not easy to find one that takes account of Spenser's version of both the 1589 and 1593 incidents, and of the Queen's known attitude to Raleigh at both times (an attitude fairly reflected in Spenser's work). But this is perhaps the most likely.

Whatever form the approach took, Elizabeth reacted strongly. But perhaps she had been flattered. At any rate, before very long Raleigh was back again at court and the Queen's help in the acquisition of Sherborne shows that he was again enjoying special favours. But when in 1592 it became known that he had been making love to Elizabeth Throckmorton, the Queen (with whom we may permit ourselves in some degree to sympathise here) took fearful offence. 'Was this the faith?' Was it, indeed? The question was more reasonable than many which Elizabeth addressed to her entourage, and it took a good deal of answering. Raleigh's first answer had been to deny the whole affair (see the letter to Cecil, p. 44). He was, like most Elizabethans, a champion liar. His second line of defence, when denial was no longer possible, was to belittle the matter: to say in fact that such things are not love but mere fancy. This is one of the lines which is taken in the *XIth and last Book of the Ocean to Cynthia*, which we have dated to the time of Raleigh's imprisonment in the Tower following the discovery of his compromising conduct. Here he seems to draw a distinction between fancy on the one hand, and on the other a love which is beyond earthly beauties:

'*my error never was forethought*
Or ever could proceed from sense of loving.'

It was (in other words) but a chance accident, and did not originate in love at all. The contrast is between something ephemeral and unimportant and

A spring of beauties, which time ripeth not,
Time that but works on frail mortality,
A sweetness which woe's wrongs outwipeth not. . . .

But by the time he came to write the preface to the *Discoverie of Guiana*, published in 1596, he had realised that the attempt to explain it away would not do, and he was talking in a different vein. The disappointments of four years had by now impressed on him that this time Cynthia's displeasure was inexorable. And indeed though he was back at court in 1597, he was never to regain the unique position in the Queen's favour which he had lost in 1591. He had been her self-confessed, but apparently hopeless lover. Now he was once again the Captain of the Guard, in close touch with the Queen, but never again wholly trusted; certainly not the sweet Adonis of ten years before.

The sequel, in the instalment of the *Faerie Queene* published in 1596, is curiously unconvincing. Timias withdraws to the remote forests

Full of sad anguish and in heavy case:
And finding there a solitary place
For woeful wight, chose out a gloomy glade,
Where hardly eye might see bright heaven's face
For mossy trees, which covered all with shade
And sad meláncholy: there he his cabin made.

His hair grows matted and uncurled, and he has no other drink 'but water, tempered with his tears', so that when Prince Arthur comes on him he thinks that 'there some holy hermit lay'. We are reminded of Raleigh's lines:

'Like to a hermit poor in place obscure
I mean to spend my days of endless doubt.
. . . My food shall be of care and sorrow made
My drink nought else but tears fallen from my eyes.

It seems likely that Spenser had them in his mind when he wrote. They were no doubt well known to Raleigh's friends, and Spenser's allusion to them would be an appropriate compliment. In the hermit's exile, the poet has in mind Raleigh's retirement to his home in the West Country, where he stayed on and off for three

years. But Spenser goes on with an allegory of the reconciliation
with Belphoebe, which is simply a piece of wishful thinking. The
desolated Timias is befriended by a dove, round the neck of which
he hangs Belphoebe's jewel.[1] The dove then flies to her, and by her
mournful plaint gradually attracts Belphoebe to return with her
to the hermit's place of refuge. There is a reconciliation, and Timias
is received back into Belphoebe's 'former favours' state':

> *In which he long time afterwards did lead*
> *An happy life with grace and good accord*
> *Fearless of fortune's change or envy's dread.* . . .

The description of this reconciliation is brief and almost per-
functory, for the excellent reason that when Book IV was published Raleigh was still out of favour. It is not surprising therefore
that, when Timias reappears in Book VI, Canto V, though the
reader is reminded that Timias has recovered Belphoebe's favour,
it is soon clear that all is not yet well. He has powerful enemies,
and they set on him the Blatant Beast, a blasphemous creature
which lives by backbiting and reviling, and which though it has
been caught and subdued by Calidore, yet in the end is once again
rampant. This Blatant Beast of Slander has given both Timias and
Serena[2] (who in the poem meet by accident, and whose common
bond is just these attacks of the Blatant Beast) severe wounds.
They are taken for care to a hermit's cell. He finds that the wounds
fester dangerously. But at last he realises that the only remedy is a
spiritual one.

> *First learn your outward senses to refrain*
> *From things that stir up frail affection.* . . .
> *Abstain from pleasure, and restrain your will,*
> *Subdue desire, and bridle loose delight.*

[1] A ring with a diamond 'which he weareth on his finger' and which was
'given him by the late Queen' was among the items taken off Raleigh's body
after his execution; see Edwards, *Life and Letters of Sir W. R.*, Vol. II, p. 496.

[2] For Raleigh's own use of the name Serena for his mistress cf. his poem 'Now
Serena be not coy', Latham, *Poems of Sir W.R.*, No. XIX. No. XX is also
described in a seventeenth-century MS. (Folger, 1. 28) as 'S.W.R. on his mistress
Serena'. Both must date from the early years of the association with his wife,
and are therefore almost certainly prior to the Spenser references. So Spenser
probably got the name from Raleigh.

In the poem this may be right enough. But for Raleigh and his Serena, it was shutting the stable door when the horse was well away. So the wounds of the Blatant Beast, of Slander and Scandal, inevitably take up a large part of this study of Raleigh's career in the critical years after he had given the Queen enduring offence. The wounds, indeed, were to prove fatal. It was slander and scandal which sent him to the Tower in 1603, and the path led eventually not only to the Tower, but again westward to Guiana, and then back to the scaffold in Westminster Palace Yard.

Raleigh and 'Love's Labour's Lost'

Many editors of *Love's Labour's Lost* have believed that there is a connection of some sort between Raleigh and this play. In recent times the scent has become hotter. The editors of the play in the *Cambridge Shakespeare* (1923)—Sir Arthur Quiller Couch and Professor Dover Wilson—reproduced his portrait as a frontispiece. They saw the connection chiefly in Raleigh's 'Academy', that galaxy of friends along with whom he studied astronomy, and along with whom he was accused of atheism. 'For 1593', they say, 'we have the following data:

(*a*) a favourite, Raleigh, suddenly fallen from power, and his friends discredited by rumours of their trafficking with Copernican astronomics and "atheism";

(*b*) a rival party—that of Essex—to which Shakespeare was vowed, in suit of his young patron the Earl of Southampton, Essex's devoted friend;

(*c*) a Christmas of 1593 during which the theatres were shut by reason of the plague;

(*d*) a play obviously topical, designed for a polite audience, abounding in shrewd hits at certain devotees of a "School of Night" presented as fantastics.'

This view was developed in 1936 by Miss Bradbrook in her *School of Night*, a brilliant sketch which is at its best in the analysis of literary effects (especially in Raleigh's poetry) and which assembles the names and indicates the personalities of those who were, or may have been, associated in that 'academe'. Miss Yates in her *Study of 'Love's Labour's Lost'* was concerned with other members of the 'school', especially Northumberland and Bruno, rather than with Raleigh himself. More recently the editor of the play in the *Arden Shakespeare* in 1951, Mr. Richard David, summarises the growth of the 'School of Night' theory, and sees as the 'central theme of the play . . . ridicule of the academic affectations of a group of noblemen;' and the words

Never durst poet touch a pen to write
Until his ink were temper'd with love's sighs

with which Berowne dissolves the academy and turns its members
back to real life, might well be a specific answer to Chapman's

No pen can anything eternal write
That is not steeped in humour of the Night. . . .

'With Raleigh himself [continues Mr. David] and some of his
protégés, such as Marlowe and the mathematician Thomas Hariot
(both "soul-loved friends" of Chapman) Roydon made up a little
"academy" for philosophical and scientific discussion which in
1592 was branded by a pamphleteer as "Sir Water Rawley's
schoole of Atheisme".' He goes on to see 'something of Raleigh
in Armado. The "Chirrah" of V, i, 33 *may* be a gibe at the Wessex
accent that Raleigh kept all his life', and 'Armado's predicament
with Jaquenetta is exactly that which brought about Raleigh's
disgrace in 1592—the taunt "the eel is quick" which so upsets him
in Act I may only be a variant of Costard's "the party is gone"
[meaning that she is carrying a child] which repeats the process in
Act V'. Yet he doubts the tidiness of this solution, and suggests a
sort of 'multiple allegory in which a fictional character can stand
simultaneously for two persons in real life, themselves exemplars
of an abstract virtue'. Thus Raleigh's academic pretensions would
be ridiculed by presenting him as the pedant Harvey, himself dis-
guised as Armado; while Holofernes is all the masters of the Raleigh school rolled into one.

In all this there is something, perhaps a great deal. The reader
may be in a better position to judge later. But the details are tan-
talisingly difficult to square with the text. When it comes to
atheism, the point is to say the least not made altogether explicit.[1]
When it comes to the Copernican astronomy, there is indeed an
allusion to the fact that ability to name the stars has only a limited
value:

These earthly godfathers of heaven's lights,
That give a name to every fixèd star
Have no more profit of their shining nights
Than those that walk and wot not what they are. . . .

[1] See however p. 120.

But this gets no one far as a convincing accusation of revolutionary astronomical views. Our first consideration must be of the evidence for the date of production, and here difficulties are immediately encountered: one, that the date as given on the title-page is itself ambiguous; a second, that the text shows signs of revision. This second difficulty involves many technicalities, and we can attempt little more here than an indication of the problem, leaving the reader to pursue it through the editions of Professor Dover Wilson and Mr. Richard David, and, on the other side, Sir Edmund Chambers's *William Shakespeare*.

The first, however, is less complex. The title-page of the First Quarto edition 'imprinted at London by W.W. for Cutbert Burby, 1598' describes the play as 'a pleasant conceited comedy called Loves Labours Lost; as it was presented before her Highness this last Christmas. Newly corrected and augmented by William Shakespeare'. This seems to give definite information of date. But it is not so precise as it appears. Dates being reckoned from one Lady Day in March to the next, the year 1598 went on till what we should reckon as the end of March, 1599. If the printing of the book had been begun in February or March of that year, 'this last Christmas' would be Christmas 1598, and the book could still be printed in '1598' according to the old reckoning of date. If it had been started in the late spring or summer of 1598, the 'last Christmas' referred to would be 1597. But with this ambiguity between the two years admitted, we seem here to have fairly firm ground for the date. The title-page tells us (and this is the one piece of information it gives which we shall not venture to question) that the play was presented before the Queen. A number of title-pages of the period describe this or that play as 'acted by the Queen's Majesty's players'. The *Love's Labour's Lost* formula, however, is somewhat unusual. Among rather more than a hundred plays, or other dramatic works, published between 1590 and the Queen's death in 1603, some dozen indicate performances in the Queen's presence. Three are entertainments or speeches designed and given in connection with royal progresses. A fourth was presented before Her Majesty by the gentlemen of the Inner Temple; surely a private performance. A fifth, the *Merry Wives of Windsor*, printed in 1602, is described on the title-page as having been 'acted both before her Majesty and elsewhere'. When compared with other title-pages of the period, therefore, that to *Love's*

Labour's Lost may give the impression that the performance recorded was a private one; and, perhaps, that when the play was published, there had been no public performance as yet. *The Taming of the Shrew* for example is printed (1594) according to its title-page 'As it was sometimes acted'; *Richard III* (1597) 'as it hath been publicly acted'; *Romeo and Juliet* (1597) 'as it hath been often (with great applause) played publicly', or again in the 1599 revision 'newly corrected, augmented and amended, as it hath been many times publicly acted'. The term 'presented', moreover, appears on only four of the hundred odd title-pages, and in three of them can be assumed to be used in connection with a private performance, while in the fourth it is specifically extended to cover both: as it hath been presented publicly (by one company) and privately (by another). This last example, *Satiromastix*, 1602, comes right at the end of the series. Perhaps in the 1590's the normal use of the term was for a private performance, and the title-page may mean that the play was given before a select audience and not in the theatre in the ordinary way. Of this, however, we we cannot be sure. Nor can we be certain beyond all doubt (*pace* Sir Walter Greg) that the phrase on the title-page 'Newly corrected and augmented' necessarily implies that 'an earlier impression has been lost', and possibly that 'it contained a corrupt text'. This may indeed be the meaning, as he showed from the title-pages of the two editions of *Romeo and Juliet* already quoted. In that instance copies of both editions are fortunately available for comparison, and the second represents a different version of the play, less corrupt than that previously published. Yet evidence for a revised acting version of *Love's Labour's Lost*, which begins, as Professor Dover Wilson in his edition of 1923 showed, with passages in which the present text gives both the original and the later versions in sequence (cf. Act IV, iii, 282–363), is accumulating, and it now seems certain that the play was revised, after June 1597, for fresh performance. Moreover, if the printer of *Love's Labour's Lost* had wished to imply: 'Playgoers will recall that this piece was acted five years ago; it has now been revised and enlarged by the author and is here for the first time printed, and in this enlarged form'—it is difficult to see what other words he would have used. The *Romeo and Juliet* comparison gives therefore some evidence, but not conclusive evidence, that there had been a previous printed edition.

And if we wish to carry scepticism to its legitimate extreme, we can return to the date. Unfortunately Elizabethan and Jacobean printers, once presented with a title-page formula, did not always bother to think up something new. The original formula of the title-page exercised a sort of spell over future editions. Let us consider another play, *Mucedorus and Amadine*, printed like *Love's Labour's Lost* in 1598. It went into many editions. In 1610 it reappeared in a fuller version, advertised on the title-page with the words 'Amplified with new additions, as it was acted before the Kings Majesty at Whitehall on Shrove Sunday night'. It was still appearing with precisely that same formula on the title-page in 1626 by which time a new king was on the throne, and the Shrove Sunday night in question was sixteen years past. But, the reader will say, *Love's Labour's Lost* is different, for here we are told that it was 'presented before her Highness this *last* Christmas'. Even that, however, is alas not conclusive. Turn, for example, to *The Shoemaker's Holiday*, Dekker's play. It appeared in 1600, 'As it was acted before the Queen's most excellent Majesty on New Year's day at night *last*, by the right honourable the Earl of Nottingham Lord High Admiral of England, his servants.' It reappeared in 1610 with the title-page saying exactly the same thing about 'the Queen's most excellent Majesty' and 'New Year's day at night *last*'. What does all this mean? It gives us, at least the solid, and most important piece of information, that some time during the period 26th March, 1598–25th March, 1599, an edition, the earliest known, of *Love's Labour's Lost* was printed. It shows that there had been an earlier version of some kind, perhaps printed (though this is not certain; it may have been simply an acting version) and suggests that this '1598' edition was in some sense at least a revised text. It shows that at some Christmas performance, perhaps privately given —but the formula is not definite on the point—the Queen was present. There is a natural tendency to assume that this must have been Christmas 1597 or 1598, but as has already been pointed out we must not claim even that as definitely established. Especially if there was an earlier printed version it is not at all impossible that the 'last Christmas' was carried forward from one edition to the other, like the 'New Years day at night last' in Dekker's play. Here scepticism is fully justified. The tendency to copy from title-page to title-page makes it almost probable that, if there was an earlier edition (as we have at least reason to suspect), the phrase 'this last Christmas' was copied from it.

The title-page of *Love's Labour's Lost*, then, is an unusual one. Another unusual feature about this play is that nothing has been discovered which can fairly be described as its source. In the vast majority of Shakespeare plays he was making sows' ears into silk purses. His habit was to take an existing story and transform it. Here again we must not be too certain of our ground. In a number of instances the source on which he is thought to have been drawing is some hypothetical lost play. In Mr. Kenneth Muir's recent study of Shakespeare's sources, though there are necessarily many queries and unproved hypotheses, as yet for only three of the plays, *Love's Labour's Lost*, *A Midsummer Night's Dream*, and *The Tempest*, the source is indicated simply as 'not known'. Perhaps it is arguable therefore that, with these three plays he wished on each occasion to write about something particular, not only to write about it in a particular way. We must hasten to add that in each of the three he can of course be shown to have *used* other material. Professor Geoffrey Bullough for example in his *Narrative and Dramatic sources of Shakespeare*, while saying of *Love's Labour's Lost* that the writer 'may have created his own plot out of miscellaneous reading and memoirs', yet goes on to print several documents as likely to have been used by Shakespeare. One of them, which he described as an 'Analogue' gives an important date, 1594/5. It is part of the *Gesta Grayorum*, the Gray's Inn Revels for that Christmas. From that seems to have come, for example, the idea of the Muscovites' disguise in Act V, scene 2. In its present form then, this scene dates from some time after those revels; it was written then, in its present form, at least as late as 1595.

Assuming, however, that Shakespeare created the plot out of his own reading, what was it that formed the plot's kernel? Here again, we must first consider the kind of entertainment he provided, quite apart from the main plot. And here no one has ever doubted that many scenes are steeped in contemporary allusions. The Cambridge editors, followed by the new *Arden Shakespeare* editor, single out the nonsensical rhymes 'which the commentators discreetly pass over in silence':

> '*The Fox, the Ape, and the Humble-bee*
> *Were still at odds, being but three:*
> *Until the Goose came out of door*
> *And stayed the odds by adding four.*'

The first two lines are spoken three times; the second pair (with a minor variation) twice. It is clear that the audience was intended to catch them and to get some special entertainment from them. This is followed up by some curious business about a 'salve'. The word is not particularly unusual, but its use in Shakespeare's plays, according to the concordances, is limited to six occurrences in this play, with one each in *I Henry IV*, *III Henry VI*, and *Coriolanus*. Here, then, the figures suggest the possibility that there was some point in it. Or there is the scene at the beginning of Act V, scene 1 in which Holofernes comments on Armado's accent: he clepeth [calleth] a calf 'cauf'; half 'hauf' and so on. In Act V, scene 2 the same pair of words is picked up again. Armado is not on the stage, nor in question. Yet does it not seem probable, after Holofernes's play with the words, that they were oddly pronounced here too? Katherine asks 'Is not "veal" a calf'? Did Longaville then correct her: 'a cauf, fair lady?' and was he in turn corrected by her, 'No, a fair lord calf.' It makes no difference to the text and is simply a matter of production. When it comes a third time, Armado is palpably the victim:

Enter ARMADO for HECTOR

BEROWNE	*Hide thy head, Achilles—here comes Hector in arms.*
DUMAINE	*Though my mocks come home by me, I will now be merry.*
KING	*Hector was but a Troyan in respect of this.*
BOYET	*But is this Hector?*
KING	*I think Hector was not so clean-timbered.*
LONGAVILLE	*His leg is too big for Hector's.*
DUMAINE	*More calf, certain.*

Our one certainty is that, in the accent of the original Armado, 'calf' was 'cauf'. Thus there are allusions to be picked up constantly: a phrase of parody here, an accent there, a gesture (no doubt) somewhere else. Anyone who has watched such a charade where the authorities of a school or college are being mocked will have some idea of the devastating agility of the mind in such circumstances. Something of that kind was happening when *Love's Labour's Lost* was played before the Queen, and a careful examination of the text shows instance after instance in which the words are in fact almost meaningless without the allusion, an allusion

which we nevertheless cannot appreciate. To take an early example: in the first scene, when the King is introducing Armado,
he says:

> *'How you delight my lords, I know not I,*
> *But I protest I love to hear him lie.'*

Armado's lying is not a particular part of the plot. Why then is it
introduced here at all? And not only here, but, very delightfully,
later on in the scene. The King is reading Armado's letter:

KING (reads) *'So it is.'*
COSTARD   *It may be so, but if he say it is so, he is, in telling*
              true . . . but so.
KING   *Peace!*

It is an exhilarating way of saying that if Armado is speaking the
truth, it is the first time he has ever done such a thing. There is
something to do with the lie or lying, which comes in thus effec-
tively in this first scene, but was in no way developed in the sequel
in Armado's words or actions. The point depends on some contemporary gossip familiar to half the audience.

In such a work the allusions may be obvious and they may be
comparatively subtle. They are an indication of what people are
reading and what they are gossiping about when the play comes to
be acted. I recall for example a Greek play in translation—said to
be the *Thesmophoriazusae*—when the house was brought down
by the chorus of women ending their strophe with the phrase
'living and partly living'. The point was taken without any difficulty at all; and if *Love's Labour's Lost* should contain allusions
to poems, which Spenser published in 1591 or 1592, that would
not be surprising—and the allusions would have been widely
appreciated.

So much for the manner of the play. But any amusing plot could
have been treated like this. Our difficulty is two-fold: first to
know to what the allusion may be, when we come on one of
these eccentric utterances; secondly to know when (as perhaps
through much of the Nine Worthies episode) knockabout is replacing allusiveness as the comic mood of the moment. With the
plot however it is another matter. It can be assumed—at least as a
working hypothesis—that, if we are here concerned with a play
that is essentially, and not merely superficially, topical, the main
plot will also be significant in its relation to some phase or incident

of the day. What was it then, with which Shakespeare began? What was the original idea from which this gay, brilliant, and swift-moving entertainment developed? A good production of it, like that done at Stratford in recent years, leaves little doubt where he began: with a scene which on the stage is superbly effective, the long third scene of Act IV. An earlier scene has already given reason to suppose, indeed, that the four lovers' vows to forswear the company of women, while they study, are going to be severely tested. Each has picked out one of the ladies in the Princess's retinue (the King the Princess herself) and has shown an unmistakable interest in her. But, unlike Armado in the underplot, they are not yet self-confessed lovers. When this scene begins, however, it is evident that they have been taken the same way as he has been. He has announced what his technique will be: 'I shall turn sonnet. . . . Devise wit, write pen, for I am for whole volumes writ in folio.' They, each one severally, without the knowledge of the other, have adopted the same plan, first Berowne, who criticised his fellows' oaths so heartily, and in taking his own, claimed that he alone would make it good. He is therefore the first victim, and his verse, in an old sing-song metre, is nevertheless not only a marvel but is given a still greater delicacy by the setting of yokels and pedants in which it is introduced. The new scene opens with his entry. He has sent one of his sonnets already, as we know, and he is in labour with another. Suddenly he espies the King, groaning, obviously with love, who proceeds to read out to himself (believing himself alone) his own magic verse; and it is hardly done when Longaville enters, clearly in the same predicament; and thinking in the same way that no one else is near, reads out his sonnet, heard and observed independently by the other two. Yet another is needed to make the bag complete. It is Dumaine, and he is of course just round the corner; he enters, equally far gone, and reads to himself a lyric even more enchanted, it seems, than those we have had already. Longaville steps forward to accuse Dumaine, the last arrival, of breaking his oath; which done, the King accuses Longaville, only to be whipped himself, by Berowne's tongue, for hypocrisy. For thirty lines or so it seems that Berowne is going to get away with it, the climax of the scene being cunningly delayed. But the moment that Costard and Jaquenetta appear, with a paper, we have no doubt that it is Berowne's. He is compromised as are all his friends, and the denouement is complete. This is a scene then, and this is a play, about love poetry. When the editor of the *Passionate Pilgrim* in 1599 raided this play, his taste was right, and he was stealing the play's essence for his book. For the play, in both plot and sub-plot, is about the writing of love poetry; Armado is in it, like the rest of them, except only that he cannot do it, while they can. And this scene gets its superlative quality from its contrasts: the contrast between the slick artificiality (on the stage completely effective) of the construction, and the poetry of the lovers. The dramatist has solved completely the problem of writing a play about poetry. Incidentally, because he is doing this, it will make little sense to apply to it the tests devised by Fleay for dating the plays. These tests depend on an analysis of the proportion of rhymed lines, end-stopped lines and doggerel metres. But this play is about that kind of thing. Poetry is the subject of the main plot. And what put it into his head to write this play about love poetry? Whose *Love's Labour* was *Lost*? To my mind there can only be one answer. Not the King's, nor Dumaine's, nor Longaville's, nor Berowne's. Matrimony for them was delayed, but so far as we in the audience can tell, this is only a postponement. Even Armado has vowed to Jaquenetta 'to hold the plough for her sweet love three years'. But the love *he* had lost is that he summed up himself when he said that he 'adored your sweet Grace's slipper'. We are not indeed specifically told that his *villegiatura* was at Sherborne. We are told that he was going 'Woolward for penance'. 'Going woolward' i.e. wearing wool next the skin, was not indeed an unusual phrase. A normal example of its use can be quoted from Raleigh himself, in the *Dialogue between a Jesuit and a Recusant* written in 1609: [the Pope] 'enforced him to yield himself and to present himself woolward and barefoot at his feet'. The commentaries may be right that there is no *double entendre* here, though it is possible that the first audience had reason to think of Wool in Dorset, not far from Raleigh's Sherborne, and one of the places visited later by the atheist commission. Whether they did or no, however, by that moment in the play the point had been made. They knew that the Cynthia poems, so notably advertised by Spenser as Raleigh's love verses to Elizabeth, and nevertheless up to that date almost entirely unknown, never having been published, were the *Love's Labour*. They had no difficulty in recognising the veracity of the proposition that that love's labour had been lost.

A clue that comes early in the play has already been indicated, though not explained. The first audience who came to see the play knew before it began that Raleigh, in the blackest disgrace, was one of the objects of its mockery. When Armado was first mentioned:

> *A man in all the world's new fashion planted,*
> *That hath a mint of phrases in his brain:*
> *One who the music of his own vain tongue*
> *Doth ravish like enchanting harmony:*
> *A man of complements, whom right and wrong*
> *Have chose as umpire of their mutiny*

they recognised the real Raleigh rather than the play's Armado; they remembered how he had spent a king's ransom on a jewel for his shoe; they remembered the streams that like a golden shower

> *Flow from thy fruitful head, of thy love's praise;*

they already spoke of him, probably as the 'mischievous Machiavel' which is one of the descriptions used for him by a ballad maker a few years later.[1] But why did the King protest 'I love to hear him lie?' Surely because what was specially in their minds was a set of verses that Raleigh had recently written when he was in the Tower, verses already quoted:

THE LIE

> *Go soul the body's guest*
> *upon a thankless errand*
> *Fear not to touch the best*
> *the truth shall be thy warrant:*
> *Go since I needs must die,*
> *and give the world the lie.*
>
> *Say to the Court it glows*
> *and shines like rotten wood*
> *Say it to the Church it shows*
> *what's good, and doth no good.*
> *If Church and Court reply,*
> *then give them both the lie.*

---

[1] The point of Act I, scene 1, l. 163, 'a refined traveller *from Spain*' is perhaps to be explained by Bond, *Works of Lyly*, 1902, Vol. I, p. 151, when he talks of 'the rather inflated metaphorical style made fashionable at the Spanish Court about this time by Luis de Gongora'.

> *Tell Potentates they live*
> > *acting by others' action,*
> *Not loved unless they give,*
> > *not strong but by affection;*
> *If Potentates reply*
> > *give Potentates the lie.*

★   ★   ★

> *Tell zeal it wants devotion*
> > *tell love it is but lust*
> *Tell time it metes but motion,*
> > *tell flesh it is but dust.*
> *And wish them not reply*
> > *for thou must give the lie.*

> *Tell age it daily wasteth*
> > *tell honour how it alters.*
> *Tell beauty how she blasteth,*
> > *tell favour how it falters;*
> *And as they shall reply,*
> > *give every one the lie.*

The answers written to this fine poem and the puns made (among others by James I ten years later) on Raleigh's name—Raw-ley—are a strong testimony to its effectiveness at the time when it was composed. And it was linked no doubt in popular talk with the way in which Raleigh had tried to lie himself through the early stages of the love affair with Elizabeth Throckmorton. So that when the King ends his description of Armado 'I protest I love to hear him lie'; and when Costard interrupts the King's reading of the first phrase of Armado's letter:

KING   *So it is.*
COSTARD   *It may be so: but if he say it is so, he is, in telling true . . . but so.*

there was no doubt about the point in the audience's mind.[1]

It may be convenient here to pick up the riddle of the 'salve' in Act III, scene 1.

[1] 'The Lie' can be precisely dated to Raleigh's imprisonment in 1592: see p. 52.

MOTH   *A wonder, master! Here's a costard broken in a shin.*

ARMADO   *Some enigma, some riddle—come, thy l'envoy, begin.*

COSTARD *No egma, no riddle, no l'envoy, no salve in the mail,*
sir . . . O sir, plantain, a plain plantain: no l'envoy, no
l'envoy, no salve sir, but a plantain!

ARMADO   *By virtue, thou enforcest laughter—thy silly thought, my*
spleen. The heaving of my lungs provokes me to ridiculous
smiling: O, pardon me my stars! Doth the inconsiderate
take 'salve' for 'l'envoy,' and the word l'envoy for a salve?

There are certainly points here waiting to be explained, and some which may never find their explanation. But figures quoted above suggest the possibility that *some* allusion lies in the word 'salve'. It seems likely that this salve reference is to a passage in the *Faerie Queene* already examined. When the Squire Timias (Raleigh here) is wounded, he is discovered by Belphoebe (the Queen), who seeks for a cure to his wounds; not an honest-to-god, down-to-earth plantain such as Costard wants for his bruise, but

> '*whether it divine Tobacco were*
> *Or Panachaea, or Polygony,*
> *She found, and brought it to her patient dear.*'

These are the 'heavenly salves' for which Timias thanked her. But what the audience perhaps remembered even more vividly was that 'sovereign salve in secret store' which Belphoebe had denied Timias.[1] If Raleigh was mocked by any phrases from the *Faerie Queene*, it must have been this; and at the time of his fall, such opportunities are not likely to have been wasted. The play here was repeating an already popular jibe at his expense.

We must at the moment consider however not the drawing of Armado's character as a whole, but his connection with the 'love poetry' theme. Somehow Moth's verses must have been linked with this theme:

MOTH (to Armado). *If she be made of white and red,*
    Her faults will ne'er be known;
    For blushing cheeks by faults are bred,
    And fears by pale white shown;
    Then if she fear, or be to blame

[1] See above, p. 91.

> *By this you shall not know,*
> *For still her cheeks possess the same*
> *Which native she doth owe.*
> *A dangerous rhyme, master, against the reason of white*
> *and red.*

ARMADO   *Is there not a ballad, boy, of the King and the Beggar?*

MOTH   *The world was very guilty of such a ballad some three ages*
since, but I think now 'tis not to be found: or if it were, it
would neither serve for the writing nor the tune.

ARMADO   *I will have the subject newly writ o'er that I may example*
my digression by some mighty precedent. Boy I do love . . .

and so on.

It can be shown that one of the finest of Raleigh's works dates
from about the time of his imprisonment in the Tower, just before,
or actually during, that imprisonment. It is one of the traditional
ballads, 'Walsingham', 'writ o'er', as Armado suggests.[1] We do not
know whether Raleigh did the same with other ballad themes.
But there is little doubt about the reference. And when at the end
of the scene, Armado exclaims:

Assist me, some extemporal god of rhyme, for I am sure I shall turn
sonnet. . . . Devise wit, write pen, for I am for whole volumes in
folio.

—we cannot but remember that the *XIth and last Book of the Ocean*
to Cynthia had just been written, with its implication of another
ten written or projected: 'whole volumes in folio' indeed.

The theme is picked up again in Act IV, scene i, where we have
the results of Armado's efforts. The accompanying letter, with the
roles reversed (for here the Don is the King Cophetua, his mistress
the beggar maid), gets a new point from the context in which it
can now be read. It is followed by the *ridiculus mus* of his poetic
composition, the end-product (as they say) of those volumes in
folio:

> *Thus dost thou hear the Nemean lion roar*
> *'Gainst thee, thou lamb, that standest as his prey:*
> *Submissive fall his princely feet before,*
> *And he from forage will incline to play.*
> *But if thou strive, poor soul, what art thou then?*
> *Food for his rage, repasture for his den.*

[1] See below, p. 172.

It would indeed be satisfactory if we could point to the parody of
any existing Raleigh poem. But, apart from 'The Lie', none was
available. Spenser had made it clear enough to the reading public
that Raleigh was writing poems of various kinds, gay and sad, for
Elizabeth. But none were published yet, at least under his name.
So parody was not possible.

And so, to clinch the matter of this verse addressed to the
Queen, we return to it in the last scene;

PRINCESS   *Speak brave Hector, we are much delighted.*
ARMADO   *I do adore thy sweet grace's slipper.*
BOYET   *Loves her by the foot.*
DUMAINE   *He may not by the yard.*
ARMADO   *'This Hector far surmounted Hannibal'*—
     The party is gone!

Enter COSTARD

COSTARD   *Fellow Hector, she is gone; she is two months on her*
     way.
ARMADO   *What meanest thou?*
COSTARD   *Faith, unless you play the honest Troyan, the poor wench*
     is cast away; she's quick—the child brags in her belly
     already: 'tis yours.
ARMADO   *Does thou infamonize me among potentates?*

Here it is, in a nutshell. Armado's approach to the Princess with
its declaration of adoration is entirely gratuitous; that is to say, it is
not integral to the plot. We have heard nothing about it before.
Hitherto it has been the King with whom he boasts to be on such
intimate terms. But now he adores the Princess. And he singles
out her slipper for adoration: 'I do adore thy sweet grace's slipper;'
why? To give Boyet his cue. He takes it: 'Loves her by the foot'—
in which the second meaning is that of the foot of a verse; Dumaine
adds 'he may not by the yard,' or (to put it politely, unlike the
bawdy *double entendre* of Dumaine), he loves her in verse because
he may not go one better; and then come the interruption of Costard to the effect that Armado is hopelessly compromised with
Jaquenetta, and Armado's furious protest about being infamonised
among potentates. The point of the play then—and surely we
must now be at least convinced that it was written to be acted to a
select private audience—lies to some considerable extent on the

taking of this allusion. And in 1593 there was certainly no obscurity about it.

I do not propose to work out in detail the passages in which
Armado appears, discussing the particular relationship of each to
Raleigh. Does the allusion to the 'traveller from Spain' carry anything more with it than a reference to Armado's high-flown
language, as suggested above? When Armado is to relate 'the
worth of many a knight from high born Spain lost in the world's
debate' is there a glance at his account of the last fight of the *Revenge* published in 1591? Probably not, but there might be. In the
letters, is Raleigh's style of speaking being accurately parodied, or
is it rather bombastic buffoonery, such as might be thought suit-
able for a man known everywhere for his arrogance? Almost
certainly the latter. The point about the accent has already been
noticed. We know that Raleigh 'spoke broad Devonshire all his
life',[1] and that Armado's accent comes in for comment from Holofernes, but once again, he would be a bold man who would say that,
philologically speaking, the parallel was precise; still that there was
an allusion here to Raleigh's intonation is likely. We know that
Raleigh used to go out of his way to emphasise that he was above
all things a soldier. So in the second scene of Act I Armado keeps
on talking of himself as the soldier in love; when he goes out after
his affair with Jaquenetta is exposed his words are that he will right
himself 'like a soldier'; he has just spoken of the 'great warman
who is dead and rotten', and we are reminded of a phrase in Raleigh's writings much later: 'If the late Queen would have believed
her men of war as she did her scribes, we had in her time beaten
that great empire in pieces.' This stress on the soldier may be an
echo of Raleigh's way of talking about himself in the 1590's.
When Armado becomes, or threatens to become Joshua, in the
Mask of the Nine Worthies, did the audience remember that
Hakluyt in one of his prefaces had referred to Raleigh as a Joshua
leading the way to a new promised land? More probably, it is a
mere coincidence. But it is not by any means impossible that
Hakluyt's phrase had been picked out for ridicule by Raleigh's
enemies already; in which case the reference here would not
have been missed. There is by-play about a duel which may allude
to a duel he had had with Essex some time before, but might be

[1] On this Devonshire accent and its consequences for Raleigh's spelling, see
Latham, *Poems of Sir W.R.*, pp. 123-4.

something different. When Armado talks of himself as 'a complete man', among the Elizabethans who as a generation showed that quality of completeness to a degree almost unrivalled except in Renaissance Italy, no Elizabethan exemplified that completeness as Raleigh did; he may have made the claim of completeness for himself as his biographers often have made it for him. He was certainly an 'Arts man', a student of the University of Oxford as he sometimes mentioned in his conversation; the point happens to be recorded in the evidence of the atheist enquiry of 1594 as made by him on that occasion. His portraits often show him in the 'thin belly doublet' which had been fashionable long before. Some of these points may have been taken by the audience, others may be due to our misunderstandings. But the audience had, besides the words, the gestures and the accent of Armado to help them. And if these last few indications of a Raleigh reference seem to amount to very little, let the reader turn to Armado's speech in Act V, scene i, in which he talks of his intimate relationships—not with the Queen indeed; perhaps that would have been going to far—but with the king:

'*Sir, the king is a noble gentleman, and my familiar, I do assure ye, very good friend. . . . For what is inward between us, let it pass . . . and among other important[1] and most serious designs, and of great import indeed, too . . . but let that pass—for I must tell thee, it will please his grace (by the world!) sometime to lean upon my poor shoulder, and with his royal finger, thus dally with my excrement, with my mustachio: but sweet heart, let that pass. By the world, I recount no fable—some certain special honours it pleaseth his greatness to impart to Armado, a soldier, a man of travel, that hath seen the world: but let that pass. . . .*'

From this we turn to the letter written to George Carew in 1589. 'If they think I am not worth the respecting they shall much deceive themselves. I am in place to be believed not inferior to any man, to pleasure or displeasure the greatest; and my opinion is so received and believed as I can anger the best of them. . . . When Sir William Fitzwilliam shall be in England, I take myself far his better by the honourable offices I hold, as also by that nearness to her Majesty which still I enjoy, and never more. . . .' Then we wonder how often Raleigh talked like this. And we are not surprised that, grotesque a caricature though Armado is, some people were amused by it.

[1] Q. reads 'important'; Cambridge editions 'importunate'.

Little has been said here so far about the 'School of Night'. This famous phrase occurs in Act IV, scene iii, in the First Quarto text:

> *O paradox! Black is the badge of hell*
> *The hue of dungeons and the School of Night.*

It was regularly emended by editors, until Arthur Acheson, working on indications which he found in Chapman's *Shadow of Night* (the original title, characteristically, is in Greek, this being its translation) and using a facsimile of the First Folio, suggested that *School of Night* might be right, and might be an alternative name for the *School of Atheism* of which mention has already been made. From this idea a considerable literature has developed, and indications have been discovered by some, and quickly rejected by others, of mocking allusions to the men like Hariot or Northumberland, who were associated with Raleigh in his 'school'. This is a special problem, which the writer of this study is in no way competent to discuss.

All that can be done here is to suggest how this part of the play's theme is connected with Raleigh. And this is important because the 'School of Night' seems to be the second of the ideas from which the plot of the play develops—the first being (as we have seen) Raleigh's love poetry addressed to the Queen and his fall from grace when he was found to be compromised with Elizabeth Throckmorton. The 'School of Night' was certainly never such a close society as Acheson seems to have considered it. The poet Chapman, one of its leading lights, dedicated one of his books to Hariot the mathematician and scholar, Raleigh's intimate and lifelong friend, and wrote a *Carmen Epicum* about Guiana. Yet in 1598 he dedicated his seven books of the *Iliad* to Essex. The truth is of course that, as can be seen also from Spenser's work, the lines of division between Raleigh's associates and those of Essex were continually shifting; they were by no means as sharp as is often implied. It also remains true, however, that in the first half of the decade 1591–1600 there was a group of men associated with Raleigh whose activities gave rise, partly because of the unpopularity of Raleigh himself, to suspicion as well as ridicule. Some of them, such as Raleigh, Hariot and Marlowe were believed to be atheists. Dr. John Dee, a learned astronomer and astrologer whom Raleigh intervened more than once to protect, was regarded as a magician, and his house was once burnt by an angry mob. The group as a whole was credited with a fanatical devotion to book learning, and an intellectual snobbery, which made them despise their un-lettered competitors:

'It is an exceeding rapture of delight'—writes Chapman in 1594—'in the deep search of knowledge . . . that maketh men manfully endure the extremes incident to that Herculean labour: from flints must the Gorgonean fount be smitten. Men must be shod by Mercury, girt with Saturn's adamantine sword, take the shield from Pallas, the helm from Pluto, and have eyes of Graea (as Hesiodus arms Perseus against Medusa) before they can cut off the viperous head of benumbing ignorance, or subdue their monstrous affections to most beautiful judgment.'

The poems that follow, in praise of darkness and obscurity, often tortuous in expression and over-elaborate in their allusions, but often written with great power, have as their background the banishing of carnal passion in the prophetic search for wisdom:

> *adamantine power is given*
> *To thy chaste hands, to cut off all desire*
> *Of fleshly sports, and quench to Cupid's fire.*

It is in this spirit that King Ferdinand, at the opening of *Love's Labour's Lost*, plans his 'little academe', whose students are told, in the first few lines of the play, that they

> *war against their own affections*
> *And the huge army of the world's desires.*

And, from one aspect, the play is a brilliant satire on the folly of such a life, in which, if the mind banquets, the body pines. The moral is, indeed, that the body quickly finds its own ways of get-ting round the regulations, and the mind gets nowhere. The King's courtiers swear to obey an arduous discipline in the search for knowledge that will bring them eternal fame. But since they are normal human beings, they all fail. A bevy of young ladies has only to appear before this stronghold of embattled asceticism for its walls to collapse like a pack of cards. In the background of the play move the pedants, sub-human, who suggest to the audience what comes of all this learning if it is seriously pursued; and the situation gets its piquancy from the fact that, in real life, the man who was the guiding spirit of the 'school' had so far forgotten himself as to fall irretrievably in love with one of the Queen's

Basan, or Basanitis regio, ober iordan, in lenght from the
torrent Iabor to the coonds of Petrha, of the Gessuris, e
Matyati. in breadth, from the hills Galaad, geir, e Hermon,
to ye sea of Galile. e Jordan.   Basan signifieth fatt e
fruitfull, exceeding in goodly oakes, e therfore was it sayd
quernis basan. It was also called terra Raphaim. id est
gigantu. Also yeare after Chodorlahomor had slayne
the kings of Sodom. e Basan. Og. veing of ye race of Raphaim
obtayned that region called Basanitidis, in wch ther
were 60 Citties wald. all wch fair the soonn of Manasse
reconered e slow Og. e his soonns. e called them Auoth Iair,
or the Citties of Iair. e were geuen by Moses to the half
tribe of Manasse.

Deut. 3.

Numb. 32.
deut. 3.
Josua. 15. e
17.

1. Edrai, the seat of Og.
2. Corozaim.
3. Cedar.
4. Astiroth.
5. Gamala
6. Galaad.
7. Pella.
8. Iabes galaad.
9. Hippos
10. Ephron.
11. Gollon.
12. Gerasa.

Raleigh the scholar; an autograph page of notes made for the
History of the World; about 1610

Maids of Honour; just as Armado, subject to the ban of Ferdinand's Court, had nevertheless carried on his intrigue with Jaquenetta, the revelation of which brings the play to its exhilarating climax.

There is still considerable controversy about the details. Arthur Acheson's book, published in 1903, continually overstates its case and claims as proved what are sometimes nothing better than the shakiest of theories. But he wrote from an extraordinary familiarity both with the sonnets of Shakespeare and with some of the poems of Chapman (though he seems never to have read the continuation of *Hero and Leander*, and this omission warps his whole judgement of Chapman's poetry), and in the present writer's view the connection that he indicates between the sonnets and Chapman is, broadly speaking, established. Later work, especially that of Miss Yates in her *Study of 'Love's Labour's Lost'* (1936) and of Miss Bradbrook in her *School of Night* (also 1936), 'a study of the literary relationships of Sir Walter Raleigh', has examined other personalities holding the views attributed to the 'school'. But the main features of the doctrines popularly associated with it by the men of that time are no longer in doubt. And they form the background of the play.

Two small further contributions to the discussion may be permissible. One of the books at which Shakespeare had almost certainly been looking when he wrote the play was the translation of Primaudaye's *French Academy*, a long and not very readable production which begins however with just such an academy of men vowed to study as the King launches in the opening scene of *Love's Labour's Lost*. This was fashionable reading in the early 1590's and is one of the items prescribed to be read in the rules of the mock 'Order of the Helmet' in the *Gesta Grayorum*, familiar to Shakespeare certainly before he produced that version of *Love's Labour's Lost* which is represented in the Quarto of 1598. It is thus interesting at least, and just possibly significant, to find that Raleigh's library when he was in the Tower in James I's reign included this same book. We now have the library list in his own autograph, and this title occurs. His 'academy' then may have been consciously modelled on Primaudaye's, as was the King's; his friends may have proclaimed as much. Otherwise the list is much as a careful reading of his life would suggest. He had, for example, a *Copernicus*, and a *Machiavelli*. He had a number of travel books, and books about America. He had books about medicine. He had books in French and Italian. What is striking about the list is that except apparently for the Works of Petrarch, to which he alluded in the fine introductory sonnet to the *Faerie Queene*, it does not contain poetry. It is possible (as has been suggested in an earlier chapter) that in his later life he became less and less interested in poetry which he had encouraged and himself practised in the 1580's and even earlier. It is possible that the sorry end of his *Cynthia* discouraged him. He had never been more than a talented amateur, though it may be guessed from the quality of his best work that he could have been a major poet. To find another explanation of this extraordinary feature of the library of a man who had once been so deeply interested in poetry, and so well known as a patron of it, is not easy.

Secondly, we may add to the 'School of Night' discussion, that there does seem to be a possible reference to Raleigh's (Armado's) atheism in Act V, scene ii:

ARMADO	*Anointed, I implore so much expense of thy royal sweet breath as will utter a brace of words.*
PRINCESS	*Doth this man serve God?*
BEROWNE	*Why ask you?*
PRINCESS	*A' speaks not like a man of God his making.*

I have avoided discussion of the further point, which is for experts to determine. The play carries with it in some scenes two versions of the same speech, in others equally obvious signs of revision. An example of the first is to be found in Berowne's famous speech on the 'beauty of a woman's face' and its inspiration, in Act IV, scene iii. It is beyond doubt that the quarto text here offers two alternative versions, and the same is true elsewhere. It has been plausibly held that the short speech of Costard at the end of Act IV, scene i, implies an earlier version, in which what he describes took place. This alteration affects an Armado, or Raleigh, scene. The theory was put forward by the Cambridge editors that the earlier version (referred to on the title-page) was to be dated to 1593, and that the printed text represented a later revision in which (to take one example only) the passage depending on the Gray's Inn Revels was part of the revision. In this battle of the bibliographical pundits the amateur bibliographer must not intervene. I have gone as far as I dare, in discussing the title-page. Here

I will only say that such a view would not seem to me inconsistent with the Raleigh allusions as I read them. They would have been topical during the winter of 1593–4, and this was perhaps the time of the first production. There are several allusions, however, which belong to the later revision,[1] and the performance before the Queen, for which this revision (including the references to the *Gesta Grayorum*) was made, took place at Christmas, 1597.

Finally, it seems worth drawing attention again to the record of the 1605[2] revival, in a letter written by Walter Cope, chamberlain of the exchequer, to Lord Cranbourne, Secretary of State:

'Sir, I have sent and been all this morning hunting for players, jugglers, and such kind of creatures, but find them hard to find. Wherefore leaving notes for them to seek me, Burbage is come, and says there is no new play that the Queen [i.e. the wife of James I] hath not seen, but they have revived an old one, called *Love's Labour's Lost*, which for wit and mirth he says will please her exceedingly. And this is appointed to be played tomorrow night at my Lord of Southampton's unless you send a writ to remove the *Corpus cum Causa* to your house in Strand. Burbage is my messenger ready attending your pleasure.

Yours most humbly
WALTER COPE'

The text of the play printed in the First Folio of 1623 was set up from a copy of the 1598 Quarto. In one place the later text substitutes 'Jove' for 'God'. An act passed in 1606 prohibited profanity on the stage, but this alteration might have been made earlier in deference to King James I's susceptibilities. There is no further trace of revision in substance in the 1623 version. The King

---

[1] In particular, it would seem that in the masque Armado was originally cast for Joshua; and that the Hector-Achilles by-play dates from the later revision, Essex *in the audience* being addressed as Achilles by Berowne:

Hide thy head, Achilles, here comes Hector in arms.

(For the point of the Achilles-Essex comparison, see p. 75.)

[2] Harold Child, in the *Cambridge Shakespeare*, gave the date as 1604. Greg (*The Shakespeare First Folio*) speaks of *two* performances at this period, a revival at court early in January, 1605, and a private performance arranged soon afterwards 'perhaps at the Earl of Southampton's'. Incidentally, in this, one of his last books, Greg seems not quite so categorical in his rejection of a revised acting version. Child printed 'revised' for 'revived' in line 5 of the letter.

himself no doubt enjoyed the play. He was already Raleigh's implacable enemy. But it must have given his host, the Earl of Southampton, a special satisfaction.

*   *   *

It has been argued here that in *Love's Labour's Lost*, Shakespeare was satirising Raleigh, the Queen's disgraced favourite: satirising him in particular for the verse addressed to her as by a lover, and satirising the predicament in which he found himself when after all the protestations which that verse contained, it became known that he was involved in an affair with one of her maids of honour.

But there is another way in which the play has a peculiarly close relationship to its period. The twenty years or so which began with the writing of Sidney's sonnets to Stella, and ended with the death of Elizabeth included the writing of some of the finest love poetry ever produced. Most of it belongs to the last decade of Elizabeth's life. Marlowe's *Hero and Leander* was an incomplete fragment when he died in 1593, but what he wrote is an incomparable piece of vivid and intense narrative, the story of two lovers' passion, forbidden because one of them had vowed her life as priestess of the goddess of love. While Marlowe's poem was being written, Shakespeare must have been working on *Venus and Adonis*, for that appeared in 1593, dedicated to the Earl of Southampton. It is a poem about the shameless lust of Venus, while the theme of its successor, the *Rape of Lucrece*, is the irresistible lust of a tyrant and its tragic ending. Though Shakespeare's sonnets did not appear in print till 1609, many of them were undoubtedly written at this time. Some have close links with *Love's Labour's Lost*. *Romeo and Juliet* appeared in print in 1597. Spenser's Sonnets belong to this same decade, as do the marvellous 'Epithalamia', the theme and manner of which suited his genius perhaps better than anything else he wrote. He had composed the 'Hymns to Beauty' and 'to Love', so their preface tells us much earlier (presumably in the 1580's) but added to them 'Hymns to Heavenly Love' and 'to Heavenly Beauty' in the early 1590's. John Donne sailed with Essex on the expedition to Cadiz in 1596 and to the Islands in 1597. His earliest work was already at this time circulating in manuscript, and Ben Jonson told William Drummond that Donne 'wrote all his best pieces before he was 25 years old' (before 1598). In addition to the work of these giants there were appearing love poems by innum-

122

erable lesser writers. The anthologies and books of music were full
of them.

   Love's Labour's Lost can be regarded as splendid criticism of the
earliest of this love poetry, and the banner, as it were, of the new
movement. The point of its criticism can be seen in the contrast
between two of Berowne's utterances about love. The first is made
when he begins to be aware that he is becoming involved himself in
love's toils, and he speaks with contempt of what is mastering him:

> *This wimpled, whining, purblind, wayward boy,*
> *This Signior Junior, giant-dwarf, Dan Cupid;*
> *Regent of love rhymes, lord of folded arms,*
> *The anointed sovereign of sighs and groans,*
> *Liege of all loiterers and malcontents,*
> *Dread Prince of Plackets, King of Codpieces,*
> *Sole imperator and great general*
> *Of trotting paritors. . . .*

This is the god of courtly love affairs, in a make-believe world; a
world in which love is a superficial, if a dangerous game. Not long
afterwards, Berowne has begun to understand what Love is in
actuality; not a love affair, any longer, but Love itself:

> *Love, first learnèd in a lady's eyes,*
> *Lives not alone immurèd in the brain,*
> *But with the motion of all elements,*
> *Courses as swift as thought in every power,*
> *And gives to every power a double power,*
> *Above their functions and their offices.*
> *It adds a precious seeing to the eye;*
> *A lover's eyes will gaze an eagle blind;*
> *A lover's ear will hear the lowest sound,*
> *When the suspicious heed of theft is stopped:*
> *Love's feeling is more soft and sensible*
> *Than are the tender horns of cockled snails:*
> *Love's tongue proves dainty Bacchus gross in taste.*
> *For valour, is not Love a Hercules,*
> *Still climbing trees in the Hesperides?*
> *Subtle as Sphinx; as sweet and musical*
> *As bright Apollo's lute, strung with his hair. . . .*

It has become fashionable to speak of 'total war'. What Berowne is now describing is total, in that sense. It is in every power, in every quality which its victim possesses. If an occasional phrase of this description comes near to what Berowne himself calls 'the liver vein, which makes flesh a deity; a green goose a goddess; pure, pure idolatry', most of it is something very different; just as is the raging passion of

> *... Among three, to love the worst of all;*
> *A whitely wanton with a velvet brow,*
> *With two pitch balls stuck in her face for eyes;*
> *Ay and by heaven, one that will do the deed*
> *Though Argus were her eunuch and her guard:*
> *And I to sigh for her! To watch for her!*
> *To pray for her!*

This is a far cry indeed from that 'sweet verse, with nectar sprinkelèd' which was the stock-in-trade of the court poet ten years before. It is the difference between make-believe and reality. In a famous sonnet, Shakespeare begins:

> *My mistress' eyes are nothing like the sun;*
> *Coral is far more red than her lips' red;*
> *If snow be white, why then her breasts are dun;*
> *If hairs be wires, black wires grow on her head.*

We recall Raleigh:

> *Those eyes for clearness do the stars surpass*
> *Those hairs obscure the brightness of the sun,*
> *Those hands more white than ever ivory was,*
> *That wit even to the skies hath glory won.*

and it is at once apparent how quickly that early work of the 1580's has dated. It is the difference between Romeo's self-conscious love-sickness for Rosaline, and his overmastering passion for Juliet. And the literary expression of either of these belongs to a different world of aesthetic expression from the other. Viewed in this context, a poem like Raleigh's 'Like to a Hermit', good though it is, is superficial—a smoke raised with the fume of sighs; whereas the *Sonnets* traverse the gamut of passion: from the serene lyricism of Sonnet XVIII (which handles incidentally in the new way the old theme of the eternal idea of love) to the passionate *odi et amo* of CXLVII:

Past cure I am, now Reason is past care
And frantic mad with evermore unrest;
My thoughts and my discourse as madmen's are
At random from the truth vainly expressed,
For I have sworn thee fair, and thought thee bright,
Who art as black as hell, as dark as night.

To take the analysis a little further, we may say that the earlier attitude is still medieval. It goes back to the discovery of romantic love as a theme for the arts, a discovery made many centuries before by the poets of Provence. In this medieval tradition Spenser had schooled himself. His work, with its apparatus of magic and chivalry, is in this also medieval; while *Hero and Leander*, or Sonnet CXLVII, are modern. And if Raleigh's *Cynthia* is to be viewed in this context, it is not altogether easy to place it. Some of the early poems, as has indeed already been suggested, rely for their effects on a sort of slickness which is superficial. With this often goes a hyperbole of flattery which is thoroughly disingenuous. But when it comes to some of the poems that we have set in the 1590's and, in particular to the *XIth and last Book of the Ocean to Cynthia*, the matter is different. 'It is not to Spenser' says Miss Latham, 'that we must look for Raleigh's fellow, but to the men of the seventeenth century . . . by his gravity, his unconventionality, and most of all by the personal note he introduced into poetry, he anticipated the turn of the century.' To judge an unfinished work of art, a sketch, is notoriously difficult. 'Between the idea and the reality falls the shadow', and in the draft, or the sketch, we are often nearer the idea than we are with the finished article. So perhaps with the *XIth and last Book*. In a final version, some of the qualities which give it power might have been revised away. But, as we have it, it is the record of an individual passion, and is a personal cry for pity, a personal appeal that the past should not be allowed to be ruthlessly forgotten, which is not only powerful but genuine.

Genuine? How much did Raleigh mean? The question will certainly be answered differently by different readers; but it is arguable that, in this one major poetical work, Raleigh was writing not only about his love for Elizabeth, but also, and mainly, about himself: about the shadow of death; about the frustration of hope, and the approach of age when none of the things he had set out to achieve had been realised. In 'Like truthless dreams' undoubtedly written some time before, he was already talking of his 'sweet spring spent', his 'summer well-nigh done'. In 'Walsingham' the approach of age has become more insistent:

> *I have loved her all my youth,*
> *But now old, as you see,*
> *Love likes not the falling fruit*
> *From the withered tree.*

The *XIth Book* returns to the same image:

> *Witness those withered leaves left on the tree*
> *The sorrow worren[1] face, the pensive mind;*
> *The external shows what may th' internal be.*

—and in the preface to the *Discoverie of Guiana* three years later he came back to it once again.

' . . . if ought might have been deserved in former times to have counterpoised any part of offences, the fruit thereof (as it seemeth) was long before fallen from the tree, and the dead stock only remained. I did therefore even in the winter of my life, undertake these travels, fitter for boys less blasted with misfortunes, for men of greater ability, and for minds of better encouragement. . . .'

It is this immense sense of frustration and despair that makes these fragments at times great poetry:

> *Despair bolts up my doors, and I alone*
> *Speak to dead walls. . . .*

or

> *The broken monuments of my great desires. . . .*

Those great desires had already, in 1592, spurred him to 'seek new worlds' in Virginia; even to aspire perhaps, in his heart of hearts, to be the consort of the Queen; and he now saw, rightly, that his hopes were in ruins, and that there could be no rebuilding.

When he wrote on such themes—whether it was in the *XIth and last Book*, or in the profoundly moving prose of the *History of the World*—Raleigh was stirred to the depths of his being. When he wrote of Elizabeth, it is, comparatively speaking, still a matter of glittering glass and tinsel:

> *This did that Nature's wonder, virtue's choice,*
> *The only paragon of time's begetting,*

[1] *worren* = worn.

> *Divine in words, angelical in voice*
> *That spring of joys, that flower of love's own setting,*
>
> *Th' idea remaining of those golden ages,*
> *That beauty braving heavens, and earth embalming,*
> *Which after worthless worlds but play on stages. . . .*

and so on. In such passages (and this is closely paralleled by another in the comparatively short compass of this single work) we are aware that the ring is not true. It had, once, been clearer:

> *Another time I likewise call to mind,*
> *My heart was he that all my woe had wrought,*
> *For he my breast the fort of love resigned,*
> *When of such wars my fancy never thought.*
> *What could it say when I would him have slain?*
> *But he was yours, and had forgone me clean.*

Then Raleigh had been telling her that he was her devoted servant. Now he was simply striving to find new superlatives of flattery.

If therefore we wish to find the real source of Raleigh's inspiration in this work, it lies not in unrequited passion for Elizabeth, but in the final disaster to ambition and the awareness—not wholly justified by the strange event—that what he sought for from life could now never be found:

> *Thus home I draw, as death's long night draws on.*
> *Yet every foot, old thoughts turn back mine eyes,*
> *Constraint me guides, as old age draws a stone*
> *Against the hill, which over weighty lies*
> *For feeble arms, or wasted strength to move.*

The *Last Book of the Ocean to Cynthia* is not a love poem but a dirge for youth and ambition; and the set of verses (written after his return to favour) which, we have suggested, was the epilogue to this extraordinary series is a courtly compliment, extravagant as the velvet cloak, dry of all feeling. It may be that when Raleigh pondered over the *History*, years later, in the Tower, it came into his mind to present this, too, to Cynthia. By that time he had had experience of a monarch who did not relent.

PART II

THE POEMS TO CYNTHIA

I

Introduction

Any attempt to link those of Raleigh's poems that are addressed to Elizabeth with particular phases of their relationship must be based in the first instance on such external evidence of the chronology of his poems as is available. The date of the long fragment at Hatfield—the *XIth and last Book of the Ocean to Cynthia*—is crucial. In it Raleigh's style is seen fully developed, and moreover it contains an explicit allusion to at least one of the earlier poems known. This date seems now established, thanks to the work done on the problem by a number of scholars. It will be considered later. What first has to be examined is any other certain date for a poem in the series. At the best, all that can normally be done is to demonstrate the existence of a particular poem by a certain date, and this can be done only with comparatively few of them. When one of Raleigh's poems appeared in print in the *Phoenix Nest*, this shows that it was in circulation at least as early as 1593, the date when that anthology was issued. But it may have been composed many years earlier. Similarly two Raleigh poems were included, not under his name, in another Elizabethan collection, *Britton's Bowre of Delights*. This appeared in 1591. It might have been tempting to assume that 'Like to a hermit' had been written during the period of exile from the court that began in 1593, especially in view of some correspondence between this poem and phrases in Spenser's later books. But its inclusion in the *Bowre of Delights* makes any such assumption impossible.[1]

[1] The *Phoenix Nest* is important for another reason also, for the study of Raleigh's poems. In 1931 Professor H. H. Hudson suggested that a substantial block of poems in the anthology which were attributed in it to no author by name, were Raleigh's. It is its editor's habit to group together the poems by an individual author except when (as with the various elegies on Sidney's death) there is reason to arrange them differently. Raleigh's elegy on Sidney is thus grouped with others on that theme. But in the block of poems noted by Professor Hudson appear several elsewhere attributed to Raleigh; the style of the group as a whole gives convincing support to the attribution, and I have little hesitation in accepting it. For the subject matter too seems, as will be seen from notes on some

The date, 1593, of the *Phoenix Nest* is, however, of relatively little use in settling the chronology of the *Cynthia* poems; for as the account given of the association between Elizabeth and Raleigh has already shown, by that time the intimate personal links between them had been broken. Almost all the *Cynthia* poems therefore are likely to have been written before that date and it is before that date that several of the allusions to them by literary critics, or by Spenser, occur. More important simply for chronological purposes (if the attribution proves acceptable) is a small group of three anonymous poems which William Byrd set to music and which appeared in print in 1589. Byrd was organist of the Chapel Royal. He certainly had access to some of Raleigh's poems, since he had printed one—the fine 'Farewell, false love'—the attribution of which to Raleigh is not seriously in doubt, in another collection the year before. I came across these three in a copy of the original 1589 edition of Byrd's *Songs of Sundrie Natures* in the library of St. Michael's, Tenbury, and was at once struck by the resemblances to some of Raleigh's work. It was only later, when attempt was made to arrange Raleigh's poems in some sort of chronological order, that their closeness in matter as well as manner to the writings I was attributing on other grounds to this period, became apparent. In the sequence as arranged in the following pages, the reader will be able to judge for himself the validity of this view. Whether or not this group is accepted, the date 1588 as the latest at which 'Farewell, false love' can have been written, is certain. 'Calling to mind' had been written by 1589 when it was quoted by Puttenham in *The Arte of English Poesie*. It seems, however, to represent a distinctly earlier phase than this. 'In vain mine eyes' is also quoted by Puttenham, and the only manuscript copy of it might be a year or two earlier than 1589. It is certainly not later.

If evidence of the stylistic changes in Raleigh's poetry apart

of the individual poems, to bear strong testimony to Raleigh's authorship. When a poem bears the marks of Raleigh's style and refers to the poet's mistress in terms that leave no doubt of her being a royal personage, it seems to be stretching scepticism too far to insist that the attribution should not be definitely accepted. Within this group is included the fine poem 'Would I were changed into a golden shower', based, like at least one other of Raleigh's poems of this period, on a poem by Desportes. Though there is another strong claimant for the poem's authorship (see the note, p. 167), I believe that it came into the hands of the editor of the *Phoenix Nest* as Raleigh's, and believe further that it is Raleigh's work.

from the *Cynthia* poems is sought, the earliest appearances of a Raleigh poem in print was in 1576, when there were published three commendatory stanzas by him in George Gascoigne's *Steele Glasse*. These are curious rather than impressive. They contain the slick antitheses, the obtrusive alliteration, and the end-stopped lines which seem characteristic of his early style. Sidney died in 1586, and Raleigh's 'epitaph', printed first in the *Phoenix Nest*, looks as if it were written at the time of Sidney's death. The allusions to the actual circumstances of his death would be most natural at that time, and stylistically the poem looks comparatively early. One other poem which can be dated with some probability (though not certainty) on external grounds is the reply to Marlowe 'If all the world and love were young'. Supposing Raleigh to have written the reply when the Marlowe was still a recent work, the date 1588–90 can be given to it, which fits in well with what is known of the mood, and the style, of Raleigh's verse at the time. It is, however, the dating of the *XIth and last Book to Cynthia* that matters most for any discussion of the development of Raleigh's style.

*   *   *

The only contemporary copies or actual autographs of Raleigh's poems that are specifically connected by their titles with the *Poems to Cynthia* are the four famous poems or fragments, in the same manuscript, in Lord Salisbury's library at Hatfield. On any account, they are the most important existing remains of Raleigh's poetic work. They were discovered in 1870, and were printed in modernised spelling by Archdeacon Hannah, sometime Fellow of Lincoln College, Oxford. Since the discovery, three views have been put forward about their date.

(*a*) Hannah's view was that, though the main fragment referred constantly to the events of 1592 when Raleigh had incurred the Queen's displeasure and had been imprisoned, yet is was written during his second imprisonment, after the Queen was dead. What seems to have convinced him of this was in the first instance the handwriting. He believed he had seen other Raleigh documents of precisely that time in which the character of the handwriting was paralleled. In view of the many different hands which Raleigh was liable to write at any one period, this argument is precarious. And Hannah's notes may not have reminded him that, towards the end, the script does in fact revert to one of the alternative hands.

Secondly, Hannah took literally the references to the 'death' of
Cynthia:

> *If to the living were my muse addressed* (l. 5)

or ll. 493–6:

> *She is gone! She is lost! She is found, she is ever fair!*
> *Sorrow draws weakly, where love draws not too.*
> *Woe's cries sound nothing, but only in love's ear;*
> *Do then by dying, what life cannot do.*

or ll. 517–20:

> *To God I leave it, who first gave it me*
> *And I her gave, and she returned again,*
> *And it was hers. So let his mercies be*
> *Of my last comforts the essential mean.*

A further reading of the long fragment, however, shows conclusively that these references to Cynthia's death are metaphorical.
Her love is dead. But she is very much alive. In one of his phrases
which equate Cynthia with the Moon, she 'from the sun reaves
[steals] power and light' (l. 251). She lacks the compassion which
would make her humanity into divinity:

> *Yet have these wonders want which want compassion,*
> *Yet hath her mind some marks of human race,*
> *Yet will she be a woman for a fashion,*
> *So doth she please her virtues to deface.* (ll. 201–4)

or—to quote two lines cancelled after l. 449:

> *Though all her thoughts be drawn back to her breast,*
> *And none remain that call thee to her. . . .*

She 'scorns the care' of the poet's 'remaining woes' (l. 281). Her
ears 'have forgotten all his past deserving', 'holding in mind but
only his offence' (l. 372). In a number of other passages the implication that Cynthia is still alive is clear. His rivals in her favour are now
enjoying the happiness that should be his (ll. 263–4, 309–10, 333).
To read the fragment as an elegy on the Queen is indeed to miss
the force of this powerful poem. It is an elegy on Cynthia's love
which derives its intensity from the chance that it might conceivably be revived; from its assertion that love is something different
from a passing fancy—in the words of Raleigh's version of the
Walsingham ballad, written about this same time:

> *But true love is a durable fire*
> *In the mind ever burning,*
> *Never sick, never old, never dead*
> *From itself never turning—*

and derives it also from the conflict in the poem between this Platonic idea of love, and the passion allowed to burst through it:

> *. . . As a man distract with treble might*
> *Bound in strong chains doth strive and rage in vain*
> *Till tired and breathless, he is forced to rest,*
> *Finds by contention but increase of pain,*
> *And fiery heat inflamed in swollen breast,*
> *So did my mind in change of passion*
> *From woe to wrath, from wrath return to woe*
> *Struggling in vain from love's subjection.* (ll. 153–160)

Elizabeth then was not dead, but still very much alive, when the poem was written. It was written, therefore, before 1603.

(*b*) Another view that has been put forward is that this fragment is the *Cynthia* of 1589 referred to in *Colin Clout's come home Again*:

> *His song was all a lamentable lay,*
> *Of great unkindness and of usage hard,*
> *Of Cynthia the Lady of the Sea.*

About this song, one of the shepherd lasses, Marin, observes:

> *. . . Right well he sure did plain[1]*
> *That could great Cynthia's sore displeasure break,*
> *And move to take him to her grace again.*

It is true that the *XIth and last Book to Cynthia* is manifestly only a draft; that does not necessarily prevent its having been finished off in another copy, and presented to the Queen. It is certainly a 'lamentable lay', and so far at least qualifies to be the song described in *Colin Clout*.

But this theory is equally untenable with that of Archdeacon Hannah. We have already observed that in the two different instalments of the *Faerie Queene*, a distinction is made between two phases in the estrangement from the Queen; in one of which the Queen has no justification for being provoked, in the second of which she emphatically has. And in the *XIth and last Book* there are

---

[1] *plain* = complain.

unmistakable allusions to the poet's fault. His 'offence' is held in mind while his 'past deserving' is forgotten (ll. 371–2). He refers a number of times to his 'error':

> *You that then died when first my fancy erred* (l. 3)

or

> *But thou, my weary soul. . . .*
> *Dost know my error never was forethought.* (l. 338)

'Once amiss hath bereaved me of all' he wrote to Cecil; and, in the *XIth and last Book*

> *One hour diverts, one instant overthrows.* (l. 231)

The *XIth and Last Book* is thus not simply a complaint of hard usage. It admits, while attempting to explain away, an 'error', a straying of the fancy, which is different from anything which we have reason to suppose for 1589. (Nor will it do, incidentally, in view of these passages, to assume with M. Lefranc, that Raleigh's marriage took place in 1588. These references to 'one hour', and 'one instant' rule out conclusively that possibility. He could scarcely have written these phrases in 1592 if Elizabeth's anger had been due to the sudden discovery that he had been married *for four years*.)

(c) The third view put forward is that the fragment dates from 1592, and is associated with Raleigh's imprisonment in that year, whatever its relationship to the *Cynthia* of *Colin Clout* (a *Cynthia* which, as we remember, was a 'lamentable lay') or the *Cynthia* of the Introduction to the Third Book of the *Faerie Queene*, which was 'sweet verse, with nectar sprinkelèd'. This third view is confirmed, first and foremost, by the nature of the other poems or drafts found with it in the Hatfield manuscript. Miss Latham says that 'it seems very probable that the verses are related'. This is an understatement. Bibliographically it is a single manuscript, all in Raleigh's autograph; and when Miss Bradbrook, in introducing an ingenious interpretation of the preliminary 'riddle' says that it was found on a 'scrap of paper' at Hatfield, her description is entirely wrong. The 'riddle' is an integral part of the manuscript[1] containing the long *Cynthia* fragment, now bound up with many other documents to form Hatfield MS.144. Miss Bradbrook has noticed

---

[1] Actually on the same piece of paper as 'My body in the walls captived;' and the watermark and wire lines identical with those of the leaf on which the *XIth Book* ends and the *XIIth* begins.

a parallel between the riddle and a letter written by Essex some years earlier, describing a conversation about Raleigh with the Queen, and she thinks that the riddle was written for Elizabeth immediately afterwards, referring to that conversation. But the close bibliographical relationship between the 'riddle' and the other three fragments is decisive against Miss Bradbrook's view. 'If Cynthia be a Queen, a Princess and supreme Keep *these* among the rest.' 'These' refers to all the fragments in the MS., and the 'riddle' goes on to refer to the intensity of feeling in which they have been written. If the *XIth and last Book* was written in 1592, so was the riddle.

The second of the short poems in Hatfield MS. 144 makes it certain that the single document of which these lines form part was written in prison:

> *My body in the walls captíved*[1]
> *Feels not the wounds of spiteful envy,*
> *But my thralled mind, of liberty deprived,*
> *Fast fettered in her ancient memory,*
> *Doth nought behold but sorrow's dying face;*
> *Such prison erst was so delightful*
> *As it desired no other dwelling place,*
> *But time's effects, and destinies despiteful*
> *Have changèd both my keeper and my fare;*
> *Love's fire and beauty's light I then had store,*
> *But now, close kept, as captives wonted are,*
> *That food, that heat, that light I find no more.*
> *Despair bolts up my doors, and I alone*
> *Speak to dead walls, but those hear not my moan.*

The contrast between the former delightful imprisonment of the Queen's love, and the dead walls of what he calls (in a letter written at the time) 'this unsavoury dungeon' the Tower, is impressive and is indeed the point of the poem. Raleigh was imprisoned twice, in 1592 and 1603. The second date is impossible for the contents of the manuscript as a whole; we are left, then, with the date 1592.

And there are other excellent grounds for dating the poems to this year. Miss Latham pointed out that the name Belphoebe, used

[1] For the accent, captíved, cf. Spenser, *Faerie Queene*, passim; also Sidney, *Astrophel and Stella*, XXIII, l. 11.

in l. 271 and l. 327 as well as *Cynthia* (l. 118) for the Queen was borrowed from Spenser, who uses it in the first instalment of the *Faerie Queene*, published in 1591; and while it is true that Raleigh might have borrowed it from Spenser when they met in Ireland, it is difficult to imagine Spenser then addressing (as he does) to Raleigh an elaborate prose explanation of it in the printed edition of the *Faerie Queene* if Raleigh not only knew it but had actually borrowed it already. Perhaps even more conclusive are the similarities between the *Cynthia* fragment and a famous letter written to Cecil just after Raleigh was imprisoned; which begins with a matter of fact request about the uniforms for the Queen's guard, but goes on much in the vein of *Cynthia*. It looks indeed as if the poem had already been running in his head when the letter was written. 'Yet have these wonders want which want compassion' says the poem; however miraculous Cynthia may be, yet unless she shows compassion, she is less than perfect. And the letter puts the same idea: 'There were no divinity but by reason of compassion, for revenges are brutish and mortal.' And when he writes to Cecil 'All those times past, *the loves, the sighs, the sorrows, the desires,* can they not weigh down one frail misfortune', he may perhaps actually have had in mind an earlier draft of the line

> *The sighs, the groans of all our past desires.*   (l. 285)

'She is gone', the letter continues 'in whom I trusted, and of me hath not one thought of mercy, nor any respect of that that was'. And the *XIth Book* says:

> *So to thy error have her ears inclined*
> *And have forgotten all thy past deserving. . . .*   (ll. 371–2)

There is no real doubt that this poem was written, in the Tower, in the late summer of 1592.

*   *   *

That the *XIIth Book*, 'entreating of sorrow', is only the fragment of a draft, is apparent, for it breaks off after only twenty lines or so when a new sentence and a new stanza have just begun. But it is also clear that the *XIth Book* itself is simply a draft. There is a number of marginal marks, some of which Miss Latham thinks were used to draw attention to rhetorical passages, as inverted commas are sometimes used in Elizabethan printed texts. Others however of a different type seem to be intended to mark breaks in the sense.

One almost demonstrably is (after l. 220), since it is drawn across from margin to margin, in a place where a break is required by the meaning. Other gaps, clearly indicated in the manuscript, which are demanded by the sense are after l. 294 (indicated by a line) and after l. 473 (where there is a small line apparently indicating a break, and a space has also been left). The impression which is given by these marks as a whole is that they show no final decisions; but are noted down reflectively at a later reading some days after the draft was first written. As the poet's eye passes down the page he marks it at places to which for one reason or another he plans to return; to recast them, to give them greater elaboration, or more precise form. For most of Raleigh's work shows a far greater degree of metrical precision than this. It is impossible to believe that, in any final form he would have left an odd line like 404, outside the rhyming scheme, or 153, similarly unrelated; or the three lines 478–80. It might possibly be argued that two other groups of three lines, 101–3, and 150–2 were intended as closing their sections; but for 478–80 no such reason can be found.

We have noticed also already a cancelled passage in the *XIth Book*, in which the second line is incomplete metrically. In two instances, it is suggested below, a line breaks off in the middle of a sentence, waiting to be completed later (ll. 425 and perhaps 461). All these points show that the poem has survived in a stage that was not final. This is one reason why there are such obscurities in the sense, here and there.

The *XIIth Book* is a mere few lines. It ends in an unfinished sentence, and the obvious explanation is that Raleigh's work on it was interrupted by his temporary release from the Tower. It would be natural enough for the papers he had left behind him to be collected and sent to the Queen's principal Secretary of State. This is the most likely story of the way in which the poems came to Hatfield. We have suggested that a report of this incipient *magnum opus* spread in court circles, and beyond them, after Raleigh's release; a report represented in Shakespeare's caricature of Armado's literary projects 'whole volumes, writ in folio' of verse addressed to Jaquenetta.

The long fragment is headed '*the XI and last book of the Ocean to Cynthia*' and the last short fragment '*the end of the books of the Ocean's Love to Cynthia, and the beginning of the 12 book entreating of sorrow*'. The twenty-one lines of this suggest a book in similar vein to the last. At any rate, Cynthia still comes into it (l. 10 and ll. 16–19), the Cynthia who can renew and can create:

> *Green from the ground, and flowers even out of stone*
> *By virtue lasting over time and date.*

The sense would suggest then that it is the *XIIth Book*[1] which is in itself *the ending of the books to Cynthia*, not the start of a completely new theme. But here again, even in the title itself, there is every sign of a draft, which would eventually have been tidied into something that made more literal sense.

*   *   *

That these two books have a different rhyming scheme seems to make it doubtful at the outset whether there was ever a coherent body of ten books in existence of the *Ocean's Love to Cynthia*. What seems rather to have happened is that in the shock of imprisonment, Raleigh who, as Cecil once rightly said could 'toil terribly' had the idea of composing a long poem about his love for Elizabeth, and began with that section which concerned its most recent history. This is what we now have in draft. No more of this particular *Cynthia* was written, though he had in mind, in it, to write the whole course of his love for her from the beginning (ll. 91–6). But in the course of the *XIth Book* he twice refers back to earlier writing about Elizabeth:

> *Twelve years entire I wasted in this war*
> *Twelve years of my most happy younger days;*
> *But I in them, and they now wasted are,*
> *Of all which past, the sorrow only stays.*
> *So wrote I once. . . .*   (ll. 120–4)

He quotes here, not from some great epic, but from a fine poem in simple sonnet form which still survives (No. XXI). Later he quotes again from some of his previous writing:

> *Thus did that Nature's wonder, virtue's choice,*
> *The only paragon of Time's begetting,*
> *Divine in words, angelical in voice,*
> *That spring of joys, that flower of Love's own setting,*

---

[1] While I have adopted Miss Latham's reading of the figures 11th and 12th books (*Poems of Sir Walter Raleigh*, p. 120), I have nevertheless still doubts about it. It may be '21st' and '22nd' books.

Raleigh the poet; verses addressed by Raleigh to Elizabeth as 'Cynthia'

Th' idea remaining of those golden ages,
That beauty braving heavens and earth embalming
Which after worthless worlds but play on stages,
So didst thou her long since describe. . . .   (ll. 344–51)

We now have a poem in which something very close to one of these phrases occurs, 'flower of love's own planting' in place of 'love's own setting'. No other of the phrases is precisely paralleled in existing poems, though there are many general similarities with one or other phrase in the series. They are perhaps collected from several different poems which he had written to Elizabeth. Incidentally, in spite of the close analogy here with the new poem, my impression is that this was written later (see pp. 206–7) and that he is here quoting an earlier, though similar, line. He often repeated himself, carrying what he had written before long in his mind.[1]

It may reasonably be inferred then that the *Cynthia* to which reference is made at these dates before 1592 is the series of Raleigh's occasional verses to Elizabeth; written in different moods; some being 'sweet verse with nectar sprinklèd', some of them descriptions of Elizabeth's beauties as Spenser suggests (cf. No. VI), some 'lamentable lays' like that to which Colin Clout alludes. Cynthia, named or not, was the subject to which most of them were directly addressed; though others were written for her amusement (cf. Nos. XV–XVII) rather than as pleas directed to persuade her. To call them 'Sir Walter Raleigh's *Cynthia*' as Gabriel Harvey did, is to speak as one might perhaps do of Catullus's love poems as his *Lesbia*. Sir Edward Dyer's *Amaryllis* was probably an analogous group of poems, addressed to, or written for, one mistress. Only one of the poems here printed (apart from the *XIth Book*, in which the name Cynthia once occurs) is addressed to Cynthia by that name. There must have been others. Those addressed to Diana nearly qualify, but do not quite make it.

But that many of the extant poems were addressed to the *Queen* is immediately apparent, and it seems possible to trace a sort of chronological sequence. The poet is at first not declaring his love

---

[1] The most striking instance of this does not seem to have been noticed before. Almost his last words as he knelt down on the scaffold were, 'No matter how the head lie, so the heart be right.' So in Bk. I, Ch. 3, § iii of the *History of the World*, he had written, 'the matter is not great which way we turn our faces [in prayer] so our hearts stand right.'

but rather the ambition to serve his mistress, to do which he will have to advance himself (No. I). When he praises her as Diana (No. IV) her nymphs deck the woods and her knights are the representatives of true honour, but she is far above ordinary humanity. She is indeed the 'power by which all powers abound', beyond time and mortality like the Platonic idea of beauty. From such ideas the transition to a love poem is an easy step. Princes have tried and failed (the poet writes) to attain what his heart is trying to achieve (No. XI); and here there is of course implied not only service, but, in some form, love. Kings have failed to obtain the grace he hopes to win. Such phrases point clearly to Elizabeth as the poems' object, and to the poet as in a sense her declared lover.

In due course, in one of them, the poet's thoughts begin to carry mistrust. 'Fain would I climb', he had told her, 'but I fear to fall.' But Cynthia shined before, and will do so again. She is masked by clouds, but through such changes (like the Platonic idea of beauty again) she remains the same. So too he may alter, but does not vary in his love. His praises of her are of one who, of right, wears a royal crown, whose 'hands conquer more than Caesar's force', whose wit turns huge kingdoms upside down. Here the suggestion that the poem might be 'any poet to his mistress' is surely an extravagance of scepticism. Whoever was the author, Elizabeth was the object. So she was also of a similar poem, where her hands 'hold the highest hearts in thrall'. Those verses must be Raleigh's, as is also 'Who list to hear...'. Almost the earliest of the series should be this last, with its superficial smartness and its alliterative jingles. With it goes the more successful 'Sweet are the thoughts....'. It is from these poems and some written evidently not much later in what Berowne would have called the 'very liver vein' that an impression is to be formed of the importance, for Raleigh, of the Queen's love at this time. There is no other evidence. In style they are to be compared with the verses from the *Steele Glasse* (Miss Latham's edition of Raleigh's poems, No. 1) or that considerable poem, the 'Epitaph on Sir Philip Sidney' (ibid., No. 4).

The second phase as we have suggested in the introductory text, begins not with the journey to Ireland, but somewhat earlier, with the rising of a rival star at court. A comparison has recently been made between Marlowe's 'Come, live with me' and Raleigh's answer to it, which notices Raleigh's 'graver, sadder tone; not less poetical because it is less care free'; 'a characteristic gravity, often allied with restraint'; and notices also the 'sincerity' by which he escapes the besetting sin of the Elizabethans, the over-elaborating on an empty theme. It is in this second phase that we begin to be aware of these qualities, as though misfortune had shown him that life was something more serious than a game of noughts and crosses. He has now to face rejection—a rejection which he once calls a 'secret murder', she who did the deed being a 'dame of state'; once again it seems an extravagance of scepticism not to accept the poem concerned as Raleigh's. This particular example is indeed transitional between one group and the next. It has not the real anguish of 'Is Love a boy?' or the bitterness and power of 'Farewell, false love...'. In the latter we catch for the first time the poet's cries against age:

> *Sith thou thy trains my younger years betrayed ...*

The theme is sometimes that which had already begun to appear in the earlier group, of a silence which his position imposes. Thus he had written (if that poem indeed belongs to the earliest group, or is like 'A secret murder' a bridge between the first and second):

> *Our passions are most like to floods and streams:*
> *The shallow murmur; but the deep are dumb.*

and

> *when discretion doth bereave*
> *The plaints that they should utter*
> *Then your discretion may perceive*
> *That silence is a suitor.*

while, not much later, comes the sonnet 'Wounded I am' with its much more powerful, and much more deeply felt lament:

> *If I complain, my witness is suspect;*
> *If I contain, with cares I am undone;*
> *Sit still and die, tell truth and be reject;*
> *O hateful choice that sorrow cannot shun.*

or, in 'My firstborn love'

> *Swell on my thoughts, till you break that contains you,*
> *My complaints in those deaf ears no more mutter,*
> *That so disdains you.*

143

It has been observed by other critics how the melancholy strain in Raleigh's nature asserts itself in his poetry. In this phase of his poetry it becomes a preoccupation with death as the impending end of his love:

> *Yet of us twain whose loss shall be the less*
> *Mine of my life, or you of your good name?*

or

> *Leave to be, and seek your heaven by dying*

or

> *at my gate, despair shall linger still*
> *To let in death, when love and fortune will.*

Thus even in a poem in many ways so different in mood from the rest, 'Would I were changed...', in which, in the French original, the 'eternal night' from which the dawn would not awaken the poet to a new day, is the ecstasy of desire, in Raleigh's version it has been subtly changed, so that it is a real death to be met:

> *So should I bring my soul to happy rest*
> *To end my life in that I lovèd best.*

'Walsingham' seems to belong to a yet more fully developed phase. In the second phase, we may think perhaps that the phrases about death and despair are still clichés. In this poem they have an unmistakably genuine ring. In this respect 'Walsingham' is best grouped with the Hatfield fragments, about which the genuineness of the feeling is often, though even now not perhaps always, apparent. What that feeling was, is a question to which an answer has been suggested already. For the moment the point is the replacement of an artificial elegance by a much more profound and individual emotion.

All this makes the last poem in our series the harder to place. The fact that Raleigh wrote it out in a notebook which he used when working on the *History of the World* does not prove that he composed it after Elizabeth's death. Indeed, it would be difficult to make sense of much of it, if it were written to the dead Elizabeth, while the discovery[1] of a musical setting for it, among a series of

---

[1] Made by the late John Boston; see below, p. 206.

madrigals manifestly composed in Elizabeth's honour during the last years of her life seems a strong argument for dating it to approximately the same time. He remembered it later, as he was to recall 'Even such is time' during the last days of his life, or the fragment of the *XIIth Book to Cynthia* when he came to draft an appeal in verse to the Queen-consort of Elizabeth's successor. My reading of its mood is one in which the passionate intensity of the late eighties and early nineties has been completely lost. The poem is a pretty, conventional compliment, written for a specific occasion, perhaps the presentation of a pageant or masque to Elizabeth: 'Now we have present made', it says, 'to Cynthia.' It is the real end of the *Ocean to Cynthia*, for in it Raleigh has ceased to be the devoted servant or the devoted or anguished lover, and is simply offering a graceful gift. Thereafter he could no longer be accused, as he could be at least through the latter part of the remainder of the series, of 'loving' Elizabeth 'by the foot'.

★   ★   ★

In the following printing of the poems, modern spelling and modern punctuation have been adopted. In the *XIth Book to Cynthia*, a greater degree of editing has been necessary, and pauses have been marked, some of which I claim in the notes to have Raleigh's authority, though others he had not indicated in the unfinished draft which is our authority for the whole. Some pauses shown by gaps in the manuscript between lines, were noted, though not marked in the text, by Miss Latham. They are not always easily seen, and where a gap should occur at the foot of a page, there may be no indication except the capital letter at the top of the next. Raleigh did not normally begin lines with capitals, and, accordingly, capitals often but not invariably suggest the beginning of a new section.

A few poems which are not yet recognised as belonging to the canon are printed in italics. In the note following each poem an atempt is made to state the evidence for the date of the poem—generally in the form of the date of its first known public appearance. An attempt is made also to explain difficulties of meaning, and this necessitates, in the *XIth and last Book*, a sort of running commentary. For the convenience of the reader, words which might cause difficulty because they are archaic or unusual are explained in the footnotes.

II

The Poems to Cynthia

1581–1587

I

Sweet are the thoughts where hope persuadeth hap,
Great are the joys, where heart obtains request;
Dainty the life, nurst still in Fortune's lap,
Much is the ease, where troubled minds find rest.
  These are the fruits, that valour doth advance
  And cuts off dread, by hope of happy chance.

Thus hope brings hap but to the worthy wight;
Thus pleasure comes but after hard assay;
Thus fortune yields, in manger oft for spite;
Thus happy state is none without delay.
  Then must I needs advance myself by skill,
  And live to serve, in hope of your good will.

Latham, No. II. There is apparently no early printed version, to help with the dating, but the style (as Miss Latham says) and the matter suggest the initial phases of Raleigh's association with the Queen, when he was climbing into favour. Stanza II: Hope brings fulfilment only ('but') to the worthy, and fortune yields only after strenuous efforts; keeping off the ambitious man, like the proverbial dog in the manger keeping off the cattle.

1581–1587

II

Who list[1] to hear the sum of sorrow's state
The depth of dole,[2] wherein a mind may dwell,
The loathèd life that happy hearts may hate,
The saddest tale, that ever tongue could tell,
But read this verse, and say who wrote the same,
Doth only dwell, where comfort never came.

[1] *list* = wants.   [2] *dole* = sorrow.

146

A careful head, first crossed with crooked hap,
A woeful wit, bewitched with wretched will,
A climbing heart, fall'n down from Fortune's lap,
A body born to lose his labour still,
A mourning mind, sore mated with despite
May serve to show the lack of my delight.

Yet more than this, a hope still found in vain
A vile despair, that speaks but of distress,
A forc'd content, to suffer deadly pain,
A pain so great, as cannot get redress,
Will all affirm, my sum of sorrow such,
As never man, that ever knew so much.

l. 9. The accepted text is 'false down from Fortune's lap' which
I cannot understand. Fall'n is an obvious emendation, too obvious
really to commend itself.

From the *Phoenix Nest* group, 1593, first identified as Raleigh's
by Professor H. H. Hudson. It is characteristic of Raleigh's early
manner, with its alliterations and jingles. The verses are in a sense
complementary to 'Sweet are the thoughts'; there the writer's life
is 'nurst still in fortune's lap'; here his climbing heart has fallen
down from it.

1581–1587

III

Calling to mind mine eye long went about
T' entice my heart to seek to leave my breast;
All in a rage I thought to pull it out,
By whose device I lived in such unrest.
 What could it say to purchase so my grace?
 Forsooth that it had seen my Mistress' face.

Another time I likewise call to mind,
My heart was he that all my woe had wrought,
For he my breast the fort of love resigned,
When of such wars my fancy never thought.
 What could it say when I would him have slain?
 But he was yours, and had forgone me clean.

At length, when I perceived both eye and heart
Excused themselves, as guiltless of mine ill,
I found myself was cause of all my smart,
And told myself, myself now slay I will:
    But when I found myself to you was true,
    I loved myself, because myself loved you.

The author of the *Arte of English Poesie*, 1589, quotes the last
two lines as an example of the figure that he calls 'Ploche or the
Doubler', and attributes them to Raleigh; so that this charming
poem (Latham, IX) can safely be placed early. It seems to show the
influence of Sidney; e.g. 'Transformed in show, but more transformed in mind' etc. The opening phrase is explained by the opening line of stanza II; it means evidently 'as I ponder, I remember
how', or words to that effect; what is now happening reminds the
poet how he has found eye and heart before offering their allegiance to his mistress instead of to himself. The third line of stanza
II: my heart betrayed to the enemy the fort of my breast, before I
was aware that the war was being fought. Last line of stanza II:
only ('but') that he was yours.

1581–1587

IV

Praised be Diana's fair and harmless light,
Praised be the dews, wherewith she moists the ground;
Praised be her beams, the glory of the night,
Praised be her power, by which all powers abound.
Praised be her nymphs, with whom she decks the woods,
Praised be her knights, in whom true honour lives,
Praised be that force, by which she moves the floods;
Let that Diana shine, which all these gives.

In heaven Queen she is among the spheres;
In aye she Mistress-like makes all things pure;
Eternity in her oft change she bears;
She beauty is, by her the fair endure.

Time wears her not, she doth his chariot guide,
Mortality below her orb is placed;
By her the virtue of the stars down slide;

In heauen Queene ſhe is among the Spheares,
She Miſtreſſe-like makes all things to be pure :
Eternity in her oft change ſhe beares,
      She beauty is, by her the faire endure.

Time weares her not, ſhe dooth his Chariot guide,
Mortality below her Orbe is plaſt :
By her the vertue of the ſtarres downe ſlide.
      In her is vertues perfeſt Image caſt.

A knowledge pure it is her woorth to know :
With *Circes* let them dwell, that thinke not ſo.

    FINIS.   *Ignoto.*

In heauen Queene ſhe is among the Spheares,
She Miſtreſſe-like makes all things to be pure :
Eternity in her oft change ſhe beares,
      She beauty is, by her the faire endure.

Time weares her not, ſhe dooth his Chariot guide,
Mortality below her Orbe is plaſt :
By her the vertue of the ſtarres downe ſlide.
      In her is vertues perfeſt Image caſt.

A knowledge pure it is her woorth to know :
With *Circes* let them dwell, that thinke not ſo.

    FINIS.   S W R

Verses written for the Queen, published in 1600 without authority:
in copy (*a*) the cancel slip obliterating Raleigh's initials is in
place; in (*b*) it has been partly removed

In her is virtue's perfect image cast.
A knowledge pure it is her worth to know;
With Circes let them dwell that think not so.

Printed in the *Phoenix Nest* 1593, but Miss Latham attributes it definitely to Raleigh on the grounds that it appeared in 1600, in *England's Helicon*, over the initials S.W.R. These initials were later cancelled, cf. No. XIV and also Pl. VI. The background of this poem is the 'Platonic' conceit of Elizabeth as the eternal idea of love and beauty; the sphere of Diana (the Moon) in the accepted cosmology of the ancients being that at which and above which there is the changelessness of eternity ('Mortality below her orb is placed'); the same conceit is the background of XI. cf. also XXVII and the *XIth and last Book of the Ocean to Cynthia*, ll. 181–8 and 348–51. The heavenly and earthly Diana are inextricably mixed in the first eight lines; not only are Diana's knights and nymphs Elizabeth's, but also 'that power by which all powers abound' seems to belong both to Elizabeth and to the Moon. In l. 10 'aye' has been emended to 'air' by Sir Edmund Chambers (cf. Latham, p. 104); it seems rather to be a synonym for the 'eternity' of the next line though the expression 'in aye' seems (to say the least of it) unusual. l. 15: the virtues of the stars (i.e. the astrological 'virtues' or powers, by which they affect things mortal) slide down through the orb of the moon (the vast transparent orb, in which the visible body of the moon was thought to be fixed) to the earth. Last line—let them live like the beasts transformed by Circe out of men. There may be an allusion to this poem in the *XIth Book to Cynthia*, ll. 348–51; but he may be quoting from verses now lost. For l. 14, cf. 'Whatsoever is under the moon and is subject to alteration' in the *History*.

1581–1587

V

The brainsick race that wanton youth ensues
Without regard to grounded wisdom's lore,
As often as I think thereon, renews
The fresh remembrance of an ancient sore;
   Revoking to my pensive thoughts at last
   The worlds of wickedness that I have passed.

And though experience bids me bite on bit,
And champ the bridle of a better smack,
Yet costly is the price of after wit,
Which brings so cold repentance at her back;
  And skill that's with so many losses bought,
  Men say is little better worth than nought.

And yet this fruit I must confess doth grow
Of folly's scourge; that though I now complain
Of error past, yet henceforth I may know
To shun the whip that threats the like again:
  For wise men though they smart awhile, had liefer
  To learn experience at the last, than never.

Before 1593 at any rate, when it was printed in the *Phoenix Nest*, and Miss Latham convincingly ascribes it to Raleigh's early manner. 'Ensues' in l. 1—i.e. the brainsick race which youth pursues or follows. ll. 7, 8: experience tells me to recognise the curb of the bit and bridle when I feel it. The image of the racing horse seems to recur from the 'race' of the first line to the 'whip' of the last but three. But the 'better smack' is difficult. The use of 'smack' for the crack of a whip seems to be later; does it mean perhaps the bridle that *tastes* better than the bridle bit I would have to wear if I offended again? 'After wit': for the adjectival use of such adverbs cf. the letter printed on p. 77 'For after revenges, fear them not . . . after fears are but prophecies.' 'Worlds of wickedness'; characteristic Raleigh also. cf. 'a world of examples'; 'world of an army'; 'worlds of enemies' from the *History*; also, from the same, for the idea of the poem: 'having learned wit by the ill-success of their folly'.

VI

Those eyes which set my fancy on a fire
Those crispèd hairs, which hold my heart in chains,
Those dainty hands, which conquered my desire,
That wit, which of my thoughts doth hold the reins;

Those eyes for clearness do the stars surpass,
Those hairs obscure the brightness of the sun,
Those hands more white than ever ivory was,
That wit even to the skies hath glory won;

Amore et virtute

LA MILITIA ROMANA
DI POLIBIO, DI TITO LIVIO,
E DI DIONIGI ALICARNASEO.

DA FRANCESCO PATRICII
DICHIARATA, E CON VARIE
FIGVRE ILLVSTRATA.

La quale a pieno intefa, non folo darà altrui ftupore de' fuoi
buoni ordini, e difciplina.

*Ma ancora, in paragone, farà chiaro, quanto la moderna fia difettofa
& imperfetta.*

IN FERRARA PER DOMENICO MAMARELLI,
A Santa Agnefe. **M D LXXXIII.**

Con licenza de' Superiori.

Raleigh the soldier; a book on military operations in the writers of anti-
quity; with Raleigh's motto in his own hand. Probably about 1586

O eyes that pierce our hearts without remorse,
O hairs of right that wears a royal crown,
O hands that conquer more than Caesar's force,
O wit, that turns huge kingdoms upside down.

    Then, Love, be judge, what heart may thee withstand:
    Such eyes, such hair, such wit, and such a hand.

At least before 1593 when it was printed in the *Phoenix Nest*, and
clearly in the early manner. Miss Latham though she keeps it in the
'conjectural' group (since its appearance among other poems in
the *Phoenix Nest* plausibly given to Raleigh is the only formal
authority for its authorship) seems, justifiably, convinced that ll.
9–12 are not an allegory addressed by any poet to any mistress, but
were written to the Queen. 'Eyes that pierce'; cf. 'eyes transpersant' in No. XXV, l. 40.

1581–1587

VII

Those eyes that holds the hand of every heart
Those hands that holds the heart of every eye,
That wit that goes beyond all Nature's art,
That sense too deep for wisdom to descry,
    That eye, that hand, that wit, that heavenly sense
    All these doth show my Mistress' excellence.

O eyes that pierce into the purest heart,
O hands that hold the highest hearts in thrall
O wit that weighs the depth of all desart[1]
O sense that shows the secret sweet of all,
    The heaven of heavens with heavenly power preserve thee!
    Love but thyself, and give me leave to serve thee.

To serve, to live, to look upon those eyes,
To look, to live, to kiss that heavenly hand,
To sound that wit, that doth amaze the wise
To know that sense no sense can understand,
    To understand that all the world may know
    Such wit, such sense, eyes, hands, there are no moe.[2]

Earlier than 1591 when it was first printed in *Britton's Bowre of*

    [1] *desart* = desert.   [2] *moe* = more.

Delights. It goes closely with No. VI and evidently belongs to the same period. In l. 8 'the highest hearts' seem to be a reference to Elizabeth's suitors. Miss Latham prints it in the group of poems conjecturally ascribed to Raleigh for the same reasons as those indicated in the note on No. VI.

1581–1587

VIII

Our Passions are most like to floods and streams;
The shallow murmur; but the deep are dumb.
So when affections yield discourse, it seems
The bottom is but shallow whence they come.
    They that are rich in words must needs discover
    That they are poor in that which makes a lover.

    Wrong not, dear Empress of my heart
      The merit of true passion,
    With thinking that he feels no smart
      That sues for no compassion;
    Since if my plaints serve not to prove
      The conquest of your beauty
    It comes not from defect of love
      But from excess of duty.

    For knowing that I sue to serve
      A saint of such perfection,
    As all desire but none deserve
      A place in her affection,
    I rather choose to want relief
      Than venture the revealing;
    When Glory recommends the grief
      Despair distrusts the healing.

    Thus those desires that aim too high
      For any mortal lover,
    When reason cannot make them die
      Discretion will them cover.
    Yet when discretion doth bereave
      The plaints that they should utter

Then your discretion may perceive
    That silence is a suitor.

Silence in love bewrays more woe
    Than words, though ne'er so witty;
A beggar that is dumb, ye know,
    Deserveth double pity.
Then misconceive not, dearest heart,
    My true, though secret passion,
He smarteth most that hides his smart
    And sues for no compassion.

l. 1. The idea's immediate derivation is probably Sir Philip Sidney, *Arcadia*, I, 127 'Shallow brooks murmur most, deep silent slide away'. There is no early printed authority for the poem but it must surely belong to the end of the early period.

1581–1587

IX

See those sweet eyes, those more than sweetest eyes
Eyes whom the stars exceed not in their grace
See Love at gaze, Love that would fain devise
But cannot speak to plead his wondrous case.

Love would discharge the duty of his heart
In beauty's praise, whose greatness doth deny
Words to his thoughts, and thoughts to her desart;
Which high conceits since nothing can supply

    Love here constrained through conquest to confess
    Bids silence sigh, that tongue cannot express.

This fragment—the original had evidently an opening four-line stanza which did not suit the composer—was set to music by William Byrd and printed in 1589. Byrd was Organist of the Chapel Royal, and certainly had access to some of Raleigh's verse; thus he published, in 1588, No. XVI 'Farewell, false love', to a musical setting. For the sentiment of this poem, cf. that of 'Wrong not dear Empress of my heart'; but this seems just that much more serious as possibly to justify its placing at least towards the end of the first period. The rhyme 'heart-desart' occurs frequently in Raleigh, cf. Nos. VII, XVIII, but seems to have been fairly common at the period. Elizabeth's greatness denying words to Raleigh's thoughts (ll. 6 and 7) would be a natural figure in view of their relationship and is paralleled by the dramatic situation imagined in VIII when the poet cannot speak his passion because his desires aim too high. I print another poem, 'Wounded I am. . . .' (No. XIV) from the same source, believing that both are by Raleigh.

1581–1587

X

In vain mine Eyes, in vain ye waste your tears;
In vain my sighs, the smokes of my despairs;
In vain you search the Earth and Heaven above;
In vain you seek, for Fortune keeps my love.

Then will I leave my love in Fortune's hand;
Then will I leave my love in wordling's band,
And only serve the sorrows due to me.
Sorrow, henceforth, that shall my Princess be.

And only joy that Fortune conquers kings;
Fortune, that rules the Earth and earthly things
Hath ta'en my love in spite of virtue's might.
So blind a goddess did never virtue right.

With wisdom's eyes had but blind Fortune seen
Then had my love my love for ever been;
But, love, farewell; though Fortune conquer thee
No fortune base nor frail shall alter me.

Until 1958 these verses were unknown except for the first four lines, and ll. 13 and 14, all of which had been printed (and definitely assigned to Raleigh) in 1589 by the writer, generally accepted as George Puttenham, of the *Arte of English Poesie*. He quotes the first stanza as an instance of 'Anaphora, or the figure of report', and quotes the other two lines a little later. The readings 'mine' in l. 1 and 'seek' in l. 4 come from Puttenham, the manuscript (Phillipps MS. 3602) in which the complete poem was discovered giving 'my' in l. 1 and 'search' in l. 4. In the second line the manuscript reads 'sightes' for 'sighs'. This doubtless reflects Raleigh's spelling of the word: he writes it 'sythes' or 'scythes'. In view of the apparent inaccuracy of the copy, I venture also to print 'serve' in l. 7, from the later 'Fortune my Foe', see l. 31, on p. 218. Palaeographically it seems easy and like Raleigh's alliteration. Phillipps MS. 3602 was examined by Raleigh's eighteenth-century biographer Oldys, who has left his note against the first stanza to the effect that he quoted the six lines [from Puttenham] in Sir Walter Raleigh's life 'from good authority [doubtless Puttenham's] as of his composition' and so 'I find this whole sonnet to have been composed by him: though I fear it is not very correctly transcribed, because of the uneven measure in some lines'. He adds, 'I take it to be the same song of Sir W.R's wch was so much in vogue in his own time and long since being often printed in Ballads etc., called Fortune my Foe, why does thou frown on me? but altered by him or somebody else.' Oldys has altered 'taken' in the manuscript, l. 11, to 'ta'en', which no doubt represents the pronunciation intended. No other entry in Phillipps MS. 3602 is later than 1587, so that it seems to push the latest possible date of the poem's composition at least two years earlier than the date, 1589, which the publication of extracts in Puttenham would allow. Moreover, it follows, in the MS., a list of the offices which were conferred on Raleigh in 1585 and which took him from court to the West Country (Lieutenant-General of Cornwall; Deputy-Lieutenant of Devonshire; Warden of the Stannaries, etc.); it is tempting to see a connection in the scribe's mind between the theme of the verses and the appointment to these offices, which involved their holder in frequent absences from the Court. See Pl. VIII for the Phillipps MS. text.

With the assistance of Miss Margaret Crum of the Bodleian Library I have run to earth a copy of the song 'Fortune my Foe' mentioned by Oldys (see above) and it is printed in an appendix (Appendix II). Its author, whom one would put some years later than Raleigh, if the smoothness of the style were a fair criterion, lacked inspiration, but seems to have borrowed lines of Raleigh's poem to make up for that deficiency. A song 'Fortune my Foe' is specified in one of Lyly's plays, and there is perhaps an allusion to it in the *Merry Wives of Windsor*. The tune is as early as the Fitzwilliam Virginal Book. Raleigh may himself have borrowed freely from some earlier version of 'Fortune my Foe'. If only this earliest version were discoverable, we might see precisely the process of a ballad being writ o'er', for the process has clearly gone on in this instance (see also above, p. 113). It is not surprising (in view of Puttenham's attribution of six lines to Raleigh all of which were included verbatim in 'Fortune my Foe') that Oldys should have ascribed 'Fortune my Foe' to Raleigh.

I have to thank the present owners of the Phillipps MS. in question (Messrs. Lionel and Philip Robinson) for drawing my attention to it as likely to have a Raleigh interest. They were indeed right. They are owed my thanks also for leave to withhold the discovery till the publication of this book.

What can be the significance of the other eight lines of verse that appear on the same page in Phillipps MS. 3602 it is hard to say. They seem to refer to the poet's royal mistress. Yet they can, at best, be only a first rough draft, and I can offer no explanation why they should have been copied out in an apparent fair copy.

1581–1587

XI

Sought by the world, and hath the world disdained
Is she, my heart, for whom thou dost endure,
Unto whose grace, sith Kings have not obtained,
Sweet is thy choice, though loss of life be sour;
    Yet to the man, whose youth such pains must prove,
    No better end, than that which comes by Love.

Steer then thy course unto the port of death
Sith thy hard hap no better hap may find,
Where when thou shalt unlade thy latest breath,
Envy herself shall swim to save thy mind,
    Whose body sunk in search to gain the shore
    Where many a prince had perishèd before.

And yet, my heart, it might have been forseen,
Sith skilful medicine mends each kind of grief;
Then in my breast full safely hadst thou been.
But thou, my heart, wouldst never me believe,
    Who told thee true, when first thou didst aspire
    Death was the end of every such desire.

Printed by Miss Latham (from the *Phoenix Nest*, and so before 1593) among the group of poems doubtfully attributed to Raleigh.

fortune hathe taken away my love
my lyves joy and my soules heaven above
fortune hathe taken thee away my princes
my worldes joy, and my true fantasies mistris

fortune hathe taken thee away from mee;
fortune hathe taken all: by takinge thee:
deade to all joyes; J only lyve to wce;
so ys fortune becomme my fantasies foe

by this Stanza; and
the two first lines
of the last, which
J have quoted in Sr
Walter Raleigh's Life;
from good Authority;
as of his Composition;
J find this whole
Sonnet to have
bein composed by him.
Thoʃear it is not
very correctly Tran-
ʃcribed, because of the
unevuen Measure
in some Lines.
        W.O.

In vayne my Eyes, in vayne yee waste yor teares;
In vayne my sightes, the smoke of my dispayres;
In vayne you searche the Earthe and heaven above;
In vayne you searche, for fortune keeps my love.

Then will J leave my love in fortunes hande;
Then will J leave my love in worldlinges' hande;
and only love the sorrowes due to mee;
sorrowe, henceforthe, that shall my princes bee.

And only joye that fortune Conquers kinges;
fortune, that rules the Earthe and earthly thinges,
hathe taken my love, in spighte of vertues mighte:
so blinde A goddes did never vertue righte.

With wisdome's eyes, had but blinde fortune seene;
then had my love, my love for ever beene:
but love farewell: thoughe fortune conquer thee;
no fortune base, nor frayle, shall alter mee.

J take it to be the
ʃame Song of Sr Wr
R's wch was so much
in Vogue in his own
tims and long since;
being often printed in
Ballads &c called
Fortune, my Foe
Why dost thou
frown on me &c
but altered by him
or some body else

Verses (here first printed) apparently addressed by Raleigh to the Queen;
this copy, not in Raleigh's hand, written not later than 1587

But I find the attribution convincing. The lady 'unto whose grace Kings (cf. also l. 12) have not obtained' is clearly the Queen; apparently the poet's choice of her is sweet to her ('unto whose grace') though it must involve for him the sourness of death. The second stanza is made up of images of the ship coming to harbour and unloading; but l. 10 is obscure. Apparently when his last breath has left him, unloaded before he can reach the hoped-for shore, even Envy herself will be moved (as anything would be, she last of all) to come and save his mind.

1581–1587

XII

TO CYNTHIA

My thoughts are winged with hopes, my hopes with love,
Mount love unto the Moon in clearest night;
And say, as she doth in the heavens move,
On earth so wanes and waxeth my delight.
  And whisper this but softly in her ears
  Hope oft doth hang the head, and trust shed tears.

And you my thoughts that some mistrust do carry,
If for mistrust my Mistress do you blame,
Say though you alter, yet you do not vary,
As she doth change, and yet remain the same.
  Distrust doth enter hearts, but not infect,
  And love is sweetest, seasoned with suspect.

If she for this with clouds do mask her eyes,
And make the heavens dark with her disdain,
With windy sighs disperse them to the skies,
Or with thy tears dissolve them into rain.
  Thoughts, hopes, and love, return to me no more
  Till Cynthia shine, as she hath done before.

From *England's Helicon*, 1600. This is not one of the poems originally ascribed to Raleigh by his initials in the first printing of *England's Helicon* (cf. above, p. 149) but is printed there from a book of Dowland's songs which had appeared three years before: 'the authors names not there set down (says the editor of *England's*

Helicon) and therefore left to their owners.' It seems to me to have the Raleigh signature all over it; for ll. 9–10 for example, cf. No. IV, l. 11 'Eternity in her oft change she bears'; or the apostrophising 'And you, my thoughts . . .' for which cf. No. XVII, l. 13 'And you my words . . .' or the characteristic 'And whisper this but softly . . .' in l. 5; 'Mount love unto the moon'; cf. his hopes in Cynthia which 'not long since the highest heaven scaled'. In *England's Helicon* the poem has three companions from the Dowland; I do not find any of Raleigh's characteristics in 'Come away, come sweet Love' but am not prepared completely to rule out the possibility of the other two ('Burst forth my tears' . . . and the well-known 'Away with these self-loving lads') being by Raleigh.

At the beginning of stanza 2: the poet's thoughts carry their own share of mistrust, at the same time as he is blaming his Mistress for mistrusting him; tell her therefore not to mistrust him; he alters but does not vary, as through her changes she also remains nevertheless the same.

1581–1587

XIII

A secret murder hath been done of late;
Unkindness found to be the bloody knife,
And she that did the deed a dame of state,
Fair, gracious, wise as any beareth life.

To quit[1] herself, this answer did she make:
Mistrust (quoth she) hath brought him to his end,
Which makes the man so much himself mistake,
To lay the guilt unto his guiltless friend.

Lady, not so; not feared[2] I found my death;
For no desert thus murdered is my mind;
And yet before I yield my fainting breath,
I quit the killer, though I blame the kind.

> You kill unkind; I die, and yet am true,
> For at your sight, my wound doth bleed anew.

Before 1593, when it appeared in the *Phoenix Nest*; included therefore by Miss Latham in her conjectural group. Miss Latham

---

[1] *quit*= acquit. [2] *feared*= afeared.

observes that 'the conceit has something of Raleigh's unexpected-
ness and violence', but the poem nevertheless gives me the impression of belonging to the early phase. ll. 6–9 (mistrust); cf. perhaps
ll. 5–6 of No. XII ('My thoughts are winged with hopes' . . .).
Several of the stories of Raleigh's early years at court are concerned
with his 'mistrust' and Elizabeth's encouragement (cf. p. 22); she
is clearly in this poem the 'dame of state' of l. 3. Miss Latham explains 'the kind' of l. 12 as referring to 'womankind'.

1587–1592

XIV

Wounded I am but dare not seek relief
For this new stroke, unseen but not unfelt,
No blood nor bruise is witness of my grief,
But sighs and tears with which I mourn and melt.

If I complain, my witness is suspect;
If I contain, with cares I am undone;
Sit still and die, tell truth and be reject;
O hateful choice that sorrow cannot shun.

Yet of us twain whose loss shall be the less,
Mine of my life, or you of your good name?
Light is my death regarding my distress;
But your offence cries out to your diffame.

    A virgin fair hath slain for lack of grace
    The man that made an idol of her face.

For the source cf. No. IX. This, like that poem, was in print at
least as early as 1589. For the general sentiment, cf. No. XIII 'A secret
murder hath been done of late', or the *XIth Book to Cynthia*, ll. 196–
200. Spenser's description of Timias's lamentation in the *Faerie
Queene*, Bk. III, Canto V, stanzas 45–7 is reminiscent of the second
quatrain; but for the idea of the last six lines compare rather the
Cynthia passage, talking of Cynthia's perfections;

    These be the tyrants that in fetters tie
    Their wounded vassals, yet nor kill nor cure,
    But glory in their lasting misery.

XV

MELIBEUS	Shepherd, what's Love, I pray thee tell?

FAUSTUS	It is that Fountain and that well
	Where pleasure and repentance dwell.
	It is perhaps that sauncing bell[1]
	    That tolls all into heaven or hell,
	    And that is love as I heard tell.

MELIBEUS	Yet what is Love, I prithee say?

FAUSTUS	It is a work on holiday,
	It is December matched with May,
	When lusty-bloods in fresh array
	    Hear ten months after of the play
	    And this is love, as I hear say.

MELIBEUS	Yet what is love, good Shepherd saine?

FAUSTUS	It is a sunshine mixed with rain,
	It is a tooth-ache or like pain,
	It is a game where none doth gain;
	    The lass saith no, and would full fain;
	    And this is love, as I hear saine.

MELIBEUS	Yet Shepherd, what is love, I pray?

FAUSTUS	It is a yea, it is a nay,
	A pretty kind of sporting fray,
	It is a thing will soon away,
	    Then nymphs take vantage which ye may;
	    And this is love, as I hear say.

MELIBEUS	Yet what is love, good Shepherd, show?

FAUSTUS	A thing that creeps, it cannot go,
	A prize that passeth to and fro,
	A thing for one, a thing for moe,[2]
	    And he that proves shall find it so;
	    And Shepherd, this is love, I troe.[3]

---

[1] *sauncing bell* = sanctus bell.   [2] *moe* = more.   [3] *troe* = trow.

Printed anonymously in the *Phoenix Nest*, 1593; it does not however, occur in the Raleigh group there, and Miss Latham does not ascribe it to Raleigh. But it was also printed in *England's Helicon* in 1600, with the initials S.W.R., originally attached to it, normally later covered with a cancel slip; cf. No. IV. There is every reason to think that in 1600 as much as ever Raleigh was disowning his poetry (which even in 1589 according to Puttenham he was reluctant to print); and these cancel slips over his initials may have been the result of a direct request to the Editor of the anthology. In the Bodleian copies in Oxford these are covered with the cancel slip, which carries the ascription *Ignoto*. There is also a manuscript ascription to Raleigh, and I doubt whether the rejection can be justified. Raleigh's manner, in the poems certainly his, is too diverse for it to be safe to say that he could not have written it. The Arcadian fashion had been started at court by Sidney's *Arcadia*; Raleigh was the 'Shepherd of the Ocean', as appears from *Colin Clout* (see p. 83). 'Cynthia' may have included poems written for the Queen's amusement, not only those directly addressed to her. For the opening line, compare the passage quoted from the *Delectable Demands*, on No. XVI.

For Miss Latham's criticism of this poem which she thinks trivial and shallow for Raleigh, see p. 171 in her 1951 edition of his poems.

1581–1587

XV

Is Love a boy? What means he then to strike?
Or is he blind? Why will he be a guide?
Is he a man? Why doth he hurt his like?
Is he a god? Why doth he men deride?
Not one of these, but one compact of all.
A wilful boy, a man still dealing blows,
Of purpose blind to lead men to their thrall,
A god that rules unruly, God he knows!
Boy pity me that am a child again,
Blind, be no more my guide to make me stray.
Man, use thy might to force away my pain,
God, do me good and lead me to my way.

And if thou beest a power to me unknown
Power of my life, let here thy grace be shown.

From the Byrd, *Songs of Sundrie Natures*, printed in 1589, cf. No. IX. I assign this conjecturally to Raleigh on similar grounds to those on which the two other conjectural attributions from this collection set to music by Byrd are made: cf. No. XIV. The use of 'still' in l. 6 (= always) is frequent in Raleigh and as Professor C. S. Lewis points out, is usual in the sixteenth century; though the meaning of 'up to now' also occurs. For these uses compare No. XX,

> *And at my gate despair shall linger still* (i.e always)

or No. XVII:

> *So let her love, and so be still* (i.e. always) *denied*

or No. XVIII:

> *Yet still accuse thy fortune for the fault*

or No. II:

> *A body born to lose his labour still.*

For the other meaning 'already' which is perhaps better here than 'always', cf. the *XIth Book to Cynthia*, l. 125:

> *My mind still feeling sorrowful success*

where 'already' is certainly the meaning. Here though Love is a boy, he is also a man, already dealing blows to those around him.

1587–1592

XVI

Farewell false love, the oracle of lies,
A mortal foe and enemy to rest;
An envious boy, from whom all cares arise,
A bastard vile, a beast with rage possessed;
A way of error; a temple full of treason,
In all effects contrary unto reason.

A poisoned serpent coloured all with flowers,
Mother of sighs and murderer of repose

A sea of sorrows from whence are drawn such showers
As moisture lend to every grief that grows;
A school of guile, a net of deep deceit,
A gilded hook, that holds a poisoned bait.

A fortress foiled, which reason did defend,
A Siren song, a fever of the mind,
A maze wherein affection finds no end,
A ranging cloud that runs before the wind,
A substance like the shadow of the sun,
A goal of grief for which the wisest run.

A quenchless fire, a nurse of trembling fear,
A path that leads to peril and mishap,
A true retreat of sorrow and despair,
An idle boy that sleeps in pleasure's lap,
A deep mistrust of that which certain seems,
A hope of that which reason doubtful deems.

Sith then thy trains my younger years betrayed
And for my faith ingratitude I find,
And sith repentance hath my wrongs bewrayed
Whose course was ever contrary to kind:
False Love! Desire! And Beauty frail, adieu!
Dead is the root whence all these fancies grew.

In print by 1588, when it was published set to music by Byrd
(cf. Nos. IX and XIV; this one is from the collection published a
year earlier). Though it was already in print at this early date, the
first line of the last stanza associates it with the second rather than
the first group of poems, as does indeed the savage rejection of
Love which is its theme. Though this poem is so finely done, it
makes its start from a series of Elizabethan commonplaces, cf. *Delectable Demands and pleasant Questions, with their severall Aunswers*
(*1566*): 'Tell me then what thing is love? It is a passion that doth
blind the spirits, removeth the understanding, taketh all the memory away, causeth ruin and loss of goods, maketh a man weak
and is the enemy of old age; the mother of all vices; the receptacle
of pensive minds; a thing without reason, without order and
stability, and the whirlpool of man's liberty.' But Raleigh has made
a powerful poem out of it.

1587–1592

XVII

My first-born love unhappily conceived,
Brought forth in pain, and christened with a curse,
Die in your Infancy, of life bereaved
    By your cruel nurse.

Restless desire, from my love that proceeded,
Leave to be, and seek your heaven by dying,
Since you, O you? your own hope have exceeded
    By too high flying.

And you, my words, my heart's faithful expounders
No more offer your jewel, unesteemed,
Since those eyes my Love's life and life's confounders
    Your worth misdeemed.

Love leave to desire, words leave it to utter,
Swell on my thoughts, till you break that contains you;
My complaints in those deaf ears no more mutter
    That so disdains you.

And you careless of me, that without feeling,
With dry eyes behold my tragedy smiling,
Deck your proud triumphs with your poor slave's yielding
    To his own spoiling.

But if that wrong, or holy truth despised
To just revenge the heavens ever moved,
So let her love, and so be still denied
    Who she so loved.

Before 1593 at any rate, when it was printed in the *Phoenix Nest* (see above, p. 131). The image of the nurse in ll. 3–4 seems to be paralleled in *Cynthia*, ll. 321–3. ll. 7–8; the 'too high flying' may be an expression of the mood described on p. 39. Certainly the poem would appear to belong to this phase. l. 6 'leave to be': i.e. give up life. l. 9: You, my verses, must cease offering your unwanted, unreturned pearls, since my Mistress's eyes, the life of my love, and the confounders of my life think little of your worth. Stanza 4 seems to imply a distinction between desire and the poet's love—by implication of a higher order; for this idea, compare the

XIth Book to Cynthia, 336, though then the allusion to the 'desire' as opposed to his real love comes only in the word 'error'. Leave love, and writing about love, to desire; leave my thoughts to swell up (without the outlet of expression) till they burst out and break that which contains them. ll. 19 and 20: his Mistress shall deck her triumphs with the spoils yielded to her willingly by her slave. Last stanza: if wrongs and holy truth despised ever move the heavens to take revenge, let my Mistress love as I have loved, and be so denied. l. 18; cf. My soul the stage of fancy's tragedy, in the *XIth Book to Cynthia*, l. 144; this image of the stage appears elsewhere also in *Cynthia*, and frequently in the *History*.

1587–1592

XVIII

Feed still thyself, thou fondling, with belief,
Go hunt thy hope that never took effect,
Accuse the wrongs that oft have wrought thy grief,
And reckon sure where reason would suspect.

Dwell in the dreams of wish and vain desire,
Pursue the faith that flies and seeks to new,
Run after hopes that mock thee with retire,
And look for love where liking never grew.

Devise conceits to ease thy careful heart,
Trust upon times and days of grace behind,
Presume the rights of promise and desart,[1]
And measure love by thy believing mind.

Force thy affects[2] that spite doth daily chase;
Wink at the wrongs with wilful oversight;
See not the soil and stain of thy disgrace,
Nor reck disdain to dote on thy delight.

And when thou seest the end of thy reward,
And these effects ensue of thine assault,
When rashness rues, that reason should regard,
Yet still accuse thy fortune for the fault.

And cry, O Love, O death, O vain desire
When thou complainst the heat, and feeds the fire.

---

[1] *desart*=desert.   [2] *affects*=affections.

The Poems to Cynthia

At any rate before 1593; this powerful poem is one of Miss Latham's conjectural group, see above, p. 151. The poet blames himself for living in a fool's paradise. His Mistress has never had any liking for him, though he still looks for her love. Stanza I, l. 3: he is apparently only now to start accusing wrongs that have often worked his grief already. Stanza 3: he is to plan fanciful thoughts, or perhaps verses, to help him forget his unhappiness, trusting on what is past and gone ('days of grace behind'); he is (poor fool) to assume as valid promises and the reward of his deserts, and measure his mistress's love by his own imagination's scale. Stanza 4: spite is daily putting his affection to flight—let him go on forcing that affection, poor fool; let him overlook wrongs done to him, and, his mind infatuate with previous delight, let him be blind to the disgrace which is soiling him. Stanza 5: when the effects of his attempt to storm the fortress are seen and his rashness is forced to regret the actions of which reason ought to have warned him, then, poor fool, let him go on blaming his ill fortune rather than his ill judgement; let him go on stoking up the fires that are scorching him.

1587–1592

XIX[1]

Would I were chang'd into that golden shower
That so divinely streamèd from the skies
To fall in drops upon my dainty flower,
Where in her bed she solitary lies;
    Then would I hope such showers as richly shine
    Would pierce more deep than those waste tears of mine.

Else would I were that plumèd swan, snow white,
Under whose form was hidden heavenly power;
Then in that river would I most delight
Whose waves do beat against her stately bower,
    And in those banks so tune my dying song
    That her deaf ears would think my plaints too long.

Or would I were Narcissus that sweet boy,
And she herself the fountain crystal clear
Who ravish'd with the pride of his own joy
Drenchèd his limbs with gazing over near;

[1] This version is based on that in the Gorges manuscript, B.M. Egerton 3165.

166

So should I bring my soul to happy rest
To end my life in that I lovèd best.

In Miss Latham's conjectural group; see above, p. 151. Raleigh's authorship however is now contested by the editor of a comparatively recently discovered manuscript entitled 'Sir Arthur Gorges his vanities and toys of youth'; a manuscript in a scribe's hand, but carrying corrections by Sir Arthur Gorges himself (B.M. Egerton MS. 3165) [It is from this manuscript that the reading here adopted for l. 3 is taken]. But the occurrence of the poem in that collection is not conclusive evidence of Gorges's authorship. Whatever the 'copy' the scribe had in front of him, it included work that was not by Gorges; after the poem numbered by the editor, Miss Sandison, 76 occurs a set of verses headed 'Of Mounsieur', which Gorges himself notes as being by Churchyard. There is moreover contemporary manuscript ascription of our poem to Raleigh (B.M. Harley MS. 7392) though that is not conclusive either. And it is not difficult to discover the reason why Gorges should have included it in the collection. It comes immediately before his own sonnet in praise of Elizabeth's chastity:

> . . . *A mind reposed whence no vain fancies rise;*
> *Desires that tend unto the heavenly throne*
> *The worlds beloved whom love cannot surprise . . .*

as if Gorges were saying, 'Here is Raleigh's disastrous poem, and here mine which smoothed things down.' I have suggested on pp. 95–6 that Spenser's use of the striking phrase 'golden shower' in the introductory sonnet to the *Faerie Queene* addressed to Raleigh, is a reminiscence of this charming poem:

> *My rhymes I know unsavory and sour*
> *To taste the streams that, like a golden shower*
> *Flow from they fruitful head, of thy love's praise . . .*

('thy' here is Raleigh, to whom the sonnet is addressed).

It is true that Spenser himself uses the phrase elsewhere in a reference to the Danae story. Both that passage (Book III, Canto XI, stanza 31) and this poem depend ultimately on a poem by Desportes for the text of which see Miss Latham, p. 161. But the relationship of the Raleigh is much closer, and there is nothing to show that in Spenser the derivation is independent and not through this poem itself. Raleigh was strongly influenced by Desportes at this stage, cf. No. XX.

Raleigh has the phrase 'golden shower' again in translating the Danae story from Horace, *Odes*, III, xvi in the *History of the World*, Book II, chapter xiii, § 4. But it became a commonplace in that context; in the St. Michael's MS. to which I refer elsewhere (see pp. 206–7) for example, there is the following variant of it:

> *Danae the fair, within a tower inclos'd,*
> *Her sweet lamenting through the clouds of sorrow*
> *To Jove her grief disclos'd;*
> *The god enamour'd with her beauty flowering*
> *Came down from heav'n a golden tempest showering.*

Another version produced in the nineties which borrows the same striking phrase is in Barnabe Barnes, *Parthenophil and Parthenope* 1593 (I quote from the unique Chatsworth copy which, from the corrections, seems to have claims to have been revised by the poet) Sonnet LXIII. [I give it in the original spelling as this is not readily accessible elsewhere]:

> *Iove for Europaes love took shape of Bull*
> *And for Calisto playde Dianaes parte*
> *And in a golden shower, he fillèd full*
> *The Lappe of Danae with coelestiall arte,*
> *Would I were chang'd but to my mistresse gloves*
> *That those white lovely fingers I might hide. . . .*

Here the debt to our poem is obvious. Barnes's dedications, incidentally, associate him at this time (in his imagination, if not in fact) with Essex and Southampton. By this time we have travelled a long distance since Sidney's:

> *Some one his songs in Jove and Jove's strange tales attires,*
> *Bordered with Bulls and Swans, powdered with golden rain.*
>
> *Astrophel and Stella*, VI, 5–6.

The literary work of Gorges and Raleigh (as has often been shown) was very closely related; for a striking example cf. the sonnet, Miss Sandison's 110, which is heavily weighted with phrases taken from the *XIth and last Book to Cynthia*; so much so that Miss Sandison seems at first to suggest that particular work as being by Raleigh himself (cf. *The Poems of Sir Arthur Gorges*, p. 230).

Miss Latham thinks that the reference in l. 10 might be to one of Elizabeth's riverside palaces. Read side by side with the other poems of this period addressed by Raleigh to Elizabeth, this one is notably more erotic in character. I have discussed this feature on p. 95. The anticipation of death, ll. 11–12, 17–18, as the price of desire at the end of stanzas 2 and 3 is typical of Raleigh. It is not implied in the French original.

1587–1592

XX

Like to a hermit poor in place obscure
I mean to spend my days of endless doubt,
To wail such woes as time cannot recure,
Where none but Love shall ever find me out.

My food shall be of care and sorrow made,
My drink nought else but tears fall'n from mine eyes,
And for my light in such obscurèd shade
The flames shall serve, which from my heart arise.

A gown of grey my body shall attire,
My staff of broken hope whereon I'll stay;
Of late repentance link'd with long desire
The couch is fram'd whereon my limbs I'll lay;

And at my gate despair shall linger still
To let in death, when Love and Fortune will.

First printed in *Britton's Bowre of Delights*, 1591; the sonnet surely belongs to the second period. It is based on a poem by Desportes, for the text of which see Miss Latham's note (Latham, p. 107). The despairing conclusion is Raleigh's addition, and is characteristic of him. Allusion is made to this poem in an anonymous letter purporting to be written in the summer of 1592; it is however a forgery: see p. 42, where Lady Raleigh's allusion to this poem in a letter written somewhat later (and certainly genuine!) is quoted. Spenser probably had the poem in mind in the passage in Book IV, Canto VII, stanzas 38–41, where he describes Timias's retreat from Belphoebe:

> *And finding there fit solitary place*
> *For woful wight, chose out a gloomy shade ...*

169

Ne other drink there did he ever taste
Than running water tempered with his tears, etc.

When Prince Arthur finds him, he thinks it must be the place where some 'holy hermit' lives.

Though this allusion is in a passage which is concerned with the 1592 incident, the fact that the poem appeared in 1591 securely attaches it to the earlier phase of estrangement. The phrase 'late repentance link'd with long desire' may perhaps be taken to suggest such a situation as is proposed on p. 93 above. Desportes has the phrase *tardif repentir*, but does not link it with 'long desire'.

1587–1592

XXI

Like truthless dreams, so are my joys expired,
And past return are all my dandled days;
My love misled, and fancy quite retired,
Of all which past, the sorrow only stays.

My lost delights now clean from sight of land,
Have left me all alone in unknown ways;
My mind to woe, my life in fortune's hand
Of all which past, the sorrow only stays.

As in a country strange without companion,
I only wail the wrong of death's delays,
Whose sweet spring spent, whose summer well nigh done;
Of all which past, the sorrow only stays.

    Whom care forewarns, ere age and winter cold
    To haste me hence, to find my fortune's fold.

To this poem there is a reference in the *XIth and last Book to Cynthia*, where the refrain is quoted followed by the words

    '*So wrote I once and my mishap foretold*
    My mind still feeling sorrowful success'

lines which seem to suggest that differences with Elizabeth prior to the disaster of 1592 had been comparatively unimportant. Raleigh quotes the last phrase 'my fortune's fold' in a letter from Sherborne: see p. 50 where the image is discussed. The reference in

the *XIth and last Book to Cynthia* puts this poem back at least before
1592 (on the assumption that that date for *Cynthia* is now accepted;
the point is argued in the introductory note to the poems, pp. 136–
138 above). This may be one of the poems which Spenser heard in
Ireland, with their recurrent refrain or 'undersong'; cf. p. 83. It
appeared in print in the *Phoenix Nest*, in 1593. There is a reminiscence of it in the *History*: 'Of all our vain passions and affections
past, the sorrow only abideth.'

1587–1592

XXI (a)

[Many desire, but few or none deserve
To win the fort of thy most constant will:
Therefore take heed, let fancy never swerve,
But unto him that will defend thee still.
 For this be sure, the fort of fame once won
 Farewell the rest, thy happy days are done.

Many desire, but few or none deserve
To pluck the flowers and let the leaves to fall;
Therefore take heed, let fancy never swerve,
But unto him that will take leaves and all.
 For this be sure, the flower once pluck'd away,
 Farewell the rest, thy happy days decay.

Many desire, but few or none deserve
To cut the corn, not subject to the sickle.
Therefore take heed, let fancy never swerve,
But constant stand, for mowers' minds are fickle.
 For this be sure, the crop being once obtain'd
 Farewell the rest, the soil will be disdain'd.]

There is good authority for supposing that this was addressed,
not to Elizabeth, but to one of her maids-of-honour, Anne Vava-
sor. It is printed here because the structure with the repeated first
lines and the refrain 'Farewell the rest . . .' perhaps provide another example of the kind of composition which Spenser had in
mind when he talked of the 'undersong' in *Colin Clout*; see note
on No. XXI.

1587–1592

XXII

As you came from the holy land,
  Of Walsingham,
Met you not with my true love
  By the way as you came?

How shall I know your true love
  That have met many one
As I went to the holy land
  That have come, that have gone?

She is neither white nor brown
  But as the heavens fair
There is none hath a form so divine
  In the earth or the air.

Such an one I did meet, good sir,
  Such an angelic face
Who like a queen, like a nymph did appear
  By her gait, by her grace.

She hath left me here all alone
  All alone as unknown
Who sometimes did me lead with herself
  And me loved as her own.

What's the cause that she leaves you alone
  And a new way doth take,
Who loved you once as her own,
  And her joy did you make?

I have loved her all my youth,
  But now old, as you see,
Love likes not the falling fruit
  From the withered tree.

Know that love is a careless child
  And forgets promise past,
He is blind, he is deaf when he list[1]
  And in faith never fast.

[1] *list* = likes.

His desire is a dureless content
    And a trustless joy,
He is won with a world of despair
    And is lost with a toy.

Of womenkind such indeed is the love
    Or the word love abused
Under which many childish desires
    And conceits are excused.

But true love is a durable fire
    In the mind ever burning;
Never sick, never old, never dead,
    From itself never turning.

This, in some ways the most moving of all Raleigh's poems, is certainly the one which makes it hardest to believe that his devotion to Elizabeth was simply an act, devised to forward his ambitions. Miss Latham and Professor F. P. Wilson have pointed to an impressive series of parallels between the images in the ballad and those elsewhere in Raleigh, particularly in the *XIth and last Book to Cynthia* and in the prose works. They have established (as I think) beyond doubt Raleigh's claim to the poem, for which claim there is good early manuscript authority (Bodleian Library, Rawlinson MS. Poet 85). I venture to disagree with Professor C. S. Lewis, *English Literature in the XVIth century*, pp. 519–20, who says: '... we attribute to him the famous 'Walsingham' poem because it is so attributed to him in the Rawlinson MS., but I should not like to do so on internal evidence. The early stanzas are clearly modelled on a popular poem and we owe all their beauty to that model. In stanza 3 we begin to get into a different, anapaestic metre. By the end this has worked up to the fine stanza "But love is a durable fire"; in the preceding stanza we had flat Tottelian morality, and sub-Tottelian cacophony, in "Of womenkind such indeed is the love".' To me the poem seems to show a striking appreciation of the flexibility of ballad rhythms, and it seems to me that in 'writing o'er' this ballad (cf. p. 113). Raleigh has produced a masterpiece. Another version of the Walsingham ballad is sung by Ophelia, 'How shall I your true love know' (*Hamlet*, Act IV, scene iii). l. 33 dureless; so in the *History* 'the false and dureless pleasures of this stage-play world'.

1592

XXIII

THE LAST BOOKS TO CYNTHIA; INTRODUCTORY VERSES (i)

If Cynthia be a Queen, a princess and supreme,
Keep these among the rest, or say it was a dream;
For those that like expound, and those that loathe, express
Meanings, according as their minds are movèd more or less.
For writing what thou art, or showing what thou were,
Adds to the one disdain, to th' other but despair.
Thy mind of neither needs, in both seeing it exceeds.

This enigmatic set of verses is an integral part of the manuscript to which the next three poems (Nos. XXIV to XXVI) belong, and cannot be dissociated from them, see pp. 136–7. This is one reason for rejecting an ingenious interpretation offered by Miss Brad-brook (*School of Night*, pp. 37–8). Another explanation is in Elkin Calhoun Wilson, *England's Eliza*, p. 313, a book I have found use-ful; but I differ from that interpretation *toto caelo*. Like Miss Latham, I find the lines exceedingly difficult, and I have, unlike her, imposed on myself by the plan of this book some obligation to attempt to explain them. It is difficult to be certain in the first place whether they are to be taken only half seriously, like the doggerel lines which Spenser writes as prefaces to his cantos, or are written with some intensity of feeling (perhaps the latter); equally difficult to know why the poet should wrap up the meaning in a riddle.

ll. 3–4 at least are understandable; they mean that the signifi-cance of a poem varies, whether it is a love poem or a hate poem, according to the writer's intensity of feeling. (ll. 1–2) If Cynthia was really a queen, not his gentle mistress (here the idea is perhaps as in l. 327 of the *XIth Book*, the contrast between the regal figure and the lover's mistress), keep (I suppose the poet is to keep) these verses among the rest he has written to her—or say that their whole relationship has been a dream of his imagination. (They are to be kept, and not given to Cynthia) because a poem's meaning de-pends on the strength of the poet's feeling's, whether those feelings are love or hatred, so to tell what he (the poet) once was, and what he is now—as he does in the following poems—is to add to the past, disdain, and to the present, despair. But his mind exceeds in both disdain and despair already. It needs no more of either.

174

'Thou', 'thy' cannot refer to Cynthia, because *her* mind cannot
be said to exceed in despair. 'Disdain' is therefore the experience of
Cynthia's disdain, added to the former Raleigh ('what thou were');
and 'what thou art' is the present Raleigh in his despair. So in the
last line, *Raleigh*'s mind is said to 'exceed' in disdain; it has far
more than its share, from Cynthia.

1592

XXIV

THE LAST BOOKS TO CYNTHIA; INTRODUCTORY VERSES (ii)

> My body in the walls captíved
> Feels not the wounds of spiteful envy,
> But my thralled mind, of liberty deprived
> Fast fetter'd in her ancient memory,
> Doth nought behold but sorrows dying face;
> Such prison erst was so delightful
> As it desired no other dwelling place.
> But time's effects, and destinies despiteful,
> Have changèd both my keeper and my fare.
> Love's fire, and beauty's light, I then had store.
> But now, close kept, as captives wonted are,
> That food, that heat, that light I find no more.
> Despair bolts up my doors, and I alone
> Speak to dead walls, but those hear not my moan.

The wounds of spiteful envy (l. 2): the wounds of what Spenser
calls the Blatant Beast. Raleigh was evidently convinced that his
real enemy was not the Queen, cf. the letter quoted on p. 49. The
prison of l. 6 is the 'ancient memory' of l. 4 in which (l. 7) his
mind used to be content to dwell. In l. 8 'time's effects' may be an
allusion to his own ageing, which is one of the themes of the *XIth
Book* as it had been of 'Walsingham': but it may simply mean in
general 'changes effected by time' in the circumstances.

For the importance of this poem in the dating of the *XIth Book*,
see p. 137. It is perhaps worth noting that these two introductory
poems are not in the formal hand used for most of the text of the
XIth Book, but in that used for the *XIIth Book*. They were probably
written therefore after he had copied the *XIth Book*, not before.

XXV

THE XITH[1] AND LAST BOOK OF THE OCEAN TO CYNTHIA

Sufficeth it to you, my joys interred,
In simple words that I my woes complain;
You that then died when first my fancy erred,
Joys under dust that never live again.

If to the living were my Muse addressed,   5
Or did my mind her own spirit still inhold,
Were not my living passion so repressed,
As to the dead, the dead did these unfold,

Some sweeter words, some more becoming verse
Should witness my mishap in higher kind,   10
But my love's wounds, my fancy in the hearse
(The Idea but resting) of a wasted mind,

The blossoms fallen, the sap gone from the tree,
The broken monuments of my great desires—
From these so lost, what may the affections be,   15
What heat in cinders of extinguished fires?

*   *   *

'The poem opens with death' (Edwards).[2] It is notable how often death intrudes into Raleigh's later love poetry. This book is no exception. In l. 1, 'my joys interred'; these are addressed by the poet, and are the 'you' of l. 3. When first my fancy erred; he is referring no doubt to his affair with E. T., or more correctly to his marriage with E. T.: see pp. 41–5.

l.5. His verse is not addressed to the living for Cynthia has died to him; her own spirit no longer enfolds his mind as in the past; and his own passion is so repressed that it is the dead speaking to the dead.

l. 11–12. I think that his fancy is in the hearse of a wasted mind, and only the Idea rests or remains with him.

The indication of a pause at l. 16 consists of a marginal horizontal line —certainly not in itself decisive—and a capital letter beginning l. 17. The mark is, in fact, introduced to draw the poet's attention again to the passage at some later reading, but I suggest that his plan often was (as here) eventually to open a gap in the final version, so as to show a pause, as I have here shown.

---

[1] For discussion of the reading 'XIth', see Latham, *Poems*, p. 120.
[2] Philip Edwards: *Sir Walter Ralegh*: 1953.

Lost in the mud of those high flowing streams   17
Which through more fairer fields their courses bend,
Slain with self thoughts, amazed in fearful dreams,
Woes without date, discomforts without end,   20

From fruitful trees I gather withered leaves,
And glean the broken ears with miser's hands;
Who sometimes did enjoy the weighty sheaves,
I seek fair flowers amid the brinish sand.

[*   *   *]

All in the shade even in the fair sun days   25
Under those healthless trees I sit alone,
When joyful birds sing neither lovely lays,
Nor Philomene recounts her direful moan.

No feeding flocks, no shepherd's company
That might renew my dolorous conceit,   30
While happy then, while love and fantasy
Confined my thoughts on that fair flock to wait;

With each of the pauses indicated below, a note is given of the manu-script 'authority' for the pause. It will be seen that I have sometimes ventured to make a pause where no manuscript authority could be shown. This is a matter of interpretation, like modern punctuation; and it is im-portant that the reader should 'beware' of it. When there seems insuffi-cient authority for the guess that Raleigh would have marked a pause, the asterisks are enclosed in brackets.

l. 17. Miss Latham compares the streams of l. 17 with those of l. 33 (which seem to be his former poems, especially no doubt in this instance the 'lamentable lays' as l. 34 shows) and l. 234 (which seem to me different; there surely the point is simply the contrast between the clear streams of his past good fortune and the standing puddles of his present state). Though the trees used to be fruitful and the soil so rich, he now can gather only withered leaves and when he looks for flowers, he finds the soil to be only sea sand. The harvest of 'broken ears' is 'gleaned' in this poem.

l. 24. *Pause marked as after l. 16 in the autograph, but no capital for l. 25.*

ll. 25-36, an obscure passage; in ll. 25-8 he never sees the sun, sitting as he is under the healthless trees of a forest with no songs of birds, joyful or sad; in ll. 29-32 he looks back to a former estrange-

No pleasing streams fast to the ocean wending
The messengers sometimes of my great woe,
But all on earth as from the cold storms bending   35
Shrink from my thoughts in high heavens and below.

✱   ✱   ✱

O, hopeful love, my object and invention,   37
O true desire the spur of my conceit
O worthiest spirit, my mind's impulsion
O eyes transpersant, my affection's bait,   40

O princely form, my fancy's adamant,
Divine conceit, my pain's acceptance
O all in one, o heaven on earth transparent,
The seat of joys, and love's abundance

Out of that mass of miracles, my Muse   45
Gathered those flowers, to her pure senses pleasing,
Out of her eyes (the store of joys) did choose
Equal delights, my sorrow's counterpoising.

Her regal looks my rigorous sighs suppressed;
Small drops of joys sweetened great worlds of woes;   50

ment when he had the 'shepherds company' I suppose of Colin Clout (cf. p. 83) who, helping him to renew his dolorous conceit (sing his 'lamentable lays'), gave him happiness (even in that charming but restricted company?).

l. 34. The pleasing streams were the songs ('that like a golden shower "flow" from thy fruitful head'; Spenser) which were thus messengers to Cynthia of the poet's sorrows; everything on earth and above it now shrinks away from his thoughts, like a plant from an icy wind. *There is no mark indicating any pause after 36: but from 37 for the next nine lines there are the marks which Miss Latham equates with the Elizabethan printer's inverted commas, and these seem to indicate the change in tone which is clear from the sense also, between 36 and 37.*

l. 39, my invention: i.e. (the source of) my inspiration; in the following line the spur of my conceit means something similar, 'conceit' being of course here 'my ideas' or more specifically 'my ideas about love'. 40 transpersant; i.e. transpiercing.

l. 42, 'my pain's acceptance' may mean the person who accepts the results of the poet's painful toiling.

178

One gladsome day a thousand cares redressed—
Whom Love defends, what fortune over throws?

When she did well, what did there else amiss?
When she did ill, what empires could have pleased?
No other power effecting woe or bliss,   55
She gave, she took, she wounded, she appeased.

★   ★   ★

The honour of her love, Love still devising,   57
Wounding my mind with contrary conceit
Transferred itself sometime to her aspiring,
Sometime the trumpet of her thought's retreat;   60

To seek new worlds, for gold, for praise, for glory;
To try desire, to try love severed far;
When I was gone she sent her memory
More strong than were ten thousand ships of war,

l. 56. *The pause here is marked in the manuscript by a gap between ll. 56 and 57.*

ll. 57–68. The general tenor of this obscure passage is the conflict which all Elizabeth's favourites experienced, between their own desire for action and glory, a desire which she partly herself inspired, and her continual last-moment refusals to let them carry out the plans. In l. 58 'love still devising' means 'Love always (cf. p. 162 for "still") being the real planner'; then, the honour of her love wounded me with conflicting ideas, sometimes transferring itself to her aspirations, sometimes was summoned by her thought's withdrawal like a trumpet which sounded retreat. In l. 62, the conflict is apparently restated: either to try desire (as we have assumed Raleigh did in 1589, see p. 95) or to try being parted far from her. The seeking new worlds is, presumably, in his Virginian expeditions, in the eighties, on which he may have wished to go; an expedition 'for gold, for praise, for glory' was that of 1592, on which Raleigh had started when he was called back as here described: see pp. 44–5.

l. 60. 'The trumpet of her thought's retreat; cf. *Willoughbie, His Avisa:*

> *The line of life his race hath run*
> *Expecting sound of death's retreat*

(Bodley Head Quarto, No. XV., p. 163.)

To call me back, to leave great honour's thought,   65
To leave my friends, my fortune, my attempt,
To leave the purpose I so long had sought
And hold both cares and comforts in contempt.

Such heat in ice, such fire in frost remained,
Such trust in doubt, such comfort in despair,   70
Much like the gentle lamb, though lately weaned,
Plays with the dug, but finds no comfort there.

       ★   ★   ★

But as a body violently slain   73
Retaineth warmth although the spirit be gone,
And by a power in nature moves again,   75
Till it be laid below the fatal stone,

Or as the earth, even in cold winter days
Left for a time by her life-giving sun,
Doth by the power remaining of his rays
Produce some green, though not as it hath done: 80

Or as a wheel forced by the falling stream,
Although the course be turned some other way,
Doth for a time go round upon the beam,
Till wanting strength to move, it stands at stay,

So my forsaken heart, my withered mind,   85
Widow of all the joys it once possessed,
My hopes clean out of sight, with forcèd wind
To kingdoms strange, to lands far off addressed,

l. 68 hold cares in contempt, i.e. think nothing of the responsibilities he was bearing; 'comforts' perhaps those advantages which he could have hoped to gain by a successful expedition.

ll. 69–73 apparently refer to the lack of real comfort or solace which he found when he got back to her. *There are, in the manuscript, signs of a gap between ll. 72 and 73, and a capital letter at the opening of l. 73. There is a mark which might suggest a pause after l. 69, but it is hard to believe that a pause there would have been Raleigh's eventual decision.*

ll. 73–104. A fine passage which is also of exceptional biographical interest; the first three stanzas compare the poet's efforts in his

Alone, forsaken, friendless on the shore,
With many wounds, with death's cold pangs embraced,   90
Writes in the dust as one that could no more,
Whom love, and time, and fortune had defaced

Of things so great, so long, so manifold
With means so weak, the soul even then departing,
The weal, the woe, the passages of old,   95
And worlds of thought described by one last sighing;

As if, when after Phoebus is descended
And leaves a light much like the past day's dawning,
And every toil and labour wholly ended
Each living creature draweth to his resting,   100

We should begin by such a parting light
To write the story of all ages past,
And end the same before th' approaching night.

*   *   *

present state with the nervous twitching of a body recently done to death; with the stray unhappy buds produced in winter; with a mill wheel still turning, till it loses its impetus, after the stream is diverted. Left in this way (l. 85) his mind has turned to ideas of voyaging to distant lands (cf. pp. 60–3); and has now begun to write 'in dust' of the long history of his love (ll. 95–96), its weal and its woe, in this last sighing breath; (ll. 97–103) like a man who starts at twilight to write the history of the world and plans to complete it before nightfall. By the time this was written then the ideas mentioned in Lady Raleigh's letter quoted on p. 63 were already forming. This poem was to be a history of *all* his love for Cynthia, (so he began at the end, and the early books were presumably never written). The image of the *History of the World* is a singular anticipation of the project eventually begun, so he says, on the inspiration of Prince Henry of Wales, son of James I.

The suggestion of a pause before l. 104 comes, again, with a horizontal mark opposite the line in the manuscript at l. 104. Here again, however, there are similar marks opposite 101 (where the intention may have been to remind him of the needs for further revision); and again between l. 92 and l. 93. But as l. 104 begins with a capital letter, the evidence for an intended pause here seems adequate.

Such is again the labour of my mind,
Whose shroud by sorrow woven now to end   105
Hath seen that ever shining sun declined
So many years that so could not descend

But that the eyes of my mind held her beams
In every part transferred by love's swift thought;
Far off or near, in waking or in dreams,   110
Imagination strong their lustre brought.

Such force her angel-like appearance had
To master distance, time, or cruelty,
Such art to grieve, and after to make glad,
Such fear in love, such love in majesty.   115

My weary limbs her memory embalmed,
My darkest ways her eyes make clear as day.
What storms so great but Cynthia's beams appeased?
What rage so fierce that love could not allay?

                    ★   ★   ★

Twelve years entire I wasted in this war   120
Twelve years of my most happy younger days
But I in them, and they now wasted are,
Of all which past, the sorrow only stays.

l. 104. 'Such is again the labour'—i.e. that described by analogy in ll. 97–103. My mind's shroud has been woven to its completion by sorrow. In l. 106 it is the mind which has seen that bright sun declined (though, grammatically, it is the mind's shroud which has seen it).

l. 107, that sun could never before descend in such a way that its beams were not still held by my mind.

l. 116, her memory was a balm to my limbs. *The pause after l. 119 is marked by the cessation, with that line, of another series of Miss Latham's 'inverted commas' which have run on from l. 112. Signs of a gap also; and l. 120 begins with a capital letter.*

l. 120. The 'twelve years entire' are presumably 1580–92, though for those who wish to date the *XIth and last Book* in 1589 there is no real difficulty since Raleigh is described as being *de curia* as early as 1576. We know nothing however of his activities at court in the 1570's, and it is unlikely that the personal relationship with Eliza-

So wrote I once, and my mishap foretold,
My mind still feeling sorrowful success,   125
Even as, before a storm, the marble cold
Doth by moist tears tempestuous times express.

So felt my heavy mind my harms at hand,
Which my vain thought in vain sought to recure;
At middle day my sun seemed under land   130
When any little cloud did it obscure.

And as the icicles in a winter day
When as the sun shines with unwonted warm

So did my joys melt into secret tears,
So did my heart dissolve in wasting drops;   135
And as the season of the year outwears
And heaps of snow from off the mountain tops

With sudden streams the valleys overflow,
So did the time draw on my more despair.
Then floods of sorrow and whole seas of woe   140
The banks of all my hope did overbear,

And drowned my mind in depths of misery.
Sometime I died, sometime I was distract,

beth began so early. 'War' is an uncomfortably vivid term for the
hopes, fears, anxieties, rivalry and disaster of the relationship. 'The
war' is the turmoil of passion which love involves, rather than
the struggle with rivals for Cynthia's favour, though both may be
implied.

l. 124. So wrote I once: the poem still survives: see p. 170. We
have assumed that it was written at the time of the first estrangement. l. 125. My mind already ('still': cf. p. 162) feeling sadness to
follow, as Miss Latham explains it.

ll. 132–60; the metrical finish of these lines is obviously still lacking. Mr. Edwards thinks that the sense is broken off owing to
Raleigh's dissatisfaction with the image of the icicle melting in the
warm sun. In l. 130 he is still apparently in the pre-disaster stage;
the disaster happens soon after but has not been made explicit yet
in the text. It might have been his joys dissolving, like an icicle in
the sun; or the snow turning to flood. Anyhow his unhappiness
increased (l. 139) and turned from a torrent to a whole sea of woe.

By l. 143 he is clearly in the Tower stage of the disaster, and the

My soul the stage of fancy's tragedy;
Then furious madness, where true reason lacked,   145
Wrote what it would, and scourged mine own conceit.

[*   *   *   ]

O, heavy heart who can thee witness bear,   147
What tongue, what pen could thy tormenting treat
But thine own mourning thoughts which present were,
What stranger mind believe the meanest part,   150
What altered sense conceive the weakest woe
That tare, that rent, that piercèd thy sad heart?

And as a man distract, with treble might
Bound in strong chains doth strive and rage in vain,
Till, tired and breathless, he is forced to rest,   155
Finds by contention but increase of pain
And fiery heat inflam'd in swollen breast,

So did my mind in change of passion
From woe to wrath, from wrath return to woe
Struggling in vain from love's subjection.   160

Therefore all lifeless, and all helpless bound
My fainting spirits sunk, and heart apaled,
My joys and hopes lay bleeding on the ground,
That not long since the highest heaven scaled.

*   *   *

reference here is probably specific, to the incident described above,
p. 46. Was 'what madness wrote', in l. 146, possibly 'The Lie',
with its almost frontal attack on the Queen (stanza 3; p. 52).
'Scourged mine own conceit', whatever precisely it means, is a
powerful phrase which looks as if it might apply to the writing of
that poem. ll. 146–7. *No conclusive indication of pause; though the
next line begins with a capital, this is his normal writing of* 'Oh'. l. 151.
What altered sense, i.e. what senses that differed in any way from
the poet's; he alone can conceive the depth of his own distress. If
this section is read in conjunction with pp. 46–8 we can hardly
doubt its vivid autobiographical character. l. 162 apaled: i.e. made
pale.

    ll. 164–5. *Here the indications of a pause are first a line in the left
margin, then the cessation of the marks against each of ll. 161–4 (// as*

I hated life and cursèd destiny;   165
The thoughts of passèd times, like flames of hell,
Kindled afresh within my memory
The many dear achievements that befell

In those prime years and infancy of love,
Which to describe were but to die in writing.   170
All these I sought, but vainly, to remove,
And vainly shall, by which I perish living.

And though strong reason holds before mine eyes
The images and forms of worlds past,
Teaching the cause why all these flames that rise   175
From forms external, can no longer last

Than that those seeming beauties hold in prime—
Love's ground, his essence, and his empery,
All slaves to age, and vassals unto time
Of which repentance holds the tragedy;   180

—But this, my heart's desire could not conceive
Whose love outflew the fastest flying time;
A beauty that can easily deceive
Th' arrest of years, and creeping age outclimb,

A spring of beauties which time ripeth not   185
Time that but works on frail mortality,
A sweetness which woe's wrongs outwipeth not,
Whom Love hath chose for his divinity,

opposed to =, *the latter being Miss Latham's 'inverted commas'), a*
mark occurring elsewhere with an individual line, 132, but not elsewhere
in a series.

l. 171. 'All these' I sought to remove, i.e. apparently the thoughts
of the past, thoughts which are now a living death to him. From
ll. 173–82 the argument apparently is, 'though reason told me that
all such earthly flames (as my desires) arising from outside causes
(unlike the elemental fire caused by nothing external) must die
like the empires of the past lasting no longer than those seeming
beauties are at their zenith ["hold in prime"]—all love being subject
to time—yet my heart, in which love was above time, could not
conceive this. This thing I loved was immortal. Time works only
on mortality.'

A vestal fire that burns, but never wasteth,
That loseth nought by giving life to all,   190
That endless shines eachwhere, and endless lasteth,
Blossoms of pride that can nor vade nor fall.

These were those marvellous perfections,
The parents of my sorrow and my envy
Most deathful and most violent infections,   195
These be the tyrants that in fetters tie

Their wounded vassals; yet nor kill nor cure,
But glory in their lasting misery
That as her beauties would, our woes should dure;
These be th' effects of powerful empery.   200

★   ★   ★

In l. 192 Miss Latham thinks that *vade* = fade (Raleigh talked,
and to some extent wrote, with a Devonshire accent) but I doubt
this. Spenser has 'vade' and 'fade' as different words actually in the
same stanza, and Shakespeare also uses 'vade' for 'disappear' in a
similar context to this. The 'vestal' fire, like that tended by the
vestal virgins is never extinguished; the word is also a compliment
to the Virgin Queen. It is like the

> '*elemental fire*
> *Whose food and flame consumes not*'

of No. XXVII. The section ends somewhat 'in the air', and would
doubtless have been tidied up considerably if it had ever emerged
into that stage. Mr. Edwards thinks that ll. 193–200 are a bitterly
sarcastic interpolation into the first draft; that the poet broke off
suddenly, perhaps thinking that he had gone too far; and that l. 201
then goes back to l. 192.

Between ll. 200 and 201; *pause indicated by gap; moreover
Raleigh in the manuscript punctuates* 'empery . . .'. *These dots have not
been used before, but hereafter are used at l. 274 (where a pause is
possible) 286 (where there is a natural pause, not otherwise marked) 335
(pause seeming unnecessary) 404 (pause difficult; but there is a line right
across the page that suggests a pause or general reconstruction of the passage planned) 416 (no natural pause) 425 (natural pause) 457 (other indications of a pause also) 441 (perhaps a possible pause) 461 (natural*

Yet have these wonders want which want compassion; 201
Yet hath her mind some marks of human race
Yet will she be a woman for a fashion
So doth she please her virtues to deface.

And like as that immortal power doth seat 205
An element of waters to allay
The fiery sunbeams that on earth do beat
And temper by cold night the heat of day,

So hath perfection, which begat her mind,
Added thereto a change of fantasy 210
And left her the affections of her kind,
Yet free from every evil but cruelty.

*   *   *

But leave her praise. Speak thou of nought but woe; 213
Write on the tale that sorrow bids thee tell,

pause) 474 (*natural pause further emphasised by a gap as well as
mark*) 482 (*no natural pause, but perhaps an unfinished passage*) 496
(*no natural pause*). *With this form of punctuation therefore, as with the
marginal lines, we have a multi-purpose mark, which does not give an
unequivocal sign of Raleigh's intention. But here the pause is well
attested.*

l. 201. 'Yet such marvels as I have been describing lack something if they lack compassion.' For the sentiment, compare the
letter quoted on p. 47. 'All wounds have scars but that of fantasy;
all affections their relenting but that of woman kind.'

ll. 205–12. As God (that immortal power) has placed (doth seat)
the waters of creation to allay the heat of fire ... so perfection,
which begat her mind, added to it change of fantasy (I suppose
change of her affections away from Raleigh) and left her the
emotions of her sex, though free from every taint except one—the
taint of cruelty.

ll. 212–13. *The signs in the manuscript of a pause here are first an
obvious gap in the manuscript between ll. 212–13, second the capital
at the beginning of 213, third, the end of the 'inverted comma' marks
which have been continuously used for the previous three stanzas.
Raleigh may have intended however to mark the pause, or an additional
break, between ll. 220 and 221, where a line runs across the page between
the verses.*

Strive to forget, and care no more to know   215
Thy cares are known, by knowing those too well.

Describe her now as she appears to thee,   217
Not as she did appear in days foredone.
In love, those things that were, no more may be,
For fancy seldom ends where it begun.   220

And as a stream by strong hand bounded in
From nature's course, where it did sometime run,
By some small rent or loose part doth begin
To find escape, till it a way hath won,

Doth then all unawares in sunder tear   225
The forcèd bounds, and raging run at large
In th' ancient channels as they wonted were,
Such is of woman's love the careful charge;

Held, and maintained, with multitude of woes;
Of long erections such the sudden fall;   230
One hour diverts, one instant overthrows
For which our lives, for which our fortunes thrall.

So many years those joys have dearly bought,
Of which when our fond hopes do most assure,
All is dissolved, our labours come to nought,   235
Nor any mark thereof then doth endure;

No more than when small drops of rain do fall
Upon the parchèd ground by heat up dried,

ll. 215–16. The idea may be that the poet must no longer try, by thinking over and over again of his past cares for Cynthia, to ensure that his cares are known; but rather to forget all the past with Cynthia and think only of the present.

ll. 221–7. The picture is of a stream which has been walled up from its original channels, finds a way through the barrier, and bursts through into its old bed.

ll. 228–36. The task of loving any woman is, he suggests, thus: a vast effort and expense, the erection of a great edifice, all swept away in a moment. One instant: i.e. that of his error, cf. p. 136.

No cooling moisture is perceived at all
Nor any show or sign of wet doth bide.   240

[★   ★   ★]

But as the fields clothèd with leaves and flowers   241
The banks of roses smelling precious sweet
Have but their beauty's date, and timely hours,
And then, defaced by winter's cold and sleet

So far as neither fruit nor form of flower   245
Stays for a witness what such branches bare,
But as time gave, time did again devour,
And changed our rising joy to falling care,

So of affection which our youth presented,
When she that from the sun reaves power and light   250
Did but decline her beams as discontented
Converting sweetest days to saddest night,

All droops, all dies; all trodden under dust—
The person, place, and passages forgotten,
The hardest steel eaten with softest rust,   255
The firm and solid tree both rent and rotten;

Those thoughts so full of pleasure and content
That in our absence were affection's food
Are razèd out, and from the fancy rent
In highest grace and heart's dear care that stood;   260

Are cast for prey to hatred, and to scorn;
Our dearest treasures and our heart's true joys,
The tokens hung on breast, and kindly worn
Are now elsewhere disposed, or held for toys;

ll. 240–1. *The only suggestion of a pause here lies in the use of a
capital letter at the beginning of l. 241.*

l. 250. She that from the sun reaves light is Cynthia, as the
moon; but in the image used, she is handing on the light and heat
to a plant, and when she diverts it elsewhere, the plant withers.

ll. 257–68. A passage in which the poet thinks bitterly of the
rivals who have displaced him; the tokens of his love once worn
are now discarded; his friends once cherished for his sake, now

And those which then our jealousy removed   265
And others for our sakes then valued dear,
The one forgot, the rest are dear beloved
When all of ours doth strange or vile appear.

Those streams seem standing puddles, which, before,
We saw our beauties in, so were they clear.   270
Belphoebe's course is now observed no more;
That fair resemblance weareth out of date.
Our Ocean seas are but tempestuous waves
And all things base that blessed were of late.

And as a field, wherein the stubble stands   275
Of harvest past, the ploughman's eye offends,
He tills again, or tears them up with hands
And throws to fire as foil'd and fruitless ends,

And takes delight another seed to sow—
So doth the mind root up all wonted thought   280
And scorns the care of our remaining woes;
The sorrows, which themselves for us have wrought

estranged. 261 reads as if it refers to a particular incident, in which one of Raleigh's gifts had been used to mock him.

ll. 269–73. The conjunction of Belphoebe with the Ocean is no doubt intended, and might have been worked up further if this particular passage had been given a more final form; the wide and deep ocean seas are now but raging waves; the former poet and Shepherd of the Ocean is now merely sound and fury; everything that was blessed before in Cynthia's eyes is now base.

ll. 275–81. For the sentiment, compare a letter written by Raleigh a little later 'Every fool knoweth that hatred are the cinders of affection.' The farmer rejoices to tear up the useless stubble from the field which was so good. So the poet's cares are scorned, his sorrows obliterated. One is reminded of the marvellous lines of Cassandra in the Agamemnon, as she leaves the stage for her death. For l. 285, compare the letter written by Raleigh in the Tower in 1592, printed on p. 138. A mark below 'groans' in the manuscript here suggests to Edwards that Raleigh was dissatisfied with the word. Would he have gone back to the earlier version?

Are burnt to cinders by new-kindled fires;
The ashes are dispersed into the air;
The sighs, the groans of all our past desires   285
Are clean outworn as things that never were.

★   ★   ★

With youth is dead the hope of love's return,   287
Who looks not back to hear our after-cries.
Where he is not, he laughs at those that mourn;
Whence he is gone, he scorns the mind that dies;   290

When he is absent, he believes no words;
When reason speaks, he careless stops his ears;
Whom he hath left, he never grace affords,
But bathes his wings in our lamenting tears.

Unlasting passion, soon outworn conceit   295
Whereon I built, and on so dureless trust!
My mind had wounds, I dare not say deceit,
Were I resolved her promise was not just.

Sorrow was my revenge, and woe my hate;
I powerless was to alter my desire.   300
My love is not of time, or bound to date;
My heart's internal heat and living fire

ll. 286–7. *Between these lines there is in the manuscript a gap, and the cessation of a series of marginal marks that have run from l. 275–286, and also the punctuation ('never weare . . .' at the end of l. 286) sometimes apparently used where Raleigh was considering a pause; cf. the note on l. 201 above.*

For the sentiment of ll. 287–306 cf. 'Walsingham', No. XXII; one sometimes wonders whether that poem was not actually written in the Tower, like this. The 'dureless trust' of l. 296 here is paralleled with the 'dureless content' of l. 33 there; though the image here of the 'bearing and not bearing sprays' is of Cynthia, whereas in 'Walsingham' 'the falling fruit from the withered tree' is the poet.

In l. 289, *where he is gone; he,* is love, not youth.

l. 295, 'conceit' as elsewhere fanciful idea or notion [of love], as opposed to the real thing. l. 297: 'My mind had wounds'; I dare not say it was deceived [but would do so] were I resolved her promise was not just. Even so, the meaning remains very obscure; what promise, and how not just?

191

Would not, or could be, quench'd with sudden showers
My bound respect was not confined to days,
My vowèd faith not set to ended hours.   305
I loved the bearing and not bearing sprays

Which now to others do their sweetness send,
Th' incarnate, snow-driven white, and purest azure,
Who from high heaven doth on their fields descend,
Filling their barns with grain, and towers with treasure. 310

Erring or never erring, such is Love,
As while it lasteth scorns th' account of those
Seeking but self contentment to improve;
And hides, if any be, his inward woes,

And will not know while he knows his own passion   315
The often and unjust perseverance
In deeds of love, and state, and every action,
From that first day and year of their joys' entrance.

.   ★   ★   ★

l. 303. Even when the spray is not actually bearing flower, I love
it, as when it is bearing; but now the sprays of pink (incarnate)
white and blue are sending their fragrance to others. Perhaps,
however, l. 308 belongs with the line after it, not with that before:
see below.

Between ll. 308 and 309 there appears to be a complete change
of idea: Cynthia has been a spray of flowers, and then becomes the
life-giving rain from heaven. If this is the meaning, the change is
violent indeed. It is possible that the change takes place between
307 and 308; the adjectives of 308 will then describe the skies which
descend in rain.

l. 312, 'scorns th' account of those'—those who or what? Those
others, perhaps, to whom Cynthia's sweetness is now sent; love
scorns account of them, looking only to itself and its own advantage (l. 313).

ll. 315-18, again very obscure. Love, so long as he knows his
own passion will not know or recognise the often and unjust perseverance of the rivals (that the reference is to them is suggested
by 'their' in l. 319.) 'So long as he knows what he himself feels, he
refuses to know—shuts his eyes to the frequent and unscrupulous
perseverance of such rivals (rivals against him) not only in their
deeds and manners of love, but in their statecraft and everything

But I, unblessed and ill-borne creature,
That did embrace the dust her body bearing,   320
That loved her both by fancy, and by nature,
That drew even with the milk in my first sucking

Affection from the parent's breast that bare me,
Have found her as a stranger so severe
Improving my mishap in each degreee.   325
But love was gone. So would I my life were!

A Queen she was to me, no more Belphoebe,   327
A Lion then, no more a milk-white dove;
A prisoner in her breast I could not be;
She did untie the gentle chains of love.   330

Love was no more the love of hiding
All trespass, and mischance, from her own glory;
It had been such. It was still for th' elect;
But I must be th' example in love's story;
This was of all forepast, the sad effect.   335

*　　*　　*

But thou, my weary soul and heavy thought,
Made by her love a burden to my being,
Dost know my error never was forethought
Or ever could proceed from sense of loving.

they have done from the first moment they came into favour.' [I
owe this explanation to Professor C. S. Lewis.]

ll. 322 on, cf. for the idea 'My first born love, unhappily conceived' (No. XVII). l. 326 improving = intensifying.

ll. 318–19, 335–6. *Originally I marked a hypothetical pause at 326–
327; but a further inspection of the manuscript shows that, in addition to
the clear gap after 318, another was intended 335–6. These are the
pauses then which the poet proposed to make.*

In l. 333, as above in 309–10 and still more emphatically in
263–4, Raleigh is thinking of his successful rivals at court.

l. 339. If Sir Robert Cecil ever read this *Cynthia* fragment
(which was in his archives and is still in the family's archives) and
if he had mentioned to Lady Raleigh l. 339 where Raleigh writes
that his 'error', i.e. his liaison with her, could never have proceeded
from, or originated in, sense of loving; if indeed he ever mentioned

Of other cause if then it had proceeding   340
I leave th' excuse, since Judgement hath been given;
The limbs divided, sundered, and a-bleeding
Cannot complain the sentence was uneven.

*   *   *

This did that Nature's wonder, virtue's choice,
The only paragon of time's begetting;   345
Divine in words, angelical in voice;
That spring of joys, that flower of love's own setting,

Th' idea remaining of those golden ages,
That beauty braving heavens and earth embalming
Which after worthless worlds but play on stages—   350
So didst thou her long since describe; yet sighing

That thy unable spirit could not find ought
In heaven's beauties, or in earth's delight,
For likeness, fit to satisfy thy thought.
But what hath it availed thee so to write?   355

She cares not for thy praise, who knows not theirs;
It's now an idle labour, and a tale

this love poem, and the circumstances in which it had been written, to Lady Raleigh, then her remark to him quoted on p. 61
from a letter 'if faith were broken with me, I was yet far away'
would be explained. But this is a pretty long shot.

In l. 342 the image in his mind is that of the quartering of the
corpse after execution. ll. 343–4: *gap in the manuscript.*

ll. 344–50. Probably a series of allusions to particular poems (cf.
351), though the only one we can nearly (but not quite) pin down
comes from a poem which I think was written later than this: the
phrase is 'flower of love's own setting', see p. 205, where I think
he was again echoing an earlier poem.

l. 349. Beauty 'braving' heavens, i.e. adding to them bravery or
splendour; earth 'embalming', adding balm to the earth. l. 350
appears to mean the kind of beauty which after worlds, worthless
as they are, but imitate in a sort of stage play. l. 355. What hath it
availed thee so to write—Love's Labours Lost, as Shakespeare put
it.

l. 356. Cynthia apparently cares nothing for the praise the poet
offers, and gets no praise from those others (his rivals). l. 365. The

Told out of time that dulls the hearer's ears;
A merchandise whereof there is no sale.

Leave them, or lay them up with thy despairs;   360
She hath resolved, and judged thee long ago;
Thy lines are now a murmuring to her ears,
Like to a falling stream, which passing slow

Is wont to nourish sleep and quietness.
So shall thy painful labours be perused,   365
And draw on rest, which sometime had regard.
But those her cares, thy errors have excused,

Thy days foredone have had their day's reward.
So her hard heart, so her estrangèd mind,
In which above the heavens I once reposed   370
So to thy error have her ears inclined

And have forgotten all thy past deserving,
Holding in mind but only thine offence
And now only affecteth thy depraving
And thinks all vain that pleadeth thy defence.   375

*   *   *

Yet greater fancy beauty never bred,
A more desire the heart blood never nourished.
Her sweetness an affection never fed
Which more in any age hath ever flourished.

The mind and virtue never have begotten   380
A firmer love, since love on earth had power;

poet's painful labours will be read as if they were the soporific sounds of a falling stream, and will promote sleep ('draw on rest') as those do, though they once had attention ('regard') paid to them.

l. 367. Her former cares for the poet have been excused, made no longer an obligation for her, by his errors. Her hard heart now only works to madden him (thy depraving) and turns a deaf ear to anything spoken in his defence. l. 374 affecteth: aims at.

ll. 375–6. *MS. page ends with l. 375; but the capital 'Yet' in 376, coupled with a series of marginal marks from l. 376 to l. 395 must be linked with some new mood or intention.*

l. 378. 'Her sweetness'—i.e. Love's sweetness.

A love obscur'd, but cannot be forgotten,
Too great and strong for time's jaws to devour;

Containing such a faith as ages wound not;
Care, wakeful ever of her good estate;⠀⠀⠀⠀⠀⠀⠀⠀⠀385
Fear, dreading loss, which sighs and joys not;
A memory of the joys her grace begat;

A lasting gratefulness, for those comforts past⠀⠀⠀⠀388
Of which the cordial sweetness cannot die—
These thoughts, knit up by faith, shall ever last;
These time assays, but never can untie,

Whose life once lived in her perrellike breast
Whose joys were drawn but from her happiness,
Whose heart's high pleasure, and whose mind's true rest
Proceeded from her fortune's blessedness;⠀⠀⠀⠀⠀⠀395

Who was intentive, wakeful, and dismayed,
In fears, in dreams, in feverous jealousy,
Who long in silence servèd, and obeyed
With secret heart and hidden loyalty;

Which never change to sad adversity,⠀⠀⠀⠀⠀⠀⠀⠀400
Which never age, or nature's overthrow,
Which never sickness or deformity,
Which never wasting care, or wearing woe
If subject unto these she could have been—

l. 385–90 are qualities which went to make up the love: care, fear of her loss (fear which sighs and is never merry because of its anticipations of loss)—all these and others like them time attempts (l. 391) to dissolve but will never be able to do so.

l. 392, 'perrellike' has generally been taken as = pearl-like. 'I think the first element is PERRIE, the collective name for precious stones, jewellery—not a *visual* image of course; the lady's heart is as precious as a casket of perrie. The double "l" could be an accidental dittography—or the mere senseless doubling we sometimes find at that period' (Professor C. S. Lewis). This is a much more real image. 'Pearl-like' seems to have little meaning here.

ll. 400–4: the sense here at first seems incomplete but is perhaps not so. In l. 399 the secret heart and the hidden loyalty are of course those of the poet, but as l. 404 shows, the disasters of ll. 400–3 are imagined as threatening Cynthia; even if she could have

Which never words, nor wits malicious,   405
Which never honour's bait, or world's fame
Achievèd by attempts adventurous,
Or ought beneath the sun, or heaven's frame

Can so dissolve, dissever, or destroy:
The essential love, of no frail parts compounded;   410
Though of the same now buried be the joy,
The hope, the comfort and the sweetness ended,

But that the thoughts and memories of these
Work a relapse of passion, and remain
Of my sad heart, the sorrow-sucking bees.   415
The wrongs received, the scorns persuade in vain.

       *   *   *

And though these medicines work desire to end   416
And are in others the true cure of liking,

suffered a change to adversity, even if old age had come upon her
or other care or misfortune (which never could have happened)
they can never alter the poet's love—any more than slander, or
fame or anything else could have done so. The tenses are awkward,
but the train of thought clear. Mr. Edwards considers that l. 404
was written in the second draft (the Hatfield MS.) not in the first;
because Raleigh thought it necessary on a second reading to make
clear there were no intentions of suggesting any susceptibility on
Cynthia's part to age or decay in any form.

The love is (l. 410) 'of no frail parts compounded', and therefore
elemental in character.

ll. 412–14. The joys of this love are now gone, except that
memory works a further relapse of passion; these memories are
the bees that suck from the poet's heart their honey of sorrow.
And the memories remain in spite of scorn and rebuff. This passage is drawn upon in a sonnet composed apparently by Sir Arthur
Gorges: cf. Sandison, *Poems of Sir Arthur Gorges*, p. 132. Gorges
was with Raleigh in the Tower at the time we assume this poem to
have been written; see above, p. 46. *Pause between ll. 416 and 417:
the authority for this in the manuscript is the punctuation in the manuscript, 'in vayne . . .'; and with the capital 'And' of 416, this seems
adequate evidence of an intended break.*

l. 417. Normally such things as the wrongs and scorns men-

The salves that heal love's wounds, and do amend
Consuming woe, and slake our hearty sighing,　　420

They work not so in thy minds long disease
External fancy time alone recureth,
All whose effects do wear away with ease.
Love of delight, while such delight indureth
Stays by the pleasure, but no longer stays.　　425

*　　*　　*

But in my mind so is her love inclosed　　426
And is thereof not only the best part,
But into it the essence is disposed;
O love (the more my woe!) to it thou art

Even as the moisture in each plant that grows,　　430
Even as the sun unto the frozen ground,
Even as the sweetness to th' incarnate rose,
Even as the centre in each perfect round,

As water to the fish, to men as air,
As heat to fire, as light unto the sun.　　435
O Love, it is but vain to say 'thou were';
Ages and times cannot thy power outrun.

tioned in l. 416 would bring desire to its end; in others they would
be the cure to love (liking), but they do not work in this way in
thy (the poet's) mind. Time can cure only external fancy—only
superficial affection.

The argument at first seems to break off unfinished in l. 425; but
the meaning is (l. 424) Love of delight stays by the object of
pleasure so long as the delight lasts, but that kind of love no longer
stays once the delight is gone; i.e. stays no longer [than that].

l. 419. The salve that heals love's wounds; a strange reminiscence of a passage in the *Faerie Queene*, examined above on p. 91.
The reminiscence need not have been conscious. But I notice in the
margin here, in the manuscript a mark (a cross which is unique to
this line); it suggests either that the phrase specially caught his eye
on re-reading, or possibly that he regarded it as particularly important to be revised away.

l. 425. *The authority for a pause, here again, is the punctuation in the*

Thou art the soul of that unhappy mind
Which being by nature made an idle thought,
Began even then to take immortal kind   440
When first her virtues in thy spirits wrought.

From thee therefore that mover cannot move
Because it is become thy cause of being;
Whatever error may obscure that love,
Whatever frail effect of mortal living,   445

Whatever passion from distempered heart,
What absence, time or injuries effect,
What faithless friends, or deep dissembled art
Present, to feed her most unkind suspect.

[*   *   *]

Yet as the air in deep caves underground,   450
Is strongly drawn when violent heat hath rent
Great clefts therein, till moisture do abound,
And then the same, imprisoned and up-pent,

MS.: 'no longer stayes . . .'; and with the capital 'But' in line 426,
this seems evidence of an intended break.

l. 426. The pronouns are difficult in this passage. Cynthia's love
is enclosed in *my* (the poet's) mind (l. 425); *thou*, o Love, art the
soul of that unhappy mind which being by nature worthless first
began to take immortal nature (kind) on it when first *her* virtues
in thy (the poet's) spirits wrought.

l. 443. From thee (the poet), therefore, that which is the prime
mover and cause of thy being, can never move; whatever failing
may obscure that love, whatever passion or absence or other
things may effect, whatever faithless friends may present to Cynthia to feed her suspicions. ll. 449–50. *In the manuscript, no indication is given of this pause.* ll. 450–4. The simile of the genesis of an
earthquake is never strictly followed up.

ll. 450–7. The comparison as it stands is between the festering
sore of love's dart in the poet's heart and the hidden pent-up dis-
turbances which bring about earthquakes; that sore will not be
known till the final dissolution of matter into dust. Rust has
already eaten the better part (of the Poet's heart, apparently)
and outgrown (that heart?); at 461 there is perhaps a breaking off

Breaks out in earthquakes, tearing all asunder,
So in the centre of my cloven heart   455
My heart to whom her beauties were such wonder,
Lies the sharp poisoned head of that love's dart,

Which till all break and all dissolve to dust
Thence drawn it cannot be, or therein known.
There mixed with my heart blood, the fretting rust   460
The better part hath eaten, and outgrown.

★   ★   ★

But what of those, or these, or what of ought   462
Of that which was, or that which is, to treat?
What I possess is but the same I sought;
My love was false; my labours were deceit.   465

Nor less than such they are esteemed to be,
A fraud bought at the price of many woes,
A guile, whereof the profits unto me—
Could it be thought premeditate for those?

of the sense, but the growth of rust over the heart seems meant.

ll. 461–2: *the indication of a pause here is Raleigh's punctuation* 'outgrown . . .'. *I read a gap also; and l. 462 starts with capital.*

In l. 462 'those' may refer to 'beauties', 'these' perhaps to the poet's anguish and the analogies of it in 460–1.

l. 465. It seems clear from l. 467 that 'love' here means 'object of love'; though the labours that were 'deceit' are also undoubtedly his. Perhaps in ll. 466–9 these two senses are inextricably mixed.

l. 469. Could the labours of my love possibly be thought to have been planned for the profits I got out of it (considering how little these were)?

In l. 465 the words 'my love was false' are underlined in the manuscript and a repeated examination of it leaves me convinced that this underline is in the original ink, i.e. belongs to this draft as he first wrote it down; whereas most of the similar marks were put in at a revision stage.

In l. 473 Miss Latham reads 'vinde' (presumably wind?) at the end of the line. If she is right the sense breaks off in the middle. I think however that what Raleigh intended was 'root and rind' a traditional phrase; cf. 'root and branch'. His 'r' and 'v' are indistinguishable.

Witness those withered leaves left on the tree.   470
The sorrow-worren[1] face, the pensive mind;
Th' external shows what may th' internal be;
Cold care hath bitten both the root, and rinde. . . .

       ★   ★   ★

But stay, my thoughts, make end; give fortune way,
Harsh is the voice of woe and sorrow's sound.   475
Complaints cure not, and tears do but allay
Griefs for a time, which after more abound.

To seek for moisture in the Arabian sand
Is but a loss of labour and of rest.
The links which time did break of hearty bands   480

Words cannot knit, or wailings make anew.
Seek not the sun in clouds, when it is set.
On highest mountains where those cedars grew
Against whose banks the troubled ocean beat

And were the marks to find thy hopèd port   485
Into a soil far off themselves remove.
On Sestos' shore, Leander's late resort,
Hero hath left no lamp to guide her love.

Thou lookest for light in vain, and storms arise;
She sleeps thy death, that erst thy danger sighèd;   490
Strive then no more, bow down thy weary eyes
Eyes which to all these woes thy heart have guided.

       ★   ★   ★

ll. 474–5. *Pause attested by gap, punctuation ('rinde . . .') and capital.*
l. 474. Make way for fortune; do not try to resist destiny.
l. 480. 'Hearty bands', i.e. bands of the heart. l. 483. The lofty
cedars which were the seaman's mark as he approached port have
been rooted up and removed to a place far away.

l. 487. Marlowe was writing *Hero and Leander* probably at this
time, at least very soon after this.

l. 490. Raleigh had suffered, like others of Elizabeth's favourites,
from not being allowed to undertake expeditions overseas which
they had wished to do, cf. l. 65. l. 492 those eyes 'by whose device
I lived in such unrest', see p. 147.

ll. 492–3. *Gap in the manuscript, and capital, l. 403.*

       [1] *worren* = worn.

She is gone, she is lost. She is found, she is ever fair!
Sorrow draws weakly, where love draws not too.
Woe's cries sound nothing but only in Love's ear.   495
Do then, by dying, what life cannot do.

Unfold thy flocks, and leave them to the fields
To feed on hills or dales, where like them best,
Of what the summer or the spring time yields;
For love, and time, hath given thee leave to rest.   500

Thy heart, which was their fold, now in decay
By often storms, and winter's many blasts
All torn and rent, becomes misfortune's prey;
False hope, my shepherd's staff, now age hath brast.[1]

My pipe, which Love's own hand gave my desire   505
To sing her praises, and my woe upon,
Despair hath often threatened to the fire,
As vain to keep now all the rest are gone.

Edwards takes the sense of ll. 493–6 to be that Cynthia's love has proved to be not the divine and eternal love which he had thought it; only death will fully realise that aspiration; such love will be found 'only by dying'. I doubt this interpretation because of the two intervening lines, which are then in a quite different key. It means rather that there is still Cynthia, eternally fair; but that his sorrows can do little to move her towards him, when they are not reinforced by her love; that only his death can satisfy her, perhaps; or alternatively move her at last to remember him.

This fine section falls into two parts, the division coming after l. 513. The last nine lines are in one of Raleigh's less formal hands in the autograph, and are on a different sheet; the final conclusion then is an after-thought or at least transcribed at a later sitting.

In 501–4 we have as before the confusion of pronouns. 'Thy' heart and 'my' shepherd's staff each refer to the poet. l. 504. 'False hope, my shepherd's staff': like 'my staff of broken hope whereon I'll stay' in No. XX. 'Like to a hermit.' In 'The scallop shell of quiet' it is the 'staff of faith'; there the scallop shell indicates a pilgrim, not a shepherd.

l. 505. 'My pipe which': which is governed by the 'upon' at the end of the next line: 'my pipe which Love's own hand', etc.

[1] *brast*=broken.

Thus home I draw, as death's long night draws on.
Yet every foot old thoughts turn back mine eyes   510
Constraint me guides, as old age draws a stone
Against a hill, which over-weighty lies

For feeble arms, or wasted strength to move.
My steps are backward, gazing on my loss,
My mind's affection, and my soul's sole love,   515
Not mixed with fancy's chafe, or fortune's dross.

To God I leave it, who first gave it me,
And I her gave, and she returned again,
As it was hers. So let his mercies be
Of my last comforts, the essential mean.   520
    But be it so or not, th' effects are past;
    Her love hath end; my woe must ever last.

l. 509. Raleigh, in the early stages of his imprisonment may have actually thought that he was going to be executed: cf. l. 496 with this line.

l. 511. I am guided by the constraint of memory, heavy as a boulder on a hill-side, which feeble arms cannot move out of the path (the stone is the memory of the past, which always confronts him).

l. 516, 'fancy's chafe'; the worries, anxieties, wear-and-tear of a passionate love affair, the 'twelve years' war' of l. 120. L. 517. 'To God I leave it'; I leave my mind's affection; which I gave to her; which she returned again to me; and which was all hers.

If anyone were arguing for this *Cynthia* as the poem alluded to by Spenser in Book III of the *Faerie Queene*, he might perhaps compare l. 495 with Spenser's version: see the quotation made from it above, p. 92. I have no doubt at all however, that whether in the poem(s) written in 1589 there were or were not many analogies to this, we have here work written in 1592.

From l. 514 onwards (a new sheet in the manuscript) a new hand, less formal, begins. It is certainly Raleigh's, but there is a break in time here, not necessarily of much more than a few hours, in the copying.

XXVI

THE END OF THE BOOKS OF THE OCEAN'S LOVE TO CYNTHIA, AND THE BEGINNING OF THE 12TH BOOK, ENTREATING OF SORROW

My day's delights, my springtime joys foredone,
Which in the dawn and rising sun of youth
Had their creation, and were first begun,

Do in the evening and the winter sad,
Present my mind, which takes my time's account,   5
The grief remaining of the joy it had.

My times that then ran o'er themselves in these
And now run out in others' happiness,
Bring unto those new joys, and new born days.

So could she not, if she were not the sun,   10
Which sees the birth, and burial, of all else,
And holds that power with which she first begun;

Leaving each withered body to be torn
By fortune, and by times tempestuous,
Which, by her virtue, once fair fruit have borne,   15

Knowing she can renew, and can create
Green from the ground, and flowers even out of stone,
By virtue lasting over time and date;

Leaving us only woe, which like the moss
Having compassion of unburied bones   20
Cleaves to mischance, and unrepairèd loss.

For tender stalks. . . .

It is difficult to judge whether the theme of this book would have been substantially different from that of the last: there seems no evidence yet of that, in spite of the change of metre. ll. 5–6. The metaphor is the presenting of the accounts; the poet's present sorrows are the debit balance. ll. 7–9. Again the loose contrast between 'these' and 'those' which we have had more than once in Book XI: cf. e.g. l. 462. Here these are 'my days' delights' which used to run to overflowing; 'those' are his rivals who now enjoy his happiness. l. 12. She still holds the same power and vigour as she has always done; like the sun which sees the birth and burial of all else. l. 15, 'by her virtue'—as it were the sun's virtue, ripening the fruit. For the details of the connection between this poem and the Petition to Queen Anne, written many years later, see Latham, p. 128; with poem No. XXXVII of her numbering.

XXVII

EPILOGUE TO CYNTHIA

Now we have present made
To Cynthia, Phoebe Flora.
Diana, and Aurora.
Bewty that cannot vade.

A floure of loves own plantinge 5
A patern keipt by nature
For bewty, forme, and stature
When shee would frame a darlinge.

She as the valley of Perue
Whose sum̄er ever lastethe 10
Tyme conquringe all she mastreth
By beinge alwaye new.

As elementall fier
Whose food and flame consumes not
Or as the passion ends not 15
Of vertues trew desire.

So her celestiall frame
And quintessentiall minde
Which heavens together bynde
Shall ever be the same: 20

Then to her sarvants leve her
Love, nature, and perfection;
Princes of worlds affection
Or prayses butt deceave her.

Title has no MS. authority.
l. 4, 'vade' Raleigh's autograph; 'fade' Tenbury MS.
l. 9, 'she' R 'she's' T.
l. 10, 'lusteth' (apparently but it might be 'lastethe') R 'lasteth' T.
l. 14, 'food and flame' R 'flame and food' T.
l. 19, 'which' corr. from 'whom' R 'whom' T.
l. 23, T and R both read 'Princes', a not unusual Elizabethan

If Love could find a quill   25
Drawn from an angells winge
Or ded the muses singe
That prety wantons will.

Perchance hee could indyte
To pleas all other sence   30
Butt loves and woes expenc
Sorrow can only write.

spelling for 'Princess': cf. No. X. Where Phillipps MS. 3602 uses this spelling.

l. 24, 'Or' R 'Our' and 'or' in different part books of T. This again is a matter of orthography, not sense.

T repeats the first stanza at the end.

The primary source for the text of this poem is the manuscript described in the introduction, identified in 1952; the lines are written on the fly leaf at the end of the notebook, and are in Raleigh's autograph. They were transcribed and printed with a photograph by Mr. George Seddon, in the *Illustrated London News* (28th February, 1953), soon after the manuscript's discovery. This led to my being given information by John Boston, a gifted young musicologist at Lincoln College, Oxford, who has unhappily since died, that he had seen the poem, set to music, in that remarkable library of music, St. Michael's, Tenbury. The manuscript in question is Tenbury No. 1163, and consists of five part books. The text is not complete in any of them but a collation of the five gives the complete text. In the brief *apparatus criticus* above, Raleigh's version is given as R, that of the part books as T.

What was the poem's occasion? The first point to be taken into account is that l. 5 appears, with a difference of only one word ('setting' for 'planting') as a quotation embedded in the *XIth and last Book to Cynthia*. Raleigh had already, then, written this poem, *or a poem which contained at least one very similar line*, by 1592. In my view, however, these stanzas are *sui generis*, quite unlike anything that we have from Raleigh dating from the 1580's or early 1590's. It is true that the image, derived from medieval versions of classical science, of Elizabeth, as being the quintessence binding the universe together, as well as the ideal 'pattern' of beauty, has been foreshadowed in other poems (e.g. No. IV, l. 12). But in these new verses the conception is surely 'Platonic' in the accepted sense of

the word. Human passion does not suggest itself. Cynthia's ser
vants are here not Raleigh himself, but 'love, nature, and perfection'. The 'Sorrow' of the last line, which can write only 'love's
and woe's expense' appears to me a formality beside the profoundly felt lament of 'Walsingham', or of the *XIth and last Book*. I
do not think that Raleigh's poetic moods before 1592 ever cor-
responded to this, and believe that it was written after his return to
favour. The occasion was some sort of presentation (l. 1), perhaps
of an entertainment, for Queen Elizabeth, and the musical setting
in MS. Tenbury 1163 may be an original part of that entertainment. One feature of Tenbury 1163 is the numbers it includes
which were printed in *The Triumphs of Oriana*. This delightful
series of madrigals in praise of Elizabeth was printed in 1601.[1] And
they were composed after 1595, as is shown by Wilbye's mention
of Guiana in No. XV:

> *The lady Oriana*
> *Was dight all in the treasures of Guiana,*
> *And on her grace a thousand Graces tended.*
> *And thus sang they: Fair Queen of peace and plenty*
> *The fairest Queen of twenty.*
> *Then with an olive wreath for peace renowned*
> *Her virgin head they crowned.*
> *Which ceremony ended*
> *Unto her grace the thousand Graces bended*
> *Then sang the shepherds and nymphs of Diana:*
> *Long live fair Oriana.*

[Text from Fellowes, *English Madrigal Verse*, 1920 edition. The
text in Tenbury 1163 does not differ from Fellowes' version,
except of course in the arrangement.]

This mention of Guiana in itself helps to link the series with
Raleigh, and it may be that his work was sung, with them, at a
ceremony performed in the Queen's honour, between 1597 and
1601; though his poem was not printed when the rest appeared,
for the same reason that Raleigh's authorship of the poems in
England's Helicon, 1600, was suppressed. 'Now *we* have present

[1] Miss Elizabeth Cole's interesting suggestion that the series was addressed to
Anne of Denmark is ruled out by the discovery that a copy was bought for
Hardwick Hall in 1601; for other evidence also see Strong, *Studies in the Renais-
sance*, Vol. VI (1959).

made' seems to suit a ceremony rather than an individual gift.

In l. 4 the copyists of Tenbury 1163 have no hesitation in giving Raleigh's 'vade' as 'fade'. Incidentally this would confirm Miss Latham's view that, in the *XIth and last Book to Cynthia*, l. 192, 'vade' is Raleigh's spelling of 'fade', following his pronunciation of the word. I am unconvinced of this, in spite of the evidence of these copyists: see the note on *Cynthia*, l. 192. In l. 10 I read 'lusteth' in the notebook, but it might be 'lasteth', as Tenbury 1163 gives it. It was however almost proverbial that May was the lusty month; cf. Malory, *Morte d'Arthur*: 'In May, when every heart flourisheth and burgeoneth, for as the season is lusty to behold and comfortable, so man and woman rejoiceth and gladdeth of summer coming with his fresh flowers . . .' or the calendar rhyme for May in a Book of Hours published by Regnault for the English market in 1537:

> *As in the month of May all thing in might*
> *So at xxx years man is in chief liking,*
> *Pleasant and lusty to every man's sight*
> *In beauty and strength to women pleasing.*

This account of Peru was perhaps a commonplace; it is to be found e.g. in de Bry, *de Natura Novi Orbis* (*Pars IX* of the *Grands Voyages*) 1602, p. 190. *Id fit in valle Yea et in montibus Villacuri; ubi in solo arido et sabuloso campi reperiuntur, toto anno admodum virentes, vernantesque.* Purchas also alludes to the climate of this valley. In l. 11 the alternative punctuation 'time conquering, all . . .' is a possibility. l. 13. This 'elemental fire' is like the 'vestal fire that burns, but never wasteth' in the *XIth and last Book*, l. 189. 'The passions ends not'; the number—singular or plural—of Raleigh's verbs often strikes one as unusual: e.g. in a letter 'Hatred are the cinders of affection'. l. 16. Cynthia's 'frame' is the very frame of the universe, that celestial sphere which (in the Ptolemaic, not the Copernican, universe) bound together the whole. l. 23. 'Princess': see the letter printed below from Miss Bradbrook. ll. 25–32, love, the god, might conceivably be able to write so as to please other senses and affections; but sorrow can write only of love's and woe's expense, of the human affections that grow and then decay. The 'quill drawn from an angel's wing' idea had been used in 1590 in the second of Raleigh's introductory sonnets to the *Faerie Queene*.

Miss Bradbrook printed the first three verses of this poem in *The Queen's Garland*, 1953. At that time she wrote to me as follows: 'The verse "then to her servants leave her" must I think reflect back on the three earlier stanzas where she is shown as a Nature-goddess, Platonically perfect and therefore the object of love to all creation. Since she rules and indeed binds the world together, its whole affection naturally inclines to her and the praises of mere mortals misrepresent her. What they can express is their own feelings of love and woe. This is how I read it, but of course, it's ambiguous and "Princes" could I suppose be masculine plural and not feminine singular, and refer to the servants.'

Why Raleigh should have written out this particular poem at that much later stage of his life—several years after Elizabeth's death—when he began the *History of the World*, remains an unsolved puzzle. But the fact may perhaps be regarded as supporting evidence for our hypothesis that the poem was the last of the *Cynthia* series, and represented his feelings, as it were 'all passion spent'. An alternative hypothesis, which cannot yet be finally excluded, is that Raleigh began to compile the *History of the World* commonplace book at an early date; this would fit in with the remarkable simile which he uses in ll. 98–103 of the *XIth Book to Cynthia*. The verses would then be a casual addition, made in the late 1590's, to a notebook already begun. But I do not find this easy to believe. Did he consider when he copied the lyric, the possibility of dedicating the *History* to Elizabeth's memory? This recollection in a new context is illustrated by his writing, on the last night of his life, lines of an earlier poem:

> *Even such is time, which takes in trust*
> *Our youth, our joys, and all we have,*
> *And pays us but with age, and dust;*
> *Who in the dark and silent grave*
> *When we have wandered all our ways*
> *Shuts up the story of our days.*

The first version (see p. 98, note 2) must belong to the early 1590's. On the night before he died, he wrote it out, with an added couplet:

> *And from which earth and grave and dust,*
> *The Lord will raise me up I trust.*

So here, much later, his thoughts may have gone back to an offering to Elizabeth, made long before.

APPENDIX I

The following account of the Cadiz action is printed, in modernised spelling, from the version first published by Raleigh's grandson in 1700. The addressee ('your Honour') is unknown. But it was evidently written within a few days of the action and is incidentally a good example of Raleigh's vivid and direct prose.

A Relation of Cadiz Action in the Year 1596

You shall receive many Relations, but none more true than this. May it please your Honour therefore to know, that on Monday being the 20th of June, the English Fleet came to an Anchor in the Bay of St. Sebastians, short of Cadiz[1] half a league.

My Lord Admiral, being careful of her Majesty's Ships, had resolved with the Earl of Essex, that the Town should be first attempted, to the end that both the Spanish Galleons and Galleys, together with the Forts of Cadiz might not all at once beat upon our Navy. Myself was not present at the resolution; for I was sent the day before towards the Main, to stop such as might pass out from St. Lucar or Cadiz along the Coast. When I was arrived back again, (which was 2 hours after the rest) I found the Earl of Essex disembarking his Soldiers, and he had put many Companies into Boats, purposing to make his descent on the West side of Cadiz; but such was the greatness of the Billow, by reason of a forcible Southerly wind, as the Boats were ready to sink at the stern of the Earl, and indeed divers did so, and in them some of the armed men; but because it was formerly resolved (and that to cast doubts would have been esteemed an effect of fear) the Earl proposed to go on, until such time as I came aboard him, and in the presence of all the Colonels protested against the resolution, giving him reasons, and making apparent demonstrations, that he thereby ran the way of our general ruin, to the utter overthrow of the whole Armies, their own lives, and her Majesty's future safety. The Earl excused himself, and laid it the Lord Admiral, who (he said) would not consent to enter with the Fleet till the Town were first pos-

[1] Spelt throughout as Cales.

sessed. All the Commanders and Gentlemen present besought me
to dissuade the attempt; for they all perceived the danger, and were
resolved that the most part could not but perish in the Sea ere they
came to set foot on Ground; and if any arrived on shore, yet were
they sure to have their Boats cast on their heads, and that twenty
men, in so desperate a descent, would have defeated them all. The
Earl hereupon prayed me to persuade my Lord Admiral, who
finding a certain destruction by the former resolution, was content
to enter the Port. When I brought News of this agreement to the
Earl, calling out of my Boat unto him, *Entramus*; he cast his Hat
into Sea for joy, and prepared to weigh Anchor. The day was now
far spent, and it required much time to return the Boats of Soldiers to their own Ships, so as we could not that night attempt the
Fleet, although many (seeming desperately valiant) thought it a
fault of mine to put it off till the morning, albeit we had neither
agreed in what manner to fight, nor appointed who should lead,
and who should second, whether by boarding or otherwise;
neither could our Fleet possibly recover all their men in before
Sunset. But both the Generals being pleased to hear me, and many
times to be advised by so mean an understanding, came again to an
Anchor, in the very mouth of the Harbour. So that night about
ten of the Clock, I wrote a Letter to the Lord Admiral, declaring
therein my opinion how the Fight should be ordered, persuading
him to appoint to each of the great Galleons of Spain, two great
Flyboats to board them, after such time as the Queen's Ships had
battered them; for I knew that both St. Philip and the rest would
burn and not yield; and then to lose so many of the Queen's Ships
for company, I thought it too [a] dear a purchase, and it would be
termed but a lamentable Victory. This being agreed on, and both
the Generals persuaded to lead the body of the Fleet; the charge
for the performance thereof (upon my humble suit) granted and
assigned unto me. The Ships appointed to second me were these:

The Mary Rose, commanded by Sir George Carew.
The Lion, by Sir Robert Southwell.
The Rainbow, by the Marshal Sir Fr. Veare.
The Swiftsure, by Captain Crosse.
The Dreadnaught, by Sir Conyers and Alexander Clifford.
The Nonpareill, by Mr. Dudley.
The 12 Ships of London, with certain Flyboats.

The Lord Thomas Howard, because the Meer honour, which he commanded, was one of the greatest Ships, was also left behind with the Generals; but being impatient thereof, pressed the Generals to have the service committed unto him, and left the Meer honour to Mr. Dudley, putting himself into the Nonpareill. For mine own part, as I was willing to give honour to my Lord Thomas, having both precedency in the Army, and being a Nobleman whom I much honoured; so yet I was resolved to give and not take Example for this service, holding mine own Reputation dearest: And remembering my great duty to her Majesty, with the first peep of day therefore I weighed Anchor, and bare with the Spanish Fleet, taking the start of all ours a good distance.

Now Sir, may it please you to understand, that there were ranged under the Wall of Cadiz, on which the Sea beateth, seventeen Galleys, which lay with their Prows to flank our entrance as we passed towards the Galleons. There was also a Fort, called the Philip, which beat and commanded the Harbour. There were also Ordnance which lay all alongst the Curtain upon the Wall towards the Sea. There were also divers other Pieces of Culverin, which also scoured the Channel. Notwithstanding, as soon as the St. Philip perceived one of the Admirals under sail approaching, she also set sail, and with her the St. Matthew, the St. Thomas, the St. Andrew, the two great Galleons of Lisbon, three Frigates of War accustomed to transport the Treasure, two Argosies very strong in Artillery, the Admiral, Vice Admiral, and Rear Admiral of Nueva Espagna, with forty other great Ships bound for Mexico and other places. Of all which the St. Philip, the St. Matthew, the St. Andrew, and the St. Thomas, being four of the Royal Ships of Spain, came again to Anchor under the Fort of Puntall, in a Strait of the Harbour which leadeth toward Puerto Reall. On the right hand of them they placed the three Frigates, on the back the two Galleons of Lisbon, and the Argosies, and the 17 Galleys by three and three to interlace them as occasion should be offered. The Admiral, Vice Admiral, and Rear Admiral of Nueva Espagna, with the Body of the Fleet, were placed behind them, towards Puerto Reall; hoping with this great strength to defend the entrance, the place being no broader from point to point, than that these did in effect stretch over as a Bridge, and had besides the Fort of Puntall to their guard. But the 17 Galleys did not at first depart with the rest, but stayed by the Town, with all their Prows bent against us as we entered; with which, together with the Artillery of the Town and Forts, they hoped to have stumbled the leading Ship, and doubted not thereby but to have discouraged the rest. Having (as aforesaid) taken the leading, I was first saluted by the Fort called Philip, afterwards by the Ordnance on the Curtain, and lastly by all the Galleys in good order. To show scorn to all which, I only answered first the Fort, and afterward the Galleys, to each piece a Blare with a Trumpet, disdaining to shoot one piece at any one or all of those esteemed dreadful Monsters. The Ships that followed beat upon the Galleys so thick, that they soon betook them to their Oars, and got up to join with the Galleons in the Strait, as aforesaid: And then, as they were driven to come near me, and inforced to range their sides towards me, I bestowed a Benediction amongst them. But the St. Philip, the great and famous Admiral of Spain, was the mark I shot at; esteeming those Galleys but as Wasps in respect of the powerfulness of the other; and being resolved to be revenged for the Revenge, or to second her with mine own life, I came to Anchor by the Galleons, of which the Philip and Andrew were the two that boarded the Revenge. I was formerly commanded not to board, but was promised Fly-Boats, in which after I had battered a while I resolved to join unto them. My Lord Thomas came to Anchor by me on the one hand with the Lion; the Mary Rose on the other with the Dreadnaught; the Marshal toward the side of Puntall; and towards ten of the Clock my Lord General Essex, being impatient to abide far off, hearing so great Thunder of Ordnance, thrust up through the Fleet, and headed all those on the left hand, coming to Anchor next unto me on that side; and afterward came in the Swiftsure as near as she could. Always I must, without Glory, say for myself, that I held single in the head of all. Now after we had beat, as two Buts one upon another almost three hours, assuring your honour that the Volleys of Cannon and Culverin came as thick as if it had been a skirmish of Musketeers, and finding myself in danger to be sunk in the place, I went to my Lord General in my Skiff, to desire him that he would inforce the promised Fly-boats to come up that I might board, for as I rid, I could not endure so great a Battery any long time. My Lord General was then coming up himself, to whom I declared, that if the Fly-boats came not, I would board with the Queen's Ship, for it was the same loss to burn or sink, for I must endure the one. The Earl, finding that it was not in his power to command fear, told me, that whatsoever I did, he would second me in person upon his honour. My Lord Admiral having also a disposition to come up at first, but the River was so choked as he could not pass with the Ark, came up in person into the Nonpareill with my Lord Thomas. While I was thus speaking with the Earl, the Marshal, who thought it some touch to his great esteemed valour to ride behind me so many hours, got up ahead my Ship; which my Lord Thomas perceiving, headed him again, myself being but a quarter of an hour absent. At my return, finding myself, from being the first, to be but the third, I presently let slip Anchor, and thrust in between my Lord Thomas and the Marshal, and went up further ahead than all them before, and thrust myself athwart the Channel, so as I was sure none should outstart me again for that day. My Lord General Essex, thinking his Ship's side stronger than the rest, thrust the Dreadnaught aside, and came next the Warspight on the left hand, ahead all that rank but my Lord Thomas. The Marshal, while we had no leisure to look behind us, secretly fastened a Rope on my Ship's side towards him, to draw himself up equally with me: But some of my Company advertising me thereof, I caused it to be cut off, and so he fell back into his place, whom I guarded, all but his very Prow, from the sight of the Enemy. Now if it please you to remember, that having no hope of my Flyboats to board, and that the Earl and my Lord Thomas both promised to second me, I laid out a Warp by the side of the Philip to shake hands with her (for with the Wind we could not get aboard.) Which when she and the rest perceived, finding also that the Repulse (seeing mine) began to do the like, and the Rear Admiral my Lord Thomas, they all let slip, and ran aground, tumbling into the Sea heaps of Soldiers, so thick as if Coals had been poured out of a Sack in many Ports at once, some drowned, and some sticking in the Mud. The Philip and the St. Thomas burnt themselves. The St. Matthew and the St. Andrew were recovered with our Boats ere they could get out to fire them. The spectacle was very lamentable on their side; for many drowned themselves; many, half burnt, leapt into the water, very many hanging by the Ropes ends by the Ship's side under the water even to the lips; many swimming with grievous wounds stricken under water, and put out of their pain; and withal, so huge a fire, and such tearing of the Ordnance, in the great Philip and the rest, when the fire came to 'em, as if any man had a desire to see Hell itself, it was there most lively figured. Ourselves spared the lives of all after the Victory; but the Flemings, who did little or nothing in the Fight, used merciless slaughter, till they were by myself, and afterward by my Lord Admiral beaten off. The Ships that abode the fight in the morning till ten o'clock, were the Warspight, the Nonpareill, the Lion, the Mary Rose, the Rainbow, and the Dreadnaught. To second these came up the Earl and the Swiftsure. And these were all that did ought against six goodly Galleons, two Argosies, three Frigates, seventeen Galleys, and the Fort of Puntall, backed by the Admiral of Nueva Espagna, and others; in all fifty-five or fifty-seven.

This being happily finished, we prepared to land the Army, and to attempt the Town; in which there were of all sorts about 5000 Foot Burghers, 150 Soldiers in pay, and about 800 Horse of the Gentry and Cavalleros of Xerez, gathered together upon the discovery of our Fleet two days before, while we were becalmed off Cape St. Mary. The Horsemen sallied out to resist the landing, but were so well withstood, that they most took their way towards the Bridge which leadeth into the Main called Puente Souse; the rest retired to the Town; and so hardly followed as they were driven to leave their Horses at the Port, (which the Inhabitants durst not open to let them in) and so they leapt down an old Wall into the Suburbs, and being so closely followed by the Vanguard of our Footmen, as when the General perceived an entrance there, he thought it was possible for ours to do the like; upon which occasion the Town was carried with a sudden fury, and with little loss; only Sir John Wingfeild was slain, Sir Edward Wingfeild, Captain Bagnoll, and Captain Medickhurt: other Men of quality few or none. For the particular behaviours of any that entered, I cannot otherwise deliver than by report; For I received a grievous blow in my Leg; interlaced and deformed with Splinters in the Fight. Yet being desirous to see every man's disposition, I was carried ashore on men's shoulders; and as soon as my Horse was recovered, my Lord Admiral sent one unto me; but I was not able to abide above an hour in the Town, for the torment I suffered, and for the fear I had to be shouldered in the Press, and among the tumultuous disordered Soldiers, that being then given to Spoil and Rapine, had no respect. The same night I returned, chiefly for that there was no Admiral left to order the Fleet, and (indeed) few or no people in the Navy, all running headlong to the sack; and secondly, because I was unfit for ought but ease at that time. At the break of day following, I sent to the General to have order to follow the Fleet of Ships bound for the Indies, which were said to be worth twelve millions, and lay in Puerte Reall Road, where they could not escape. But the Town new taken, and the confusion great, it was almost impossible for them to order many things at once, so as I could not receive any answer to my desire. The Afternoon of the same day, those that were Merchants of Cadiz and Seville, offered the Generals two millions to spare that Fleet, whereupon there was nothing done for the present. But the morning following, being the 23rd of June, the Duke of Medina caused all that Fleet of Merchants to be set on fire, because he was resolved that they must needs have fallen into our hands; so as now both Galleons, Frigates, Argosies, and all other Ships of War, together with the Fleet of Nueva Espagna were all committed into ashes, only the St. Matthew and St. Andrew were in our possession. Much of the Ordnance of the St. Philip hath been saved by the Flemings, who have had great spoil. There is embarked good store of Ordnance out of the Town, and the two Apostles aforesaid are well furnished, which (God willing) we purpose to bring into England. The Town of Cadiz, was very rich in Merchandise, in Plate and Money: Many rich Prisoners given to the Land Commanders; so as that sort are very rich. Some had Prisoners for 16000 Ducats, some for 20000, some for 10000; and besides, great Houses of Merchandise. What the Generals have gotten, I know least; they protest it is little. For my own part, I have gotten a lame Leg, and a deformed. For the rest, either I spake too late, or it was otherwise resolved. I have not wanted good words, and exceeding kind and regardful usance; but I have possession of naught but poverty and pain. If God had spared me that blow, I had possessed myself of some House.

Raleigh's signature, about 1585; reproduced from Plate VII, with the obliteration removed

'Fortune, my Foe'

This song, a mention of which I first saw in Oldys's note quoted on p. 155 is extant in a unique copy dated by the Short Title Catalogue (No. 22926) 1640? The 'Lover's Complaint for the loss of his Love' and the 'Ladies comfortable and pleasant answer' are printed in the original in parallel columns. Spelling of the broadside is here followed:

THE LOVER'S COMPLAINT

Fortune my foe, why dost thou frown on me
And will thy favour never better be?
Wilt thou I say for ever breed my pain
And wilt thou not restore my joys again.
Fortune hath wrought my grief and great annoy
Fortune hath falsly stoln my love away;
My love and joy whose sight did make me glad
Such great misfortunes never young man had.
Had fortune took my treasure and my store,
Fortune had never griev'd me half so sore,
But taking her whereon my heart did stay,
Fortune thereby hath took my life away;
Far worse than death my life I lead in woe,
With bitter thoughts still tossed too and fro,
O cruel chance, thou breeder of my pain,
Take life or else restore my love again.
In vain I sigh, in vain I wail and weep,
In vain mine eyes refrain from quiet sleep,
In vain I shed my tears both night and day.
In vain my love my sorrow do bewray.
My love doth not my piteous plaint espy,
Nor feels my love what griping grief I try;
Full well may I false fortune's deeds reprove,
Fortune that so unkindly keeps my love.
Where should I seek or search my love to find,

When fortune fleets and waves like the wind
Sometimes aloft, sometimes again below,
This tottering fortune tottereth to and fro.
Then will I leave my love in fortune's hands,
My dearest love in most unconstant bands,
And only serve the sorrows due to me,
Sorrow, hereafter, thou shalt my Mistress be.
And only joy, that sometimes conquers Kings,
Fortune that rules on earth and earthly things
So that alone I live not in this woe,
For many more hath fortune served so.
No man alive can fortune's spight withstand
With wisdom skill, or mightly strength of hand,
And midst of Mirth she bringeth bitter Moan,
And woe to me that hath her hatred known.
If wisdom's eyes had but blind fortune seen,
Then had my love, my love for ever been;
Then love farewell, though fortune favour thee
Nor fortune frail shall ever conquer me.

THE LADIES ANSWER

Ah silly soul, art thou so sore afraid?
Mown not my dear nor be not so dismaid,
Fortune cannot with all her power and skill,
Enforce my heart to think thee any ill.
Blame not thy chance, nor envy at thy choice,
No cause thou hast to curse, but to rejoyce.
Fortune shall not thy joy and love deprive,
If by my love it may remain alive.
Receive therefore thy life again to thee,
Thy life and love shall not be lost by me,
And while thy heart upon thy life do stay,
Fortune shall never steal the same away.
Live thou in bliss, and banish death to Hell,
And careful thoughts see thou from thee expel;
As thou doth wish thy love agrees to be,
For proof whereof behold I come to thee.
In vain therefore do neither wail nor weep:
In vain therefore break not thy quiet sleep,

Wast not in vain thy time in sorrow so,
For why thy love delights to ease thy woe.
Full well thy love thy privy pangs doth see,
And soon thy love will send to succour thee:
Tho well thou mayst false fortunes deeds reprove
Yet cannot fortune keep away thy love.
Nor will thy love at fortunes back abide,
Whose fickle wheel doth often slip aside,
And never think that fortune beareth sway,
If vertue watch, and will not her obey.
Pluck up thy heart suprest with brinish tears,
Torment me not but take away thy fears;
Thy Mistress mind brooks no unconstant bands,
Much less to live in ruling fortunes hands.
Though mighty kings by fortune get the foyl,
Loosing thereby their travel and their toyl;
Though fortune be to me a cruel foe,
Fortune shall not make me to serve thee so.
For fortune's spight thou needst not spare a pin,
For thou thereby shall neither loose nor win,
If faithful love and favour I do find,
My recompense shall not remain behind.
Dye not in fear, nor live not discontent.
Be thou not slain where never blood was ment
Revive again, to faint thou hast no need,
The less afraid, the better shalt thou speed.

'Fortune my foe' was a four line stanza tune (cf. Chappell, *Old English Popular Music*, Vol. I, p. 76). The tune is at least as early as the Fitzwilliam Virginal Book. Wm. Lilly gives the first stanza, with the variant in l. 2, 'And will my fortune never better be.' A ballad 'Of one complaining of the mutability of Fortune' was licensed to print by John Charlewood, 1565–6. There may be an allusion to some form of the song in *Merry Wives of Windsor*, Act III, scene iii, l. 60 (Cambridge Shakespeare) '. . . if Fortune thy foe were not, Nature thy friend'. The present version gives the impression of being somewhat too slick for the 1580's in spite of the close correspondence with the Raleigh lines, p. 154.

APPENDIX III
(see pages 98 and 209)

Poems to Serena

NOTE: The two poems following were addressed by Raleigh to 'Serena' (see footnote, p. 98); the first by name, the second according to MS. Folger, l. 28, which gives the title as printed opposite. 'Serena' is certainly Elizabeth Throckmorton, who became his wife, and the date of the poems is certainly about 1592. They are reprinted here partly for the reader's convenience—since reference is made to them in the text; partly that he may observe the contrast in manner between the straightforward love poetry addressed by the poet to his mistress, and the elaboration and platonic distance of the poems addressed to the Queen. The only exception among the latter is 'Would I were changed' No. XIX, discussed on p. 95 and pp. 167–9.

(a)

TO HIS LOVE WHEN HE HAD OBTAINED HER

Now Serena be not coy;
Since we freely may enjoy
Sweet embraces: such delights,
As will shorten tedious nights.
Think that beauty will not stay
With you always; but away;
And that tyrannizing face
That now holds such perfect grace,
Will both changed and ruined be;
So frail is all things as we see,
So subject unto conquering Time.
Then gather Flowers in their prime,
Let them not fall and perish so;
Nature her bounties did bestow
On us that we might use them: And
Tis coldness not to understand
What she and Youth and Form persuade
With Opportunity, that's made
As we could wish it. Let's then meet
Often with amorous lips, and greet
Each other till our wanton Kisses

220

In number pass the days Ulysses
Consumed in travel, and the stars
That look upon our peaceful wars
With envious lustre. If this store
Will not suffice, we'll number o'er
The same again, until we find,
No number left to call to mind
  And show our plenty. They are poor
  That can count all they have and more.

(b)

S.W.R. ON HIS MISTRESS SERENA

Nature that washed her hands in milk
  And had forgot to dry them,
Instead of earth took snow and silk
  At Love's request to try them,
If she a mistress could compose
To please Love's fancy out of those.

Her eyes he would should be of light,
  A Violet breath, and Lips of Jelly,
Her hair not black, nor over bright,
  And of the softest down her Belly,
As for her inside he'd have it
Only of wantonness and wit.

At Love's entreaty, such a one
  Nature made, but with her beauty
She hath framed a heart of stone,
  So as Love by ill destiny
Must die for her whom nature gave him
Because her darling would not save him.

But Time which nature doth despise,
  And rudely gives her love the lie,
Makes hope a fool, and sorrow wise,
  His hands doth neither wash, nor dry,
But being made of steel and rust,
Turns snow, and silk, and milk to dust.

The Light, the Belly, lips and breath,
  He dims, discolours, and destroys,

With those he feeds, but fills not death,
    Which sometimes were the food of Joys;
Yea Time doth dull each lively wit,
And dries all wantonness with it.

Oh cruel Time which takes in trust
    Our youth, our Joys and all we have,
And pays us but with age and dust,
    Who in the dark and silent grave
When we have wandered all our ways
Shuts up the story of our days.

Piscator in Exodum.

Maurus in Genesin, et Exodum.

Le imagini de dei Caetari

Histoir des Histoires.

L'Alamont les voiages.

Gouncales de China.

Coyal histoir ecclesiastiq.

Jhon do Seras histoir des Francd vol 5

Jeur de colloson de la embassadeur

Antiquites francois par præsident fauchet

Dermer Troubles de france

Lacademie francois

Naissance duvee & chequt destates

Part of Raleigh's library list; about 1609. Note the entry referring to the 'French Academy'; see p. 119

TIME CHART

Spanish War	Essex	Raleigh
		At Oxford (1568). Service in France. Possibly at Middle Temple : a time (1575).
1575		
		(Disgrace of Leicester, on ¤ revelation of his marriage the widow of the Earl Essex, 1579.)
1580 Drake's voyage round the world; attacks on Spanish shipping in the Pacific.		Some years' service in Irelar to December, 1581. (1582) At court in confiden of Queen. Mission to A¤ werp with Leicester. (1583) Backs Gilbert's expe¤ tion to Newfoundlar Raleigh knighted. (1584) Granted charter Governor of Virginia; fi¤ colonists return with Drak 1585.
1585 Drake's W. Indies expedition. Sack of Santiago, Cartagena, etc. Leicester commands exped. to Low Countries; Battle of Zutphen; death of Sidney. Expedition to Cadiz, 'Singeing of K. Philip's beard' (1587). Armada (1588). Failure of Drake-Norris exped. against Spain (1589).	Distinguished, aged 19, at Zutphen. Becomes Master of the Horse (1587). Appointed K.G. (1588).	(1585) Becomes Lord Ward of Stannaries. First return to Parliament. Small sett¤ ment left in Virginia ¤ Grenville, disappears. (1587) New Virginia settl¤ ment led by John Whi¤ Raleigh becomes Captain the Queen's Guard.
1590	Marries Sidney's widow (1590). Commands force to assist Henri IV against Spain (1591).	(1589) First temporary di¤ grace; visits Ireland. (1591) Queen grants Ralei¤ lease of Sherborne Castl R's *Report* of Grenville fight printed.
Last fight of the *Revenge* in the Azores (1591). Privateering exped. to attack Spanish shipping; Raleigh succeeded in command by Frobisher (1592).		(1592) Sails on expedition ¤ molest Spanish shipping; r¤ called. Marriage; disgra and imprisonment. Release September, but disgrace co¤ tinues till 1596. (1593) Intervenes in Parli¤ mentary Debate on su¤ sidies.
1595 Drake's disastrous. exped. to W. Indies, and death. Essex's expedition to Cadiz in association with Howard and Raleigh (1596). Islands voyage to Azores; Essex accompanied by Southampton; Raleigh takes part (1597).	Commands expedition to Cadiz (1596). Commands Islands Voyage (1597). Made Earl Marshal after being aggrieved by Howard's promotion (1598). Fails to quell Irish Revolt (1599). Tried for his failure but released (1600). Abortive rising, and execution (1601).	(1595) Expedition to Guiana (1596) On expedition ¤ Cadiz. Reinstated at Cour Publication of *Discoverie Guiana*. (1597) On Islands Voyage. (1601) Speech in Parliament against Spain. (1603) Detention from Jul¤ 20th, trial and condemn¤ tion. Reprieved on day ¤ execution, but imprisone permanently in Tower.
1600		
Elizabeth dies; peace with Spain (1603).		

TIME CHART

Spencer, Marlowe and Nash* (printing dates)	Shakespeare (printing dates)	Lyric Poetry, Anthologies, etc. (printing dates)

[Note: Books and poems often circulated widely in manuscript before they were printed.]

Spenser: *Shepheard's Calendar* (1579).

Nash's *Anatomie of Absurdity* (1589).
(1590) Marlowe's *Tamberlaine*; Spenser's *Muiopotmos* (*Mother Hubberd's Tale*); *Faerie Queene*, Bks. I–III.
Spenser's *Complaints* and *Daphnaida* (1591).
Nash's *Pierce Pennilesse his Supplication to the Divell* (1592).*
Nash's *Apologie of Pierce Pennilesse* (1593).
Marlowe's *Edward III*. Death of Marlowe (1593).
Spenser's *Colin Clout* printed (prefatory letter dated 1591), 1595.
Faerie Queene, Bks. I–VI (1596).
Prothalamion (1596).
Nash's *Have with you to Saffron Walden* (1596).
Death of Spenser (1599).

Death of Nash (1601).

Venus and Adonis (1593).
Rape of Lucrece (1594).
Titus Andronicus (1594).
Romeo and Juliet
Richard II } (1597).
Richard III
Henry IV Pt 1
Love's Labour's Lost } (1598).
Passionate Pilgrim (1599).
Henry IV Pt 2
Henry V Pts 1 and 2
Merchant of Venice } (1600).
Much Ado
Midsummer Night's Dream (1600).
Merry Wives of Windsor (1602).
Hamlet: 1st ('bad') Quarto 1603.

Byrd's *Psalmes, sonets and songs* (1588).
Puttenham's *Arte of English Poesie* (criticism) (1588).
Byrd's *Songs of Sundrie Natures* (1589).
Sidney's *Arcadia* (posthumous) (1590).
Sidney's *Astrophel and Stella* (posthumous) (1591).
Britton's *Bowre of Delights* (1591).

Phoenix Nest (1593).
Chapman's *Shadow of Night* (1594).
Chapman's *Ovid's Banquet of Sence; A Coronet for his Mistress Philosophy*, etc. (1595).
Chapman's *Seaven Bookes of the Iliades*; also *Achilles' Shield* (1598).
Marlowe's *Hero and Leander*; also issued same year (1598) with Chapman's continuation.
England's Helicon (1600).

* c.f. *Love's Labour's Lost*, Cambridge Shakespeare, p. xxii.

(i) Index of First Lines

(ii) General Index